soul covers

Refiguring American Music   A series edited by Charles McGovern and Ronald Radano

Michael Awkward

soul covers

Rhythm and Blues Remakes

and the Struggle for Artistic Identity

(Aretha Franklin, Al Green, Phoebe Snow)

Duke University Press   Durham and London   2007

© 2007 Duke University Press

Printed in the United States of America on acid-free paper ♾

Designed by C. H. Westmoreland

Typeset in Scala with Impact display by Tseng Information Systems, Inc.

Library of Congress Cataloging-in-Publication Data appear on the last printed page of this book.

For my belles, Camara and Leah

contents

. . . .

acknowledgments

The characters that skilled soul singers interpret and temporarily embody come to life in and as part of intimate sonic tapestries, addressing current, former, or potential lovers to whom they communicate their innermost thoughts in graphic detail. The musical sounds and verbal textures used to register these thoughts then become objects of evaluation—appreciation, sympathy, recognition, comprehension, befuddlement, and derision—for eagerly solicited eavesdroppers, for whom evaluation comprises a crucial feature of the bountiful entertainment that soul provides. Whatever their authors, professional and layperson alike, say about these acts of address and reception, I have long suspected that they are less likely to train their analytical tools on the songs that have the deepest meaning for them, partly because the depth of their—of our—investment serves to imbue such material with the power to transcend the parameters upon which these types of discussions generally rely. Such transcendent songs, essentially privatized because they seem to represent deeply pleasurable or agonizing moments of our own lives, stab, shake, challenge, expand, enrich, salve, and heal our hearts, minds, and souls; like bottomless pain and incomparably sweet sensations, their description falls outside of the purview of even the broadest notions of critical analysis. And if there is, as the Persuaders claimed, a thin line between love and hate, a bridgeless space, as wide as the unspecified sea referenced in so many pop songs, may separate our most lucid interrogations of R & B music from our deepest emotional investments.

My efforts to consider some of the implications of three singers' engagements of familiar songs have been greatly assisted by studies by and conversations with deeply informed, profoundly engaged music lovers. In addition to the singers and authors of the works I discuss in the following pages, I want to thank my former colleagues Chris Flint, Robin Kelley, and Farah Griffin, whose willingness to communicate the depths of their engagement in music liberated me to consider my own. In similar ways, I am indebted to two other music lovers: Mark Anthony Neal, who I hope will see this book as an adequate substitute for the study of Philly International Records that I claimed to be writing and that he once gently chided me to get to work on, and Michelle Johnson, whose vast knowledge and good sense make her one of the two people I know—if self-knowledge counts in such assessments—who recognizes Bloodstone's "Never Let You Go" as a singular achievement of 1970s soul.

I truly appreciate those family members and longtime friends whom I have thanked elsewhere, privately and publicly, for their encouragement, concern, and support, people who, I am sure, are tired of seeing their names connected to my projects. Also, I am grateful to those people who invited me to discuss sections of this book at institutions located, among other places, in Barcelona, Ann Arbor, Boston, Philadelphia, and Hampton, Virginia. And I thank the anonymous readers solicited by Duke University Press, for compelling me to clarify my arguments, Assistant Editor Courtney Berger, for aiding my navigation of the process, and especially Executive Editor Ken Wissoker, for his continued faith and timely suggestions, both of which inspired me to push myself and, hence, this project, in fruitful directions. After its tentative beginnings at the University of Pennsylvania, where I discussed seventies soul, Al Green's autobiography, and an earlier draft of the chapter on *Call Me* with insightful students, *Soul Covers* took shape at Emory University. I am indebted to staff, students, and colleagues there, especially Yolande Tomlinson, who researched aspects of Aretha Franklin's and Dinah Washington's careers; Robert Patterson and Aida Hussen, whose assistance with courses on black masculinity, American autobiography, and Toni Morrison gave me time to think and write; and a remarkable collection of scholars of Afro-American literature—Rudolph Byrd, Frances Foster, Larry Jackson, and Mark Sanders—whose community I hope I enriched during my time in Atlanta.

The two people most responsible for helping me are my daughters, Camara and Leah. They served as unpaid research assistants and have embraced, with what I choose to hear as minor protest, their membership in an exclusive group of people with all of the following attributes: can sing all of Solomon Burke's greatest hits, are deeply informed (Al) Greenophiles, understand the terrible injustice of *Rolling Stone*'s exclusion of the Temptations from its initial list of rock 'n' roll "Immortals," and know that both Aretha Franklin and Phoebe Snow recorded "Do-Right Woman, Do-Right Man." Their love sustained me more than they'll ever know, in the beginning and, as one of our favorite songs puts it, "right to the end."

"how the parts relate to the whole"

Books examining black popular music of the 1960s and 1970s often speak of it as a sonic and lyrical extension of the social, cultural, and political upheavals of that transformative period. In fact, the most illuminating of these investigations, including *The Death of Rhythm and Blues, Sweet Soul Music, Soulsville, USA, Just My Soul Responding, What The Music Said*, and *A Change Is Gonna Come*, explore how people in the business of making and selling soul—performers, songwriters, producers, and record company executives—responded to and helped to shape national debates about and perspectives on such topics as civil rights, class conflicts, racial integration, regional identity, gender inequality, and black power.

This book draws much of its inspiration from the seriousness with which these studies have approached the task of illuminating the socio-political implications of the music. I want to say at the outset, however, that unlike the authors of these studies, I have not sought to construct an overarching perspective on or theory about the cultural meanings or historical significance of the subcategory of R & B with which I am primarily concerned. I strategically avoid doing so because a great deal of intellectual energy has already gone into devising intriguing analyses whose goals include positioning the music as a manifestation of both integrationist and black nationalist impulses, paradigms, and activities. As I believe will become evident in the following pages, along with contemporary theories of popular music, race, and gender, and techniques of textual literary analysis, vital aspects of these studies inform *Soul Covers*, which aid my efforts to produce nuanced, cogent, well-informed, and persuasively contextualized interpretations. But my treatment of the music has also been influenced by the skepticism of our own age concerning grand social, political, and cultural narratives, by which I mean interpretations of the constitutive qualities of a group, nation, or epoch that strategically privilege a segment or aspect of that entity, using it to represent the whole (or what analysts believe that whole should ideally be) and to render illegitimate those segments or aspects that do not fit neatly into that schema. As a consequence of that skepticism, I'm generally more inclined to recognize the limitations of attempts to codify *the* indispensable, definitive meaning of soul (or of the age in which it emerged and upon which it is said to reflect) than I am to embrace any overarching theory of its cultural significance and, certainly, to strive to create my own. In dealing with a particular subcategory of soul, it is clear to me that to reduce it, let alone the vast cultural field that R & B represents, to a meaning or even a unified set of meanings—to say, for example, that the soul cover reflects its age's competing notions of integration, black nationalism, freedom, communal values, gender roles, or romance—is, in effect, to simplify it to such an extent that it becomes, for open-eyed (and -eared) observers, a small, barely unrecognizable thing.

As a complex cultural entity, soul music is, because of its production, consumption, and analysis by an enormous array of people, attitudinally progressive, moderate, *and* conservative simultaneously. It is ideologically engaged *and* relatively indifferent to sociopolitical concerns; it is forward-thinking with respect to representations of race and gender and, hence, to changing ideas about acceptable social interactions (including in the realm of romance) *and* aggressively resistance to such changes; it is a well-guarded arena of black nationalist interrogation *and* a site with porous borders whose invasion by white American, West Indian, African, Latino/a, and British participants, along with its concomitant corruption by nonindigenous practices, mark it as an incontestably multicultural, transracial, and international sphere. If theorists of race and gender are persuasive in their contentions that, for example, no single definition of racial or gender identity continues to be persuasive, if it is now correct to speak of cultural constructions of whiteness and of masculinities, then it follows that we create, promote, and embrace notions of *the* predominant meaning of a cultural entity such as R & B at our own investigative peril. Such formulations are possible and persuasive only when we intentionally misperceive the music's vast expanse in order to serve our necessarily limited perceptions and interpretative agendas. My goal in this study is not to theorize or, for that matter, even to arrive at a plausible assessment of the music's general social meaning, but to investigate how albums by three artists with distinct relationships to soul—Aretha Franklin, Al Green, and Phoebe Snow—can be said to employ songs with a discernible cultural history to negotiate aspects of the ideologically inflected public and private personae these singers seek alternately to project, protect, and resist.

My inquiry focuses on a twelve-year period (1964–1976) following rock 'n' roll's emergence, an emergence that was coterminous with efforts to end governmentally sanctioned racial segregation. A question relevant to the concerns of this study has been raised frequently about singers from rock's earliest period as different from one another as Elvis Presley (the undisputed King of the pre-Beatles, pre-Motown period) and Pat Boone, whose "cleaned-up, hit cover versions . . . outsold the arguably superior versions by the original [black] artists: Little Richard's 'Tutti Frutti' . . . and 'Long Tall Sally' . . . , Ivory Joe Hunter's 'I Almost Lost My Mind' . . . , and Joe Turner's 'Chains of Love'" (*Rolling Stone Encyclopedia* 104): how should we view their appropriation (or *theft*, to echo Little Richard's persistent claim) of songs and aspects of the styles of black performers whose recordings were generally not played on stations aimed at white listeners? In the wake of efforts during the 1950s and 1960s to desegregate America's public spaces, including its airwaves, the concept of theft seems inadequate to describe what, by the mid-1960s, had become a *cultural exchange* of musical texts. On the one hand, the Pat Boones who "cleaned up" music that whites had had to transgress carefully patrolled racial boundaries in order to hear were replaced by acts such as Johnny Rivers ("Baby, I Need Your Lovin'"), Rare Earth ("Get Ready"), Dr. Hook ("Only Sixteen"), Rita Coolidge ("(Your Love Keeps Lifting Me) Higher and Higher"), and Art Garfunkel, James Taylor, and Paul Simon ("What a Wonderful World"), who interpreted tunes originally performed by blacks (the Four Tops, the Temptations, Sam Cooke, and Jackie Wilson respectively) that constituted, for them and for countless other nonblacks, what Motown's publicity machine sagely termed "the sound of young America." And, on the other, songs written and originally performed by whites were being interpreted by black artists, including: Stevie Wonder's "Blowin' in the Wind," Aretha Franklin's "Bridge Over Troubled Water," Wilson Pickett's "Sugar Sugar," Earth, Wind, & Fire's "Where Have All the Flowers Gone," Isaac Hayes's "By the Time I Get to Phoenix," Al Green's "For the Good Times," and the Isley Brothers' "Love the One You're With."

Whatever we make of these active transgressions of the color line, we can find precedence for them in earlier periods of the twentieth century, when, in the case of songs such as "I Can't Give You Anything but Love," "For All We Know," "Embraceable You," "My Funny Valentine," and "How Long Has This Been Going On," entry into the American Songbook was determined in part by how many artists, representing a variety of musical styles, chose to interpret them. While it is impossible or, at the very least, intellectually imprudent to exclude race from any consideration of cultural exchange involving dominant and subordinate groups, it is also problematic to fail to consider the fact that mass-distributed artistic texts become part of the public domain and, as such, are available to be utilized in any (legal) manner their consumers and interpreters desire. Depending on how we evaluate the quality of the appropriations, it is possible to argue that the Hollies' "He Ain't Heavy, He's My Brother" and Nina Simone's "Young, Gifted, and Black" became Donny Hathaway's; that Buddy Holly's "That'll Be the Day" and Betty Everett's "You're No Good" became Linda Ronstadt's; and that Rod Stewart's "Maggie May" (the first 45 I bought) and the Jackson Five's *Maybe Tomorrow* (my first album purchase) became mine.

All sorts of ideological concerns, of course, swirl around such acts of consumption, interpretation, performance, and ownership. In my own case, I was aware of the degree to which my racial identity and cultural authenticity were confirmed by my Motown purchase and challenged by "Maggie May," despite my recognition of familiar sonic elements in the raspy grain of Stewart's voice. But we cannot respond effectively to such issues, let alone satisfactorily address the analytical problems they present for us, simply by relying on notions of theft and victimization that justifiably inform discussions of the history of black-white relations, whose most persistent feature has been the material, moral, and psychic profit whites have accrued from the labor of blacks. In my estimation, Boone's right to remake "Tutti Frutti" cannot be denied, although his effort should be measured in accord with a variety of criteria and found lacking, for example, by rock 'n' roll enthusiasts, for whom Boone's talent is suspect at best and, perhaps more important, Little Richard's original is sacrosanct. But by the same token, fans of the Hollies have every right to find Hathaway's soulful take on "He Ain't Heavy" insufficiently attuned to the group's rock aesthetics and, hence, inferior to the original or, for that matter, to the Osmond Brothers' more faithful version that appeared on the flip side of their Jackson Five–inspired hit single "One Bad Apple."

I have chosen to focus on soul covers primarily for two reasons: (1) many of what I view as the best of them were produced during the period in black popular music in which I am most interested and (2) they constitute—to invoke formulations that describe how art responds to and incorporates earlier works—fascinating examples of repetition and revision. Because they are generally engaged in processes of textual alteration, covers provide me with opportunities to revisit and expand upon ideas I have considered with regard to Afro-American literature, a field in which I have toiled professionally for more than two decades. *Soul Covers* constitutes an essential part of my efforts to investigate intertextual relations in a variety of genres that make up black expressive culture. (In an earlier study, I explored thematic and formal relations between works by black female novelists, and in a future project, I will examine film adaptations of Afro-American novels.) Since, for example, as many scholars have claimed, notions of intertextuality greatly assist our attempts to comprehend the significance of similarities between texts by Zora Neale Hurston and her literary descendant Alice Walker, I believe it is fruitful to utilize such notions in a consideration of Aretha Franklin's tribute to Dinah Washington. So despite my reliance of historical and critical studies of ʀ & ʙ and theoretical analyses of popular music in my attempts to conceptualize *Soul Covers*, the readings I've produced are clearly and intentionally the product of a scholar of literature, just as, despite their reliance on the notions of black cultural production found in the work of prominent theorists of literature, Samuel Floyd's and David Brackett's analyses of the history of black American music and of James Brown's "Superbad," respectively, are demonstrably the work of scholars with musicological orientations.

In fact, along with theoretical notions of intertextuality, I draw on literary sources and critical methodologies in several instances to unpack the possible meanings of biographical, autobiographical, and lyrical material I engage. In tracing connections between Franklin's efforts to dispute claims that she is a quintessential blues figure and her unpersuasive rejection of Washington as a model, for instance, I utilize Harold Bloom's theories of influence which consider artistic identity to be a function of battles waged by aspirants against their precursors. In the course of my investigations of the role a born-again Al Green insists the natural world plays in his life and songs, I discuss Ralph Emerson's "Nature," which offers suggestive insights into its meanings for Christians generally and for artists in particular. So while I rely heavily on a variety of sources, to the degree that this is an interdisciplinary study, it is one which reflects my belief that many texts, tools, and paradigms drawn from literary studies can help elucidate other types of expressive cultural narratives, including soul covers.

By "interdisciplinary study," I mean specifically the efforts of scholars, many of whom are dissatisfied with the rigidity of the traditions in which they were trained, to arrive at and communicate meaning by utilizing eclectic clusters of investigative strategies drawn from critical theory, cultural studies, and disciplines often viewed by their methodologically more conservative departmental colleagues with at least some suspicion, if not downright contempt. Those clusters allow scholars to speak to a potentially broad range of similarly disaffected readers about texts and issues that their disciplines' gatekeepers would deem it imprudent for them to scrutinize. Rather than pretend that it is not challenging for me, given my limited musicological knowledge, to discuss songs as music, I've chosen, in this investigation of a subject I know thoroughly but not, if you will, technically, to utilize texts and analytical approaches over which I can claim a modicum of professional mastery. I operate from the assumption that if Simon Frith is correct that "songs are more like plays than poems" (quoted in Longhurst, 172), the strategies that have helped to unlock complicated dramatic, prose, and poetic meanings can be useful, in concert with staples of R & B interpretation (including examinations of autobiography, biography, historical context, and ideology), in exploring features of the particular category of soul narratives with which I am concerned.

⊙ ⊙ ⊙

In order to justify the trajectory of their investigations of soul, analysts often use their prefaces to suggest how early, life-altering encounters help to shape the contours of the studies they go on to produce. For example, Gerri Hirshey connects her fascination with James Brown, which began when she was an enthralled junior high school girl witnessing his "three-cape, collapse-and-resurrection exit" from the stage of *The Ed Sullivan Show*, to "a fan's notion of freedom" (xi, xvi) inspired by Brown and the other performers whose lives and careers *Nowhere to Run* goes on to detail. Consequently, she represents soul as a transgressive musical form that seeks to obliterate social boundaries (including race), positioning it as a perfect musical complement for the era's progressive social, political, and cultural activities. And, more than a decade later, Mark Anthony Neal describes *What the Music Said*, his investigation of black popular music, as an extension of "communally derived critiques of the African-American experience" (xi) to which he was a witness in barbershops, beauty shops, and kitchens in which he spent extensive amounts of time as a child in the South Bronx.

   With such examples in mind, I want to embark upon a brief autobiographical excursion of my own in order to ground this study's approach to a portion of the Soul Songbook. My first relevant experience occurred when, as a nine-year-old, I peeked in my older sister's diary and discovered her neat transcription of the words of the Originals' seductive ballad "Baby I'm for Real." While I was both excited to have access to my sister's secret musings and afraid that she'd exact some sort of unimaginable revenge if she caught me, I was agitated during this surreptitious encounter primarily because the lyrics baffled me. As I read them, I couldn't understand why the male persona assumes the female addressee doesn't understand him. Why, I wondered, is she about to go away? Why does his telling her that he wants to be her only man bring little tears to her eyes? Why does he believe that she assumes that his stated feelings are inauthentic, despite his elaborate protestations to the contrary? What makes him so sure he knows precisely how she feels about him and what she's thinking? How does he know that, in the perhaps distant future, he'll want to keep his promise never to leave her, and why does he believe that she needs to hear that sort of promise? Laid out, in my sister's familiar handwriting, were secrets whose decoding was crucial to a young boy who was compelled and confused by their insights into the meanings of gender and their impact on the mysterious world of romance.

By the time that I'd learned that the song was cowritten and produced by Marvin Gaye, I understood that comprehension of the lyrics depended on my awareness of societal notions concerning the nature and consequences of men's and women's allegedly divergent investments in romantic love's exclusive, everlasting qualities. In their communication of the belief that men typically resist such attachments while women are strongly desirous of them, songs such as "Baby I'm for Real" suggest that men who become smitten, despite masculinity's strictures against such manifestations of psychic and emotional weakness, must offer elaborate promises of unflagging devotion ("Never never never never gonna leave you baby") to prove their sincerity to the skeptical, already heartbroken female objects of their desire. But more important, especially in the context of this project, my sister's transcription of this song indicated to me that what singers and musicians were trying to communicate *mattered* in ways which transcended the mere—and, in the case of "Baby, I'm for Real," truly significant—sonic pleasures of appealing words, voices, and instruments working in conjunction. Beyond the scope of both the aural and strictly verbal registers of the song were answers to questions whose pursuit was essential to my attempt to connect the meanings of this gendered narrative to the ways of the world out of which it emerged. In essence, I later understood, as a consequence of my interactions with the Originals' song and other appealing complementary narratives, I was being indoctrinated into an ideology of romance and of gender relations, performances, and expectations that masqueraded as timeless, as natural as sunrise, and as right as rain.

Because of my fascination with the mesmerizing sounds of powerful voices hoping against hope to communicate all of the textures of longing, ecstasy, passion, and pain, I was never able to engage what I considered a great soul ballad in the "distracted and inattentive" way that Theodor Adorno insists that we interact generally with popular music. Indeed, I could often be found—to borrow his description of classical music enthusiasts whom he contrasts with easily distracted pop consumers—"sitting down and giving it all [my] attention, and seeing how the parts relate to the whole" (quoted in Longhurst 13, 8). Soul sounds uncovering dimensions of love lost and found, broken and fixed, debilitating and elevating possessed a type of dramatic narrative vivacity for me that television, movies, and the books I was mature enough to read typically did not. And because I was indeed curious about "how the parts relate to the whole," I heard or imagined, for example, the sound of rain crashing against a window while I listened to David Ruffin's anguish in "I Wish It Would Rain," just as I would sometimes wonder if the lover of "My Girl" (who'd given the Temptations' singer the sensation of feeling sunshine on a cloudy day) had left him and become the reason he was crying tears he felt he needed to hide.

In part as a consequence of this desire for continuity, I was fascinated by the phenomenon of the answer song, those quickly churned out, generally amusing responses to still-popular hits I heard frequently during my childhood. One such song, Barbara Mason's "From His Woman to You," a response to the Stax classic, "Woman to Woman," rejected the efforts of Shirley Brown's persona to normalize the lengths to which she is willing to go to keep her man. After we hear the familiar click of a rotary phone and two rings, Brown's persona responds to a muffled "hello" by telling a woman named Barbara that she'd found her name and telephone number when she was rifling through her untrustworthy man's pockets. Pleading for sisterly understanding, she implores Barbara to abandon her relationship with the man she loves and for whom she has purchased countless dollars worth of material goods. But rather than inspiring empathy or guilt, Brown's impassioned performance—hers is truly one of soul's great voices—prompts Mason (who'd revived her career after her teenaged success with "Are You Ready," a song of sexual initiation, with a series of mature takes on the challenges of romantic love, including "Bed and Board," "Who Will You Hurt Next," and "You Can Be With the One You Don't Love") to declare her persona's pity for the woman who perceives nothing wrong with trying in essence to purchase devotion. Despite her relative youth and lack of gainful employment, Barbara responds to the call (which Mason's record replicates) by asserting that, unlike Shirley, she can give "him [the loving] he needs when he needs it, and that's all he expects from me." Seeking sisterly understanding, "Woman to Woman" inspires, instead, a contemptuous retort from a younger woman who resolves, despite her awareness of her rival's pain, to keep seeing—and sexually satisfying—the man they have been sharing.

Whatever information we might glean about changing gender roles during the early 1970s from Brown's song, where the persona assumes the traditionally male role of provider, Mason's response makes it clear that Shirley is unsuccessful in her efforts to use her economic clout to compel her kept man (or his outside woman) to embrace notions of romantic exclusivity upon which American ideologies of romance are based and which ground—and help to explain—the desperation animating "Baby I'm for Real." Considering, among scores of other textual relations, the Temptations' songs as "parts" of a "whole" narrative of a single romance, and following the thematic implications of "Woman to Woman" and "From His Woman to You" to their logical extreme, I learned to conceive of R & B as an extended debate about how men and women do and should behave, what attitudes were deemed warranted, and which ones were likely to cause harm, deep embarrassment, and a desire for seclusion.

⦿ ⦿ ⦿

With these notions of soul as a terrain of contentious dispute about the gendered politics of romance at the forefront of my thinking, I began in the early 1990s to prepare myself to write a book about R & B. The topic I'd originally intended to explore was inspired by my conflicted responses to the following lines of "Ain't No Way," perhaps my favorite Aretha Franklin song: "I know that a woman's duty is to help and love a man / And that's the way that it was planned." How, I wondered, could I love a song whose notions of the divinely decreed fate of women to be men's necessarily subordinate helpmates I rejected? Did my attraction to the song mean that, underneath the progressive bluster of my engagements in feminism, my ideas about gender were more traditional than I believed and often claimed? Were the song's engrossing sounds separable from the meaning of its words? Was I so compelled by Re Re's amazing voice and its seemingly heartfelt promises of endless devotion that I could simply ignore, or at least try to bracket, the gender politics that inspired them?

While I kept Franklin as a subject, I abandoned the idea of foregrounding interpretations of conflicted responses. I did so largely because I saw only three possible ways of assessing reactions, conflicted or otherwise, to music of a bygone era, none of which particularly appealed to me: (1) a summary of surveys quantifying soul's impact on its listeners; (2) a self-reflexive account of my own responses to individual songs; and (3) an approach that sought to theorize, like reader response criticism that was in vogue in literary studies during the 1970s and 1980s, how listeners did, or ought to, interact with the sounds, narratives, and ideologies of soul music. Instead of continuing to compile a list of songs that engendered ideological discomfort or other types of ambivalence on my part—a list of great songs that included the Commodores' "Brick House," The Ohio Players' "Skin Tight," Joe Tex's "Hold On," and an assortment of the moaning-and-groaning tunes from the 1970s (Marvin Gaye's "You Sure Love to Ball," Teddy Pendergrass's "Easy, Easy, Got to Take It Easy," and New Birth's "It's Been a Long Time")—I worked to increase my general critical knowledge of R & B, hoping that my reading and careful listening would yield an appealing and workable topic.

Ultimately, however, I couldn't suppress the desire to confront, in some fashion, songs and artists about which my responses were in conflict with how people whose opinions I generally respected (including music critics, friends, and members of my family) insisted I should feel. By 1997, as I was working on two other projects, I had settled two areas of investigation: the highly praised albums Al Green produced between 1971 and 1974, and the universally ridiculed early work of a young Aretha Franklin. Green interested me precisely because the appeal of the majority of his classic songs, which was readily apparent to music historians and his rabid, primarily female, fans (including my mother), had escaped me. Many of the same critics who dubbed Green "The Last of the Great Soul Men" condemned Franklin's early work, a fact which, frankly, made me suspicious, largely because they failed to demonstrate that their assessments were grounded in a serious scrutiny of the songs themselves. If I couldn't hear the greatness they—and millions of record buyers—ascribed to Green, neither could I believe the narrative they'd constructed insisting that Franklin produced nothing of enduring value until she was signed to Atlantic Records in 1966 by Jerry Wexler, taken down south, and sat before a well-tuned piano and a microphone to begin the recording of what became the monumental *I Never Loved a Man the Way I Loved You*. I became even more skeptical of this narrative when I read Wexler's own acknowledgment that "she made a lot of great records on Columbia," where he believed her career floundered because "they didn't focus on an idea—a *sound* in the studio" and, hence, "went all over the [musical] map" (Bego 82).

Beginning my evaluative quest with Green's *I'm Still in Love with You* and a compilation of Franklin's Columbia recordings from Sony's *This Is Jazz* series, I found myself eventually—and thoroughly—compelled by the combination of intelligence, daring, and boyish masculinity that informed Green's "Simply Beautiful," "One of These Old Days," and the album's title track, and by the power, clarity, and nuances of Franklin's voice on songs like "Drinking Again," "Nobody Knows the Way I Feel This Morning," and "Today I Sing the Blues," and by her playful renderings of "Trouble in Mind" and "Muddy Water." As I dug deeper into his work, I recognized that among the most fascinating features of his albums from *Al Green Gets Next to You* through *Explores Your Mind* were his interpretations of familiar songs, including "I Can't Get Next to You" (Temptations), "How Can You Mend a Broken Heart" (Bee Gees), "Funny How Time Slips Away" (Willie Nelson), and "Unchained Melody" (Righteous Brothers). My growing fascination with that aspect of Green's recordings led me to focus on Franklin's tribute to Dinah Washington, and specifically on the question of how a talented young artist, struggling to make her professional mark, refashioned songs associated with a legendary, just-deceased predecessor into vehicles of self-expression. I settled on *Unforgettable: A Tribute to Dinah Washington* and on *Call Me*, Green's fourth solo album, as subjects, and on a compelling point of comparison: in addition to "Funny How Time Slips Away," *Call Me* features "I'm So Lonesome I Could Cry," which was written and originally recorded by Hank Williams, whose "Cold, Cold Heart" Franklin follows Washington in remaking. Because these albums prominently feature interpretations of songs originally recorded by whites, and because of the numerous examples and discussions of whites remaking R & B songs, it seemed to me important that this book include an investigation of a white performer.

While there are certainly white artists that have been more successful on the R & B charts (including Pat Boone!) and who have been more widely embraced by enthusiasts (especially Teena Marie), none, in my estimation, is a better subject for this study than Phoebe Snow. Unlike Marie, her repertoire of soul covers is extensive: from Sam Cooke's "Good Times" on her first album to the Four Tops' "Baby, I Need Your Lovin'" on her most recent, from minor R & B hits like Barbara Acklin's "Love Makes a Woman" to major ones like the Emotions' "Best of My Love," from Franklin's classic "Do-Right Woman, Do-Right Man" to the Temptations' "Shakey Ground." But I've chosen to focus on her remakes of Billie Holiday's "No Regrets," the Supremes' "Going Down for the Third Time," and "There's a Boat That's Leaving Soon for New York" from *Porgy and Bess*, which appear on her 1976 gold LP *Second Childhood*, because I was intrigued by the choice of a white singer to cover, on a single album, a set of songs the blackness of whose sounds and cultural perspectives have long been debated. In her choices, as well as in her discussions of her responses to familial salutations by black fans and to being mistaken for a light-skinned black woman, Snow's work speaks to the complexities of racial performance and cultural style in the post–civil rights era where, even if Afro-Americans continue generally to occupy a marginal status in the nation, elements of black culture—especially its sounds—are widely, openly, and enthusiastically embraced.

Like Franklin and Green, Snow provides me with an opportunity to consider the implications of conflicted responses. I dealt with such responses frequently during the late 1970s, when Jewish friends at Brandeis complained about the nasality of her voice whenever I played her music and joked about setting me up with a kinky-haired woman with whom we went to school whom they dubbed "the fake Phoebe Snow" (she did resemble the singer quite a bit), while blacks often played her albums—especially *Second Childhood*—went to see her in concert, and considered her a talented soul performer. Clearly, she is nowhere near as consequential an artist as this study's other subjects. But because I focus on how song covers illuminate or challenge aspects of artistic identities, Snow's stature and, for that matter, others' perceptions of the quality of her efforts concern me less than her negotiations of social constructions of race and gender through her interpretations of black songs. Indeed, if uncontested artistic achievement were my primary criterion for selection, I would have explored, for example, one of Franklin's monumental Atlantic albums—perhaps *I Never Loved a Man the Way I Love You*—instead of one which relatively few R & B enthusiasts have embraced. But because of my interest in the implications of conflicted responses, both my own as well as those of other listeners and of the artists themselves, I've chosen to examine music that enables me to map, resolve, and move beyond the tensions between perception and reception that arise, among other places, in the three artists' autobiographical remarks and in their performances of others' songs. While Franklin's first Atlantic release is endlessly fascinating and may well be not only her finest LP, but one of a small handful of the most impressive R & B albums ever recorded, and while it contains remakes of songs by Sam Cooke ("Good Times," "A Change Is Gonna Come") and Otis Redding ("Respect"), it is impossible for me to locate within it or its reception anything close to the sorts of compelling interpretative conflicts that can be said to animate her performances on *Unforgettable*.

Perhaps this study will encourage others to listen attentively to the clarity, power, maturity, and unadulterated beauty of a young Aretha's voice when she was in the process of trying to become the Queen; by the time she achieved this stature, according to Wexler, "heartache and drinking"—and I would add, age and smoking—had begun to take "their toll" on her incomparable instrument (215). Perhaps my focus, via his own discussion of his life and work, on the centrality to his self-conception of his southern identity will expand the now-constricted and, I believe, hopelessly redundant, nature of critical examinations of Al Green's art. Perhaps *Soul Covers* will even encourage a reconsideration of Phoebe Snow's frustratingly uneven contributions to American popular music, and inspire others to recognize, in the words of music critic Robert Christgau, that "none of her sisters sing the postblues like Snow—neurotically, that's what she's about, but with incisive power" (*Guide to the 1980s* 376).

I am hopeful, but experience has made me something of a realist about such matters. No amount of encouragement or repeated playing of her music on my part compelled some of my friends—including my college roommate, Dan, who quickly grew as annoyed by her voice as I became with James Taylor's—to recognize Snow as "one of the most gifted voices of her generation," to hear that "her rich, throbbing alto, with its stratospheric outer limits, is a genuine phenomenon," or to appreciate her "tough, gutsy emotionality" (*The New Rock Record Guide* 473) in the ways that my younger sister (who'd first heard her music on WDAS, Philly's R & B station) was able to do. Nor can I get my stubborn older sister to hear Franklin as something other than a screamer or to recognize that Green's songs don't all "sound the same." But what I'm fairly certain this study can do is to compel readers for whom R & B is both intellectually engaging and spiritually enriching to consider soul covers as vehicles through which artists explore how they are different than other singers and who, precisely, they want and believe themselves to be.

In looking at these artists' extensive commentary about their own lives, I demonstrate that a complicated but informing relationship exists between personal experiences and the songs these self-conscious performers produce and reproduce. In my analyses of songs, specific albums, and narratives of their lives and careers, I bring together information gleaned from song lyrics, autobiographical statements, and historical studies to challenge the limitations of oft-repeated formulations. As a result, I am able to speak expansively about connections between, among other things: Franklin's reported blues-filled life and her combative entry into a regal black vocal tradition; Green's conflicted location at the sacred/secular divide and his sense of himself as a "country boy"; and Snow's truncated period as an important singer-songwriter and her own—and others'—sometimes vexed interrogations of her right, as a white female, to "sing the postblues."

When I'm singing a song, I live in the lyrics. Before I even go to the studio to cut a record, I study the words and the music to create a character in my mind based on the person in the song. I try to imagine how they got to the point emotionally of singing the words.—**Gladys Knight**, *Between Every Line of Pain and Glory*

The analysis of popular music reveals that there are in fact many levels of meaning having to do with music, lyrics, images, and movement as negotiated by individuals with specific social and cultural biographies.—**Richard Middleton**, introduction to *Reading Pop*

Introduction

"I live in the lyrics"

On Truth, Intent, Image, Identity,

and Song Covers

The famed soul singer Al Green is featured as part of a duet on "Put It on Paper," a song concerned with a couple's decision to marry that is the title track of former Sounds of Blackness vocalist Ann Nesby's 2002 album. The woman (sung by Nesby) refers to herself as "a little old fashioned" because she is in a monogamous union and is not "shackin' up," and Green sings the part of the "old school brother" who is in love with her; as evidence of his commitment he tells her, "I wanna change your name." This duet is preceded on the album by a short "Al Green Interlude," on which Green performs his other well-known public role: that of the Reverend Al Green. Presumably troubled by the preponderance of the types of unholy alliances that the song's characters ultimately reject, and apparently unable to find biblical justification for his participation in the explicitly secular project, Green seems initially incapable of articulating a coherent thought or finishing a sentence.

For those listeners aware of Green's decades-long struggle to sing pop songs without feeling that doing so directly conflicts with his ministerial calling, this "Interlude" may appear to be little more than the effort of a guilty preacher to overcome his ambivalence about participating in another purely secular endeavor. Indeed, it is only in response to entreaties from Nesby and the song's producer, Timothy Lee, that confirm his sacred role—particularly Lee's enthusiastic "Go on, say it Reverend"— that Green's sense of comfort noticeably improves, and he goes on to offer a brief recitation on the institution of marriage. The biblical pretext he identifies for the secular song he had no hand in writing is St. Paul's assurance that the Lord blesses the "undefiled" "marriage bed," a promise that inspires God's followers to put their faith in his blessings "on paper" by entering into holy matrimony. Subsequently manifesting an unmistakable joy of recognition and a practiced enthusiasm, Green is spurred on by his minicongregation's familiarity with the relevant line of Scripture—"Whosoever findeth a wife findeth a good thing"—and its familiar calls ("Come on, come on Preacher") inspire from him a biblical exegesis that motivates and apparently helps him to rationalize his participation: "A good wife is from the Lord."

Whatever else it does, the "Al Green Interlude" offers a poignant example of the attempts of an acclaimed singer to discover points of confluence between the story of a song and the narrative of his life that would enable him to embody the persona whose perspectives he is being called upon to convey. His efforts resonate, in interesting ways, with sentiments on the art of emotive performance found in the autobiography of another celebrated soul star, Gladys Knight. In this excerpt, Knight discusses both her thespian-like preparations and the psychic difficulty she experienced in conjunction with one particular performance:

> When I'm singing a song, I live in the lyrics. Before I even go to the studio to cut a record, I study the words and the music to create a character in

my mind based on the person in the song. I try to imagine how they got to the point emotionally of singing the words. Then, to stay in that emotional state and in character when I am in the studio, I often record in darkness.

I couldn't get into the character that I found in the song that Berry Gordy wanted me to record near the end of 1970. She was not someone I felt I could identify with. The song was "If I Were Your Woman." The lyrics are the words of a woman who is in love with a married man. She is a bold thing, singing, "If I were your woman and you were my man, you'd have no other woman, you'd be weak as a lamb."

. . . I had never been that aggressive in going after a man. It just wasn't my style. I was taught that the man pursued the woman.

I thought the lyrics were too suggestive for my image, or for me personally. (201–2)

Despite her disapproval of the persona's allegedly "bold" pursuit of "a married man," a brazen act in conflict with how she perceived herself ("me personally") and the wholesome self she presented to the general public ("my image"), despite her belief that she failed, before and during her 1971 recording of "If I Were Your Woman" with the Pips, to "get into the character," Knight was nonetheless able to deliver one of her most acclaimed performances. If the famed vocal group's 1971 recording of the song succeeds despite her inability to inhabit the character, she acknowledges that, "As I've grown older, and a little bit more self-assertive, I've grown to like it and understand it more" (202).

Strangely, Knight's declarations suggest that she does not, indeed, "understand" a crucial aspect of "If I Were Your Woman," which would have led her to find its persona anything but truly "bold" and the song's lyrics something other than "too suggestive." In the first verse, the persona does appear to be addressing the object of her affection, audaciously offering a man whom she knows is already involved with another woman a guarantee of a fulfilling union that will include exhausting sexual pleasure. However, later in the song, her words indicate that she is not, in actuality, speaking directly to the man she claims to love: "You're part of me, and *you don't even know it* / I'm what you need, but *I'm too afraid to show it*." As these lines demonstrate, the bold initial words are not those of an assertive woman in pursuit of a man who is being mistreated by an insensitive mate, but instead express desires she cannot communicate; they are one side of an imagined conversation with the man for whom she pines in secret. On some level, of course, Knight must be aware of the dissonance between imagined assertiveness and actual timidity, but her earlier embarrassment at and disapproval of the character's thoughts apparently so dominate her perception that she ignores indisputable evidence that her character's promise of lusty lovemaking merely reflects what music critic Dave Marsh calls her "*idea* of cheating with someone else's man" (340, my emphasis).

If we utilize the full range of what Knight presents us as evidence of her own evaluations of the song—her engrossing performance, in which her voice moves from soft and measured to loud, pain-filled, and impassioned; her discussions of her wholesome "image" and her resistance to changing social mores generally and to women's liberation in particular—"If I Were Your Woman" evinces the utility of close readings of pop lyrics to our understanding both of the affective power of the words and sounds of songs and of the cultural milieu upon which they reflect. In addition to its possible biblical resonances—Knight herself connects her difficulty with the character to a childhood spent as "the little church mouse of [Atlanta's] Mount Moriah" (201)—the song's image of a "weak . . . lamb" also signifies the state from which she wishes to free the object of her desire and to which she hopes to reduce him with her elevating love and assertive lovemaking. Her character is in silent conflict with dominant precepts of her "crazy" world, which insist that it is better for a "diamond" of a man to accede to being publicly "treat[ed] like glass" by a hard-hearted mate than it is for the woman who really appreciates him to offer him her heart, body, and soul. Consequently, it could be said that she is struggling to "pick . . . up" two discouraged people, her torn-down ideal man and herself, and perhaps because of her awareness of the forces—societal norms and her own reticence—she must confront to deliver him from the arms of an "unkind" woman, she communicates her perceptions with increasing urgency, even apparent desperation.

Whatever else we make of Knight's seemingly contradictory interpretations or, for that matter, of Green's "Interlude," they compel us to consider the role lyrical analysis can play in singers' own assessments of the nature and appropriateness of their emotional and intellectual engagement with songs, if not necessarily in the quality and specific contours of their performances. For Knight, the shock of "bold" references to lusty, self-assured female sexuality apparently leads her, almost thirty years after her initial performance, to remain "in darkness" about the fact that her song's persona is, as the songwriters present her, the very embodiment of nonaggressive femininity she both valued and sought to project as part of her youthful "image."

Like Simon Frith, I believe "that words matter to people, [and] . . . are central to how pop songs are heard and evaluated" (159). Given the propensity of both listeners and performers to interpret the meanings of the words of songs in line with their own emotional, spiritual, and psychological economies, it seems to me that when we consider a song as what Frith calls a "speech act" or "words to be analyzed in performance" (158), we can best assess the sometimes complicated relationship between the content and form of narratives that detail human emotion and behavior. Clearly, awareness of the self-perceptions and crafted images of recording artists is crucial when we attempt to understand their musical output, because, among other things, these constructed selves provide us with interpretive keys we can use to analyze their formulations of their songs' meanings. But as is indicated by the struggles of distinguished soul singers to read lyrics in terms of their own values and histories, we need also to be attentive to points of apparent dissonance between the purported selves, crafted images, and performed characters that come together, sometimes in quite problematic ways, in various public interpretations of songs. Given the instability of all three of the modalities of identity into which singers like Knight and Green tap ceaselessly, it may very well be the case that the quality of our interpretations depends on our willingness to come to terms with the fact that, for self-conscious recording artists, listeners, and critics alike, reading is what semiotician Robert Scholes calls a "two-faced activity."

Scholes points out that "every text that comes to us comes from before our moment in time," and is accessible in subsequent moments only when we examine it in terms of its place on the complicated "web of textuality" "in which we hold our cultural being and in which every text awakens echoes and harmonies" (6). Consequently, reading inevitably "looks in two directions. One direction is back, toward the source and original context of the signs we are deciphering. The other direction is forward, based on the textual situation of the person doing the reading. It is because reading is almost always an affair of at least two times, two places, and two consciousnesses that interpretation is the endlessly fascinating, difficult, and important matter that [it] is" (7). At their most persuasive, interpretations of songs and other texts involve both "seek[ing] original truth or original intent"—the potentially divergent meanings, for example, that the authors, lead and background singers, and producer of "If I Were Your Woman" sought to convey—and exercising the critical "freedom" to situate them as part of "a textual world that is always being written" (6–7), even if such creative investigation yields notions of truth that conflict with those of the texts' originators. In other words, however dedicated investigators are to discovering textual truth and artistic intent, their conclusions—reactions, in part, to the aspects of the text that experience has taught them to deem analytically significant—will inevitably reflect their predilections and interpretive practices, formed at a variety of different moments, more accurately than the text's "origins." When, for example, Knight sees her character in "If I Were Your Woman" as engaged in brazen action rather than in wishful thinking, like her passive, falsetto-voiced male counterparts in songs from the period such as Bloodstone's "Natural High" and the Temptations' "Just My Imagination," that reading clearly results from her exaggerating the import of parts of the lyrics and ignoring others. As we have seen, her autobiographical accounts of her history, image, and self help us to recognize what motivates her choices as an interpreter and performer of the narrative and, perhaps, the distance between them. If it is the case, as Scholes insists, that "the person who reads a text is never the person who wrote it—even if they are the 'same' person" (50), Knight's formulations reflect the fact that the vocalist who interprets a familiar song is never the same person who originally sings it, whether or not he or she composed it.

Throughout this study, I am concerned with the ways in which the notions of "self," "image," and "performance" delimit the possible meanings of already known songs which three singers, Aretha Franklin, Al Green, and Phoebe Snow, seek to claim, in moments after their original production, appearance, or popularity, as essential elements of their expressions of their identities, musical and otherwise. I focus on song covers by artists who were in the process of developing distinctive images when they recorded them and who, as a consequence, seek to reshape familiar material in ways that reflect what critical discussions of them and their own autobiographical statements indicate are constitutive aspects of their musical personae and personal lives. My goal in dealing with these artists' versions of songs associated with a diverse cast of major twentieth-century American musical figures that includes Dinah Washington, Hank Williams, Tony Bennett, George Gershwin, the Supremes,

Billie Holiday, and Willie Nelson is to describe and to create ways of examining their "web of textuality." Song covers help to illuminate how texts "awaken" and can themselves become "echoes and harmonies" for singers attempting to shape, validate, and rationalize their social identities and artistic images.

I take seriously the arguments of scholars of popular music who insist that, when readers look at lyrics in isolation from their accompanying sounds, what emerges, in all likelihood, will be what musicologists like Brian Longhurst call a "crude form of analysis" (169). Recognizing that pop songs are, as Frith reminds us, "stories" or "implied narratives" that feature "a central character . . . with an attitude, in a situation, talking to someone (if only to herself)," I look at how, when artists perform familiar songs, that performance can alter not just their sounds, but the attitudes of their central characters, and, hence, their overall meanings. If, in their efforts to make them conform with who they are or claim to be (and not to be), singers can radically alter the fundamental meanings of familiar songs, Scholes's notion that no cultural text possesses (and, I would add, no listener or singer can discover in it) a single, unassailable "truth" would seem to be correct (7).

In determining the meanings of songs like "Put It on Paper" and "If I Were Your Woman," it is essential that we recognize the "creative" responsibilities of the listener who cannot uncover "original truth" and who is thus forced to choose from among a variety of plausible—if not, given his or her experiences, equally persuasive—possibilities. That choice, for the analyst of song covers and artistic images, is made easier if he or she is attentive to the "analytic distinction" Frith makes between "a song's composer, performer, and protagonist." If, as he indicates, "a protagonist's character is determined by the composer (by the way the music is constructed) but interpreted by the performer," listeners must, in seeking to assess "what the relationship is of these two processes," devise credible answers to the question "What does an interpreter do?" that allow them to participate effectively in acts of narration and interpretation that are necessarily both descriptive and inventive (200, 199). In the case of talented artists, Frith asserts that part of what interpreters must do is to recognize that "songs . . . clearly 'belong' to their singers, not their writers. Interpretation in this context does not mean realizing what the composer . . . meant, but using the music to show what interpretation means" (200–201).

Looked at from the vantage point of singers, "interpretation" connotes, among other things, the ability to shape songs in ways that conform to, confirm, and, at times, intentionally conflict with their images. Those images, which are always in part "inventions," reflect prevailing social conventions and are the product of skillful manipulations of well-publicized or presumptive experiences by agents, record companies, and others—especially the singers themselves—who collectively engage in the construction of the public personae of these performers. As Frith asserts in a formulation that confirms the logic of Knight's description of her efforts to embody her characters, whether or not a well-established singer is performing her own compositions, listeners assume that she taps into a store of significant personal experiences:

> In pop, biography is used less to explain composition (the writing of the song) than expression (its performance): it is in real, material, singing voices that the "real" person is to be heard, not in scored stylistic or formulaic devices. . . .
>
> . . . . [A]s listeners we assume that we can hear someone's life in their voice—a life that's there despite and not because of the singer's craft, a voice that says who they really are, an art that only exists because of what they suffered. (185–86)

Ultimately, if Frith is correct, the "analytic distinction" between "a song's composer, performer, and protagonist" becomes essentially irrelevant. If the song's author is not its performer, or his or her life story is not already well known—typically, we do not consider, for example, whether and how the Supremes' songs of love and heartbreak, composed by the renowned team, Holland-Dozier-Holland, represent key experiences in any or all of the male writers' personal lives—the composer is bound to be erased from consideration by the listener and replaced, as the possible origin of truth and intent, by the singer, whose constructed "image" and "self" are then deemed the sources of narrative meanings. When their performances are especially powerful, our understanding of singers' experiences often shape our readings even of songs that are already firmly entrenched within the catalogs of other artists, because success, in this context, is seen as the capacity to transform familiar songs into vehicles through which they can express their personal joys and suffering. Think, for example, of Otis Redding's bemused reaction after hearing Aretha

Franklin's version of "Respect," a song he composed and originally recorded: "I just lost my song. . . . That girl took it away from me" (Guralnick 332).

The three albums that this study primarily engages, Franklin's *Unforgettable: A Tribute to Dinah Washington* (1964), Al Green's *Call Me* (1973), and Phoebe Snow's *Second Childhood* (1976), contain noteworthy song covers and, in Green's case, the start of what will become an enduring pattern of self-referential intertextual gestures. In my examinations, I am concerned with issues Frith raises: the relationship between singer, (auto)biography, and interpretation; the degree to which a song's "meaning" can be discerned by attending to the "sounds" that accompany the lyrics; the ability of talented singers both to shape a song in ways that reflect their own artistic concerns or identity and to maintain their "personal distance" from material and the performance of it; and, more generally, "what performance means." In pursuing these topics, I focus in part on what Frith describes as a largely ideological consideration in the process of arriving at "critical musical judgment" as it relates to

> the distinction between "the cover version" and "the version." The cover version is almost always heard as bad—this is now the usual attitude to the white pop versions of black songs and records in the 1950s, for example. . . .
>
> "Version," by contrast, refers to a situation in which the "copy" is taken to improve on the original, to render it "bad" by revealing what it could have been. Here, reversing the previous argument, black covers of white origins are routinely valued positively (Ray Charles singing "I Can't Stop Loving You"), and rock arrangers are taken to make pop songs more interesting (Vanilla Fudge's "You Keep Me Hanging On," Phil Collins' "You Can't Hurry Love"). The fact that Ray Charles puts his personal stamp on Don Gibson's song is obviously a good thing. Imitation, in short, is as much an ideological as a musical matter; the critical response depends on an account of whom is imitating whom and for what attributed reason. (69–70)

This formulation of "critical musical judgment" identifies the ideological nature of such racially inflected acts of reiteration and revision as Ray Charles's, Vanilla Fudge's, and Phil Collins's covers, all of which, in Frith's view, constitute memorable "versions" that "improve on the original."

Questions that come to mind in response to Frith's assertions include: If they deem Franklin's "Respect" to be superior to Redding's, will listeners, led to her albums by her appearance as a reverential fan and engaging guest vocalist in the documentary *Standing in the Shadows of Motown*, recognize Joan Osborne's remake of Redding's "These Arms of Mine" on *How Sweet It Is*, her 2002 album of interpretations primarily of R & B music from the 1960s and 1970s, as a "version" rather than merely a "cover"? If record buyers judge Michael McDonald's career-revitalizing *Motown* albums strictly as "cover" efforts, will that judgment make them less likely to appreciate his sumptuous reconstruction of Freddie Scott's "Hey Girl" a decade earlier? And to introduce the specific queries that give shape and direction to the following chapters: How do we categorize the remakes of songs associated with the then recently deceased Dinah Washington by a young Franklin, who came to be known as the Queen of Soul following her transcendent 1967 album, *I Never Loved a Man the Way I Love You*, but who, in 1964, seemed unlikely ever to approach her former idol's commercial success and critical acclaim? How do we assess the interpretations of songs originally performed by and/or typically associated with black artists by Phoebe Snow, a Jewish woman who was deemed to possess Negroid features and a bluesy voice, the combination of which led some to assume that she was herself black? And, in considering Al Green's *Call Me*, deemed by critics to reflect his struggles to accommodate his yearnings both for the divine and for the secular—and sexual—how do we both investigate manifestations of that struggle and connect them to a self-described country boy's versions of quintessential (white) country songs by Hank Williams and Willie Nelson, his use in his compositions of themes and imagery consistent with those found in these "versions," and his referencing of titles of his own celebrated singles in one of these compositions? In order to explore such matters, I consider, among other things, the singers' perceptions of the meanings of race, gender, region, and religion, and their notions of musical identity as authentic self and created—and creative—"image," as socially constructed and aggressively policed, as imagined, preordained, invented, in process, and divinely inspired. I am interested, in particular, in how these singers utilize familiar songs as sonic and lyrical canvases upon which they test, display, and promote their evolving notions of the connections between their musical and experiential selves.

⊙ ⊙ ⊙

Analyses of writers' echoes of the compelling words, ideas, images, and themes of their predecessors are among the most common and, hence, most rigorously investigated forms of literary study. As Thais Morgan argues, the analysis of intertextuality, the "apparently infinite play of [a text's] relationships with other texts," does not lead scholars to posit "completely neutral 'facts'" concerning textual relations; instead, like discussions of bad song covers and transcendent versions, the theory and practice of intertextual study are "fraught with 'value judgments'" (239). If "'influence' remains the most tenacious critical metaphor in the pedagogy and theory of literature today" (and, I would add, in discussions of new musical artists), its tenacity has in large part to do with the fact that "the burden of debt"—the certainty that "text A influences text B when the critic can demonstrate that B has 'borrowed' structure(s), theme(s), and/or images(s) from A" (240)—establishes, among other things, a necessarily hierarchical relationship between source and derivative antecedent. And in some critical formulations, it is precisely that "burden of debt"— James Baldwin's to Richard Wright, for example, or Gloria Naylor's to Toni Morrison—that compels emerging artists to acknowledge, compete with, strive to repress, and attempt to improve upon, the achievements of their seemingly indomitable forebears.

Looked at in light of these formulations of literary textual relations, we could say that song covers seem both less "fraught" and equally anxiety-ridden. Because, with rare exceptions, covers tend generally to be word-for-word—if not, of course, note-for-note—copies of well-known performances, few of the questions that inevitably attach themselves to analyses of literary borrowing appear appropriate to address in this context. While we can debate the extent to which Baldwin's delineation of poisonous father-son relations in his first novel, *Go Tell It On the Mountain*, is a rewriting of Wright's concerns with perverse paternity in *Black Boy*, there is no question that Stevie Wonder's "Blowin' in the Wind" is a remake of the Bob Dylan–penned original. However, like LeRoi Jones, we may feel compelled to determine which of these recordings we prefer and to attempt to justify our preferences. As he recounts in *Black Music*, Jones finds Wonder's cover vastly superior because he prefers the sounds of its music and of the Motown singer's voice. These preferences lead him to argue that the original is "abstract and luxury playing around stuff [while] when Stevie Wonder sings it, [it] . . . becomes about something that is actual in the world and is substantiated by the life of the man singing it. That is, with Dylan it seems just an idea. A sentiment. But with Wonder . . . , you dig that it is life meant. In life" (206–7). Whatever else we might say about Jones's analysis, including whether or not we share his perceptions of the relative qualities of these recordings, clearly it is "fraught with 'value judgments,'" including his views on racial suffering, before and during the revolutionary 1960s, and its effective—and affective—performance.

Two of Jones's assumptions resonate with my own perspectives concerning Franklin, Green, and Snow: (1) that aspects of the singers' selves are communicable in, reflective of, and have the potential to enhance, their renderings of others' songs, and (2) as opposed to models of literary inheritance where, even when the responsive text is widely embraced, the canonized source is generally deemed superior, covers seem unavoidably to provoke comparisons whose outcome—the result of necessarily subjective assessments of people with strong, often easily discernible, investments—is always potentially in doubt. To evaluate, for example, Carole King's, James Taylor's, or Roberta Flack and Donny Hathaway's rendition of King's composition "You've Got a Friend" (or, for that matter, Hathaway's live solo version of the song), listeners typically assess which rendition most closely conforms to their developing or already fully developed musical tastes.

Song covers, then, are a different species of intertextual activity than their literary counterparts, but the most engaging and imaginative of them do not strive merely to pay tribute to and replicate beloved performances. Indeed, versions can serve as ways for skillful artists to develop and display distinctive styles and voices. Note, for instance, Green's description of his "version" of "How Can You Mend a Broken Heart," where he insists that, while it "had been a major hit for the Bee Gees . . . , they might just as well have given it right over to me and saved themselves the trouble. I'm not a bragging man, but I *owned* that song from the opening refrain. . . . To my mind, the Gibb boys had written a masterpiece . . . and it was up to me to make it immortal. But you'll have to make up your own mind about such matters" (270–71). Green's perception of the superiority of his rendition, which he ascribes to the effectiveness of his "near-whispered pleading" and ability to give "each word the weight and wisdom that would come from a sadder-but-wiser penitent" (271), results from his certainty that he communicates the anguish and deep regret contained in the lyrics much more effectively than the Bee Gees. In his analysis, published nearly three decades after the fact, Green notes—and calls on his readers, in all likelihood fans already enamored of his soulful, "pleading" version of the song, to evaluate—his success in discovering the narrative potential of "masterpiece" lyrics that "the Gibb boys" were mature enough to compose but not skilled enough to perform. In this instance, then, the version serves as a way for a singer both to illuminate inexpertly performed dimensions of the song's narrative and to crystal-lize the style and "image"—the vulnerable sufferer who becomes, during his most successful period that encompasses *Call Me*, his quintessential "character"—with which he chose to represent himself professionally.

To return to "Put It on Paper," which refers to bygone days when Green was the brightest R & B star on the musical scene and to one of his earlier songs: it is significant that the singer expresses the perspectives of his persona by using the deeper registers of his voice, whose submersion had been essential to the development of his signature style. That choice obscures his contemporary persona's aural connection to the boyish char-acters in the sweet-voiced, "old school" singer's hits such as "Let's Stay Together" and "I'm Still in Love with You," the types of narratives of en-during love "Put It on Paper" thematically emulates.

For reasons we might deem interpretively significant—his use of an identifiably masculine sound to distinguish his voice from Nesby's deep, powerful tones; the possibility that the vulnerability that his seventies style conveys is inappropriate for men in an era when, according to the song, monogamy, discretion, sensitivity, and respect for females are not highly valued traits; the likelihood that age has deepened his voice and made sustaining boyish tones more difficult—Green, in fact, sounds very little like his old self. If the song's sounds and the singers' spirited de-livery, along with the aforementioned "Interlude" and Nesby's aside "I wanna be pleasing in God's sight," suggest more of a stylistic and the-matic connection to gospel than to Green's classics, the singer who in the "Interlude" seeks biblical precedence encourages us to consider it in the context of his own recordings when he exclaims, "Let's get married today," the most prominent line of his 1974 hit.

Looked at in a cursory way, the intertextual reference is interesting, appropriate, and sly, the sort of intriguing associative gesture that, as we will see, Green first used on *Call Me*. But if we take seriously the contrast between "old school" and contemporary values and the task of exploring the song's "web of textuality," we may conclude that, intentionally or not, Green's act invalidates this rather simplistic juxtaposition and complicates our tasks as readers. "Put It on Paper" extols monogamous values that the song—and the contemporary black urban culture that it claims to reflect—associates implicitly with Green's (hey)day generally and with "Let's Get Married" in particular. However, as a living remnant, as it were, of "old school" values romanticized in the duet in part because they are devalued within the informing cultural environment, the character in Green's original marriage narrative, which is as caught up as the twenty-first-century tune in the tensions between monogamy and promiscuity, is also unable to meet the challenges posed by religious and social ideals. In "Let's Get Married," Green's character proposes marriage largely because of his own general malaise and in response to his growing ennui and dissatisfaction with joyless promiscuity; having reached a point where he is "not too crazy about the idea / Of having nothing to do" and is "tired of playing around / [With] a girl in every town," he is baffled by the lukewarm response to his proposal by a woman who appears uncertain about whether this much traveled womanizer can transform himself into a faithful husband.

The desire of Green's persona in "Let's Get Married" to encourage the privileged but skeptical member of his stable to "give me your hand" appears similar to the male character's urgent request in "Put It on Paper" to his girlfriend to "change your name." However, unlike the twenty-first-century "brother," Green's "old school" love man—seen not through the rose-colored lens of a simplistic cultural history but as a social actor articulating his perspectives—seems cut from the same cloth as the contemporary men from whom his counterpart in the duet distinguishes himself. Green's more recent use of the line "Let's get married today" is uttered by a character who, despite and because of his own strategic, romanticized recollections of "old school" attitudes, appears to be in an infinitely better position to be a good husband than his predecessor.

Interestingly, on April 4 of the same year that "Put It on Paper" was released, Leonard Pitts's syndicated column connected that very line to George Bush's "proposed changes in Bill Clinton's 1996 Welfare Reform Act," which would "earmark $200 million in federal money to fund state programs that promote and maintain healthy marriage." Depicting a social reality that is identical to that of the characters in the Nesby-Green duet, Pitts insists that contemporary urban America is a place in which "husbands and wives have been supplanted by 'my baby's daddy' and 'my kid's mother' . . . , children, who thrive on stability, predictability and routine, find themselves largely bereft of all those things because of the hedonism, selfishness and immaturity of some fathers and mothers[, and] . . . commitment is a four-letter word." Pitts begins his declaration of support for the proposal in the following way: "'Let's get married today.' Al Green sang that in 1973. These days, it's George W. Bush on lead vocals." While, for many, the image of Bush stepping into the musical shoes of the Last of the Great Soul Men may be chilling, more important for my purposes here is the fact that the persona of this song, far from being an ideal candidate for marriage, could indeed be seen as a product of the very sexual revolution on which both Pitts and right-wing ideologues blame the woeful state of the traditional family in the first place. Pitts argues that cultural "soldiers," who should be commended for supporting minority, women's, and gay rights, also "taught us that we could do away with responsibility and commitment and that our nation, our families, our children, would pay no price as a result."

The male persona of "Put It on Paper" is clearly motivated by "very serious" feelings for his mate, unlike his predecessor, for whom the idea of marriage "sound[s] strange," but who resolves that he "might as well" settle down with a woman he professes to love as an afterthought and whose tears, which he promises "to wipe away," are in all likelihood the result of his womanizing. Exemplifying the ease with which songs can be misinterpreted, Pitts's 2002 reading of "Let's Get Married" suggests that he is so seduced by Green's hypnotic voice and the propulsive beat that he romanticizes and cannibalizes its narrative to the extent that all that remains of it is a seductive line from its chorus and none of the reasons that the woman should respond to this proposal with an emphatic "no." But to the degree that such uses—including that of Green's persona in "Put It on Paper"—are the results of interpretation, the conclusions of any responsible analytical model would be that these readings are, at best, partial and misleading. Looked at as intertextual analyses, where the "original" "truth" or "intent" of the formulation of marriage in the early 1970s song fades to the interpretive background in favor of the strategic bending of the words to fit "the textual situation of the person doing the reading" (Scholes 7), Green's and Pitts's twenty-first-century readings of the line "Let's get married today" reflect its meanings only insofar as they confirm the intersecting webs upon which rest the "images" of the singer as an old-school romantic and of the American inner city as an unstable, hedonistic, immoral mess.

⊙ ⊙ ⊙

According to Richard Middleton, a noted scholar of popular music, "the ubiquitous phenomenon of covers, undoubtedly grasped by listeners as a species of 'interpretation,' is merely the most striking exemplar of a wide-spread 'practical criticism' pursued through musicians' exploitation of stylistic intertextuality" (11). When they are undertaken by singers with the requisite skill and resolve to "sound like nobody . . . except me" (Wexler 203), to use soul icon Wilson Pickett's phrase, covers can be said to constitute modes of critical "interpretation." In other words, because of their capacity to manipulate the lyrics, sounds, and meaning of familiar songs within identifiable "stylistic" fields such as R & B, talented singers perform acts of "interpretation" and "practical criticism" that enable them to (re)imagine, create, and develop their own artistic personae.

For example, "Respect" helped Franklin to establish a persona of a powerful, take-no-mess soul sister, which she utilizes in several of her classic performances. Her producer, Jerry Wexler, insists that her remake of Redding's hit far surpasses the original both commercially and aesthetically. Following on the heels of her first Atlantic release, "I Never Loved a Man (The Way That I Loved You)," her cover certainly helped to cement her status as the most significant black female singer to emerge following the death of Dinah Washington. After interpreting Redding's song, transforming it into what Wexler considers an "ethnic and feminist" "touchstone" that both recognized and demanded women's increased socioeconomic power, Franklin was quickly installed as the Queen of Soul, whose work is said to manifest a blues woman's bawdy resilience, a gospel singer's willingness to raise a powerful noise, and a liberated woman's insistence on gender equity. Franklin's theft of "Respect," like Green's assumption of ownership of "How Do You Mend a Broken Heart," suggests that the highly competitive nature of pop music performance can perhaps best be recognized and explored in those moments when song covers clearly serve both as modes of revision and as opportunities for artistic self-making.

⊙ ⊙ ⊙

As I have indicated, my discussions of the albums *Unforgettable: A Tribute to Dinah Washington*, *Call Me*, and *Second Childhood* investigate Franklin's, Green's, and Snow's responses to already known songs as part of their efforts to create, confirm, and resist aspects of their emerging images and artistic personae. I do not accept uncritically the meanings that music critics attach to these singers when they assess their work: of Franklin as traumatized blues sufferer whose recordings before her first Atlantic album are essentially irrelevant to our understanding of her career; of Green's work as marked predominantly by an unresolved tension between sacred and secular imperatives; and of Snow as a tormented singer-songwriter whose relationship to black music is less constitutive of her musical identity than her more clearly autobiographical folk-pop efforts. Instead, I operate from the assumption that these perspectives, when they are taken as full explanations, limit our capacity to explore either the nuances and unanticipated twists and turns in these singers' work or manifestations of their self-conscious chafing in the face of such necessarily confining expectations. And because my analyses attempt to expand the possible ways we can examine these singers, they each begin with extensive discussions and analyses of their autobiographical remarks that point to illuminating alternate avenues of exploration: Franklin's combativeness and rejection of the label of blues sufferer, Green's country aesthetics and desire to create thematically unified albums, and Snow's ambivalent responses to her participation in black music.

I approach Aretha Franklin's *Unforgettable* in terms of formulations of intertextuality that suggest that artistic self-creation is a contentious process whose goal is the supplanting of predecessors. When Dinah Washington died in late 1963, Franklin—a former prodigy who, after her stirring debut in 1961, had produced a string of unremarkable albums—seemed unprepared to join the line of transcendent black female singers that includes Bessie Smith, Billie Holiday, and Ella Fitzgerald. Having been deemed "the next one" by Washington herself, but having failed to that point to produce recordings that proved indisputably that she was worthy of such praise, Franklin's remakes of songs associated with the recently deceased Queen of the Blues can be seen as her attempt to demonstrate that she was indeed ready to wear her idol's crown. Looked at in light of theories of artistic influence, Franklin's efforts can be said to reflect her awareness that, to fulfill Washington's prophesy, she would have to demonstrate that she was capable of improving upon her predecessor's efforts. *Unforgettable* contains three categories of interpretation: (1) songs such as "What A Diff'rence a Day Makes" and the title track on which Franklin comes close to approximating the older singer's style; (2) tunes such as "Nobody Knows the Way I Feel This Morning" and "Evil Gal Blues," where her readings reflect a lack of artistic maturity and eventuate in less compelling performances than Washington's; and (3) two tracks, "Cold, Cold Heart" and "Drinking Again," where the combination of engrossing lyrics, subtle delivery, and overpowering emotionality enables her to improve upon Washington's recordings and to create templates for her subsequent regal performances. Emphasizing the latter two categories of remakes, I demonstrate that, by the time she signed with Atlantic two years later, Franklin was fully prepared for that role in part because she had used some of her predecessor's signature tunes to identify the range and contours of her own gifts and, through her still unsurpassed coalescence of vocal styles—including blues, jazz, gospel, R & B, and soul—to expand the possibilities of the black female voice.

As I've suggested, assessments of Al Green's musical career generally focus on his struggles to resolve the question of whether it is sinful for a minister who received his religious call at the height of his commercial popularity to continue to perform his greatest hits and to make new secular music. While Green uses the topic of the sacred-secular divide to bracket his autobiography, *Take Me to the River*, he also speaks there of his desire to be a great artist who, "at a time when the singer/songwriter was just beginning to be a force in the music business . . . , wanted to be up there with the best of them" (261). Considering the first instance of bold self-reference in his work, his singing of the titles of three of his own hits during the fadeout of the middle song of *Call Me*, "Your Love Is Like the Morning Sun," I suggest how his most critically acclaimed album can be looked at specifically in light of his desires to be an artist "up there with the best of them" in part because, like many of the greatest achievements in the form of his era, it aspires to be musically and thematically coherent. Seeking formal coherence, Green brings together putatively irreconcilable aspects of his history, self, identity, and image: secular and sacred music or, more specifically, his image as a vulnerable male desperate for the love of a good woman and his long-suppressed belief that earthly happiness is possible only for those who make themselves vulnerable to the love of God; his desires both to create sophisticated art and to maintain the level of commercial success he'd achieved with songs like the ones he references during the aforementioned fadeout, "Tired of Being Alone," "Let's Stay Together," and "I'm Still in Love with You"; and his sense of himself both as a cosmopolitan black artist and as a forlorn country boy whose covers of "I'm So Lonesome I Could Cry" and "Funny How Time Slips Away" (and, as important, rewritings of these songs in his own compositions) are essential to his articulation of a mode of black masculinity that is both radical and utterly traditional.

The final album I examine, Phoebe Snow's *Second Childhood*, helps to shed light on a period in American cultural history when one of the consequences of the mainstreaming of R & B was an attempt by large numbers of whites to master its sounds and, hence, many of its most significant songs. Because they recognize that listeners' perceptions of what Richard Middleton calls "musicians' exploitation of stylistic intertextuality" are greatly impacted by prevailing American ideologies of race, scholars argue that our comprehension of the phenomenon of song covers requires, among other things, a willingness to scrutinize a given historical period's justifications for and notions of the permeability of color line. If, according to Frith, "imitation . . . is as much an ideological as a musical matter," if "critical response depends on an account of whom is imitating whom and for what attributed reason," by his own account, by the time Snow's album appeared, white "imitations" of black songs (including, to use an example he cites, Vanilla Fudge's 1968 remake of the Supremes' "You Keep Me Hangin' On") were no longer "almost always heard as bad" because they could be connected to notable efforts during the 1960s to challenge centuries of white attempts to naturalize American racial segregation. By focusing not on Snow's folk-pop compositions on *Second Childhood* (a top forty album on *Billboard*'s pop, R & B, and jazz charts), but on her three covers, I consider the complex encounters of a blues, jazz, and R & B enthusiast with black cultural aesthetics at a time when, because of or despite such desires to achieve a truly integrated America, there was lingering resistance, at least in some ideological hot spots on the dark side of the street, to whites' performing—and profiting from— black musical styles. Interestingly, the songs that Snow remakes had figured prominently in debates about race and cultural performance: "No Regrets," on which Billie Holiday approaches a Tin Pan Alley love song in a manner that relocates it, in Angela Davis's words, "in a specifically African-American cultural tradition and simultaneously challenges the boundaries of that tradition" (165); "Going Down for the Third Time," a largely unknown track by the Supremes, the cultural blackness of whose music has been frequently challenged (including in Frith's assessment of race and song covers, where it is labeled "pop"); and "There's A Boat That's Leaving Soon for New York" from *Porgy and Bess*, a beloved but controversial musical, the cultural authenticity of whose sounds and representations is frequently called into question because their famed primary author, George Gershwin, was white. By remaking this fascinating set of what we could call *boundary songs*, Snow, whose tightly curled hair, olive skin, wide facial features, large frame, voluminous soul covers, and jazz-, soul-, and blues-tinged voice have led some fans to assume she is a light-skinned black, can be said to test, among other things, both the fluidity and the rigidity of the category of race as it had been applied over the course of the first three quarters of the twentieth century to American popular musical performance.

These chapters consider song covers as mechanisms through which talented singers construct and reflect their still evolving artistic and social identities. I engage remarks uttered by these singers about their own lives and careers both in published memoirs, in the case of Franklin and Green, and soul-searching commentary offered by all three of these figures, but especially Snow, who has spoken extensively to journalists and music critics about her struggles to feel comfortable with her looks, voice, musical tastes, and the implications of professional success and failure. I'm less concerned with either confirming or challenging the veracity of their recollections than with how they facilitate a discussion of the singers' contributions to, confirmations of, and confrontations with their images. Whether or not Green really hated "Let's Stay Together" until it became a hit, or Snow really only listened to rock when she was a child, or Franklin really doesn't remember why she and her first husband were not married by her minister-father matters infinitely less than how Green's sense of himself as a country boy, Snow's notions of the sociocultural implications of the sound of her voice, and Franklin's representations of her conflicted relationships with other artists manifest themselves in, and help to illuminate, the meanings of their songs and albums.

Brian Longhurst insists that "analysis needs to consider how the meaning of a text may relate to the overall meaning that has been created by a star" (185). What makes autobiographical narratives particularly useful in that regard is the information they provide about how the stars themselves respond to others' assessments of their "overall meaning," which they work quite energetically both to shape and, as important, to resist. If, Frith argues, "a pop star is like a film star, taking on many parts but retaining an essential 'personality' that is common to all of them and is the basis of their popular appeal" (199), the selves these singers construct, in formal autobiographies, interviews, and other professional appearances, are essential to our understanding not of who they were necessarily at the time they recorded these albums, but how they wished to be perceived as artists and what they wanted us to believe about their real lives. All three singers were engaged in significant personal struggles at the time these albums were made: Green had descended into hedonism that wracked him with guilt so profound that he felt compelled, for reasons he wasn't fully aware of at the time, to write and record "Jesus Is Waiting"; Snow was mourning the death of the boyfriend who oversaw her blues and jazz education, striving to suppress her self-doubt and questions about whether she should be delving so deeply into black styles, and courting bliss because of her pop, jazz, and R & B success, the birth of a child, and a marriage to a handsome man she believed had a sweet disposition; and Franklin had been unable to harness her transcendent gifts and was saddled with a domineering husband and, I believe, the fear she would never reach the artistic heights that had been prophesied for her. As the following chapters demonstrate, these projects, and the soul covers they contain, were not only important for their careers in a variety of ways, but central to their ongoing efforts to construct—and re-construct—themselves.

[Dinah Washington] said, "Rev. C. L. Franklin has a twelve-year-old daughter up in Detroit named Aretha. She's the next one. You watch." — *The Autobiography of Quincy Jones*

Aretha was crushed when she heard of the death of her idol. Even though Aretha was being sold as "The New Queen of the Blues," she stated to the press, "The Queen of the Blues was—and still is—Dinah Washington!" Recording an album of Dinah's hits was a natural choice for Aretha. She . . . loved evoking the moody expressiveness of her favorite star. Aretha's *Unforgettable* album is without a doubt her most artistically successful Columbia LP. — **Mark Bego,** *Aretha Franklin: The Queen of Soul*

My mentor, Clara Ward . . . , and Daddy remained my dominant influences. — **Aretha Franklin** and **David Ritz,** *Aretha: From These Roots*

But when it comes to unjustly criticizing me in public, let's stop the B.S. — **Aretha Franklin** and **David Ritz,** *Aretha: From These Roots*

"she's the next one"

Aretha Franklin's *Unforgettable: A Tribute to Dinah Washington* and the Black Women's Vocal Legacy

In *Queen of the Blues*, a biography of the singer Dinah Washington, who "from 1949 to 1958 . . . joined the ranks of Bessie Smith, Billie Holiday, Sarah Vaughan, and Ella Fitzgerald as one of the most popular blues and jazz singers of all time" (Bego 34), Jim Haskins discusses his subject in a way that suggests the sometimes pernicious effects of the tendency of fans and critics to evaluate new artists as virtual replicas of earlier performers so as to satisfy their own, seemingly insatiable need for artistic continuity:

> Dinah . . . had to contend with the pressures of stardom and with the inevitable comparisons with Bessie Smith, whom Dinah resembled somewhat in appearance, as well as in style. Old-timers who were nostalgic for Bessie kept looking for a new Bessie in Dinah. And none other than John Hammond, record producer and star-finder, said, "Dinah's stage behavior is very similar to Bessie's. I am struck by it each time I hear her sing. [But] she's no Bessie, not yet." Dinah knew that there were other, private comparisons between her and Bessie—that they were both unattractive, rough-hewn, and moody—and she disliked the comparisons, good and bad. Still, there were bases for them. (60)

According to Haskins, Washington created herself in large part by appropriating aspects of the styles of established performers whom she found compelling. Indeed, he insists that she utilized as models such entertainers as Roberta Martin, who "started that fad of the gospel sound on the piano"; Bette Davis, from whose engrossing cinematic characters she learned to speak "beautifully"; and the "mesmeriz[ing]" Billie Holiday, whose subtlety and economy of vocal gestures she so admired as a young singer that she ultimately "tone[d] down her own [extravagant] presentation, trying to see if she, too, could hold an audience with the sheer power of her singing" (18, 21). While openly acknowledging the other influences, Washington disliked the Smith comparison for three reasons: first, the resemblance between the two singers, in the estimation of onlookers so ready to seize upon apparent affinities, was such that they ignored the differences between the firmly established and emerging artists; second, the link was based largely on what she knew others thought were unappealing physical and behavioral traits; and third, given the "nostalgic" lens through which such affinities are gazed, she must have felt that others would conclude that she was unable to match the artistic acumen of her predecessor.[1]

This comparison troubled Washington, who was struggling with a quandary faced by many emerging artists: how to construct a sufficiently individuated mode of self-expression while employing, and even calling attention to her utilization of, cultural codes and styles whose guiding principles informed not only her aesthetic choices and formal concerns but also her listeners' notions of her prospects for future significance. But

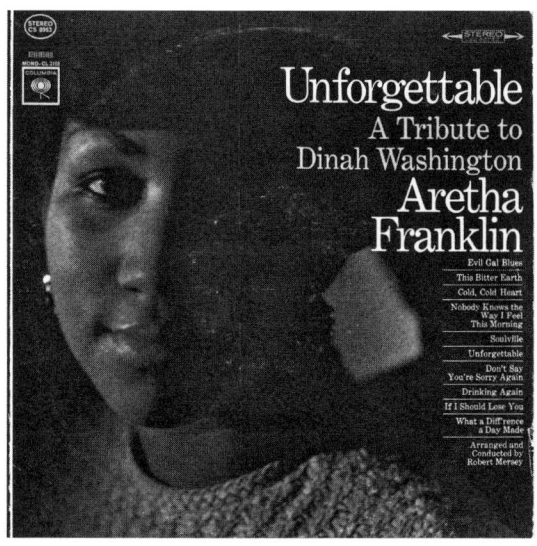

Aretha Franklin's best efforts in her tribute album to Dinah Washington reimagine songs closely associated with her idol and allow the gifted twenty-one-year-old to discover the full range of her own soulful voice.

however problematic such comparisons proved to the young Washington, it would appear that—to cite a more recent example—the situation of Natalie Cole was even more daunting because of her connections to two already famous singers. She was burdened, in particular, by the legacies of her iconic father, the smooth crooner Nat "King" Cole, which she confronted in her celebrated tribute album, *Unforgettable: With Love* (1991), and of this chapter's subject, Aretha Franklin, who succeeded Washington as the dominant black female singer and after whom Cole patterned her own vocal style. In her autobiography, Cole relates an early manager's contention, offered after her performance of "a string of Aretha Franklin songs one night," that if she hoped "to establish [her] own distinctive sound," she should stop singing songs associated with her "idol," whom he believed she "sound[ed] too much like." Subsequently, Cole sought "to finesse a little bit . . . and still interpret . . . in [her] own way, without outright stealing" from Franklin's style (103). Soon thereafter, she was chosen by Marvin Yancy and Chuck Jackson to record material that became *Inseparable*, her first album, precisely because, having failed to interest Franklin in their songs, the producers changed their emphasis from recording the established Queen to "looking for the *next* Aretha" (108).

During her three years of phenomenal success, Cole felt compelled to deny that she "had really begun to believe that [she] was the new Queen of Soul" (131) because golden record sales, critical acclaim, and promotional efforts by Capitol Records and by her producers, Yancy and Jackson, who "had been hyping her around the music world as 'the next Aretha Franklin'" (O'Neill 232), all led people to believe that she posed a serious threat to her idol's reign. This threat is perhaps best exemplified by the fact that at the 1975 Grammy Awards, where Cole "became the first black ever voted Best New Artist" (O'Neill 231), her initial single, "This Will Be," was deemed to contain the Best Female R & B Vocal Performance, "a category," notes Cole, "that Aretha Franklin had won every year for the past nine years." She adds, "I took away what would have been her tenth" (131). Although her facts here are a bit askew—Franklin had won eight, not nine, consecutive Grammys, and was not nominated in the category in the year of Cole's initial victory—her emergence at the point when her idol's popularity had begun to wane positioned her, in the minds of music critics and fans (and, apparently, of the older singer herself), as the first serious rival for the symbolic title Queen of Soul, to which Franklin had held exclusive claim since a Chicago deejay conferred it on her after the release of her debut Atlantic album, *I Never Loved a Man the Way I Love You*, in 1967.[2]

In the following discussion, I examine Franklin's *Unforgettable: A Tribute to Dinah Washington* (1964) as a compelling manifestation of this singer's early attempts to master the nuances of black vocal traditions. Her lengthy apprenticeship at Columbia during the first half of the 1960s, where her encounters with commercial and aesthetic failure were perplexing and dispiriting, clearly forced her to assess both the field itself and her potential contributions to it. Among the choicest fruits of these assessments is her first "album concept" (Franklin and Ritz 82), a collection of interpretations of songs closely associated with an idol who, before her death in 1963 at age thirty-nine from an imprudent mixture of diet and sleeping pills and hard liquor, was so highly esteemed that, more than thirty years later, she remained one of the twenty most popular acts in the history of the genre, sandwiched between the Four Tops and Earth, Wind, and Fire (Whitburn, *Singles* 621). I am particularly interested in considering her tribute as evidence of how the young Aretha, whose dominance of the field of black singing had been prophesied by Washington herself before she was a teenager, responded to evidence that she had not mastered her craft sufficiently to garner either commercial success or widespread critical acclaim.

As we have seen, Cole responds to the "immense anxieties of indebted-ness" (Bloom, *Anxiety* 5) by avoiding tunes associated with her idol while seeking the artistic "finesse" to reference Franklin's style without imitating it. By contrast, the young Aretha is quoted in her tribute's liner notes as saying that she recorded *Unforgettable* to honor a singer with whom she wished she had "been close personal friends," and to give "people some idea of the way [she] felt and [would] always feel about Dinah" as an artist and as one of the many famous adults who visited her childhood home because of their fondness for her father, Reverend C. L. Franklin. Her anxieties concern not mimicry, as do Cole's, but discovery of the limits of her own prodigious gift that obliged her to approach the songs in "the way they felt best, whether [the results] happened to be similar [to] or different" from Washington's recordings. Staking a claim to a place within the regal black female line, Franklin uses her idol's songs to construct "a distinctive voice . . . differentiated from its precursors" (Bloom, *Anxiety* 148) through interpretations of work associated with the Queen of the Blues.

Indelible Marks and Erasable Imprints

The explanations that singers and producers construct to justify their tributes to other artists are often as arresting as the discs themselves. This genre—which in the vast field of black music includes Motown's covers of songs by the Beatles, Marvin Gaye's of those by Nat "King" Cole, and contemporary artists' tributes to Curtis Mayfield, Stevie Wonder, and Luther Vandross—displays a pull of tradition, nostalgia, and influence as profound as, for example, the stirring commemorative tracks that mark and mourn Gaye's own passing (including Maze's "Silky Soul Singer," Teena Marie's "My Dear Mr. Gaye," the Commodores' "Night Shift," and Diana Ross's "Missing You"). If we exclude from our consideration the proliferation of tributes to young artists such as Norah Jones and Ashanti—the lasting significance of whose recordings is still very much in question—this genre seems generally to reflect efforts on the part of singers and musicians to acknowledge the work of infirm, recently deceased, under-appreciated, or highly esteemed predecessors whose music represent a high point in what is often an obsolescent style. In addition, tributes generally reflect a cagey selectivity on the part of the performer, who chooses songs on the basis of personal taste, the extent to which they can be made to fit his or her style, and their familiarity to the general public.

Focusing on the issue of selectivity enables us to consider both the nature of performers' recognition of earlier artists and their uses of such projects to initiate, preserve, or crystallize the specific directions of their own careers. In the case of Regina Belle's *Reachin' Back* (1995), an album of songs originally recorded in Philadelphia during the 1970s by Teddy Pendergrass, the Spinners, the O'Jays, the Stylistics, Blue Magic, and the Delfonics, her selection of romantic tunes such as "Could It Be I'm Falling in Love," "Just Let Me Make Love to You," and "You are Everything" and her exclusion of songs featuring turgid social commentary such as "Ghetto Child," "For the Love of Money," and "People Make the World Go Round" are noteworthy. For those who associate R & B music produced in this city during the 1970s with examinations of social inequality, with (in the words of Philadelphia International Records' company motto) a sociopolitical "message in our music," her concentration on love songs might seem at least curious. Belle's (re)collection of Philly sounds, then, is not only partial, as all such tributes are by necessity, but appears to depoliticize the city's black musical output. It is not that she distorts or recklessly reimagines the music of her formative years—years that are generously referenced through her inclusion in the disk's insert of photographs of herself at various stages of development—but that, in her choice of lush love songs whose chief architects are Kenny Gamble and Leon Huff and their frequent collaborator, Thom Bell, she constructs the city as a romantic setting where the politics of romance exists as a crucial musical subject alongside economic inequity, racial unity, interracial and intraracial strife, familial dysfunction, and materialist excess.

A track on Belle's second album, *Stay with Me* (1989), conflates Donny Hathaway's "Someday We'll All Be Free" and Marvin Gaye's "Save the Children," demonstrating that she was not uninterested in the types of messages that Philadelphia songs of social protest represent. Given that demonstrated interest, we might speculate that her extended nostalgic journey to an earlier point in the history of her chosen field of artistic expression constitutes a critical response on Belle's part to the directions of black popular music after the 1970s, when the City of Brotherly Love ceased to be the epicenter of recorded soul. The work of an artist who entered the scene in the mid-1980s, a period notable both as a low point for R & B vocalists and for the emergence of politically engaged rap as a dominant form, *Reachin' Back* offers Belle a way to connect herself to obsolescent modes of singing, revive a style of expressive romantic satisfaction, longing, and pain imperiled in the age of songs with titles like "Do Me Baby" and "Rub You the Right Way," and contest a reduction of 1970s Philadelphia music to a largely political register that serves implicitly to devalue remarkable records that emerged during her childhood and helped to shape her notions of the aesthetics of romance.

Because Belle does not discuss her project in detail, however certain I am of the implications of her choices and of the musical environment in which it appeared, my analysis of her intentions—which, according to her, was simply to "make an album that would remind folks of the blue light that hung in their basements or slow dancing with one's first love" (VH1 Biography)—is, at best, plausible conjecture. Other projects, however, provide significantly more in the way of explanation, including Dee Dee Bridgewater's *dear Ella* (1997), a tribute to the jazz stalwart that appeared a year after Fitzgerald's death. This album's liner notes, authored in part by Bridgewater herself, include the types of reverential comments younger people generally construct in response to acclaimed figures in their chosen fields. She acknowledges, for example, reacting "like a true fan" during her initial encounter with the legendary artist, whose incomparable work she had long admired, and her heartfelt commitment both to the older singer and to the imperiled music that connects them, a commitment that is encapsulated in her observation that "Ella Fitzgerald epitomized jazz singing, a style that seems destined for near-extinction as we move toward the 21st century. While there are some promising young jazz singers who've taken up the challenge of what we term today traditional jazz singing, the pickings are slim." Positioning herself as spiritual and artistic heir, Bridgewater speaks of experiencing "such a profound sadness that it almost frightened [her]" when she learned of Fitzgerald's death, like she might have felt if she'd "lost a member of [her] own family," and admits she had thought of her as "immortal, like a child does with its parents." And though recognizing Fitzgerald as part of a group of canonical female jazz vocalists (she places her "along with other great ladies we've lost, like Billie Holiday, Sarah Vaughan, [and] Carmen McCrae"), Bridgewater contends that "it is Ella who left the most indelible mark" because she was the best exemplar of the obsolescent art of "traditional jazz singing."

According to notions of artistic succession such as those described by literary critic Harold Bloom, potentially great younger artists strive to establish their own preeminence because they fear that the work of precursors will always be deemed more cogent, thematically compelling, and aesthetically satisfying than anything they can create, and that they will forever be seen as disciples of a "major figure" who have failed to create themselves. If artists are to become truly powerful in their own right, they must move beyond idol worship to discover and create their own voice by situating themselves energetically in terms of—but also, and perhaps more important, in marked conflict with—their forebears' daunting example. "Weaker talents idealize," Bloom declares, while the "strong . . . wrestle with their strong precursors" (*Anxiety* 5).

Unlike Dee Dee Bridgewater, Claude Carriere—who authors the other section of the liner notes to *dear Ella*—is sufficiently attuned to the "perilous undertaking" in which the younger singer is involved to construct what is essentially a countertext that emphasizes her prodigious gifts (he insists that Bridgewater possesses "one of the greatest voices in jazz today," informed by a "lively intelligence") and her capacity, through "her own interpretations" of Fitzgerald's songs that are "imprinted" in "our memory," to cause us to forget these luminous earlier performances "very quickly" as "we find ourselves tasting the new versions, and wondering at the treasures of the imagination that the singer and her directors have deployed for our benefit." For Carriere, then, the truly exceptional tribute album is anything but an exercise in preservation, obeisance, and fidelity. Instead, it is an opportunity for younger artists to present themselves as no longer "true fans" striving to honor their idols' performances, but as highly skilled craftspeople struggling to release the listener's "imagination" from the tenacious hold of their predecessors. Employing their vocal and intellectual resources to reshape their predecessors' texts, younger artists seek to refashion the "imprint" of the listener's "memory" in order to establish their own artistic significance.

If Bloom is correct that "strength comes only from a triumphant wrestling with the greatest of the dead" (9) and not from timid recapitulation of an earlier artist's performances, themes, forms, and voice, and if Carriere is correct that his subject strives to surpass her idol, it is Bridgewater's "wrestling" with Fitzgerald's achievements, not her purported efforts to preserve our memory of them, that makes *dear Ella* truly worthwhile.[3] For a number of reasons, including Fitzgerald's justifiably exalted stature in the pantheon of American vocalists, fans of "traditional jazz singing" are unlikely to feel that this tribute is the work of a singer who is able to transcend her sources. Nevertheless, taken together, Bridgewater's and Carriere's conflicting assertions establish the parameters (what, following Robert Scholes's formulations that I discussed in the introduction, we could call a "two-faced activity")—reverential, preservationist recapitulation, on the one hand, and, on the other, combative reinvention—that mark the tribute album in particular, and the cover song generally, as a distinctive interpretative genre.

Somewhat ironically, in the era that inspired the aforementioned attempts by Belle and Bridgewater to preserve favored vocal practices, Dinah Washington's reputation as a major artist is being kept alive in part by Columbia, a company for which she never worked, which has made Franklin's *Unforgettable* widely available to record buyers interested in the Queen of Soul's musical origins. Franklin's reissued tribute is considered the finest album she recorded during her often frustrating apprenticeship that spanned the first half of the 1960s, and includes the original liner notes to which I refer above. Authored by songwriter and jazz historian Leonard Feather, these notes are prefaced by a 1963 declaration by Washington that the younger singer, the daughter of her "good friend," Reverend Franklin, "has got soul." Over and above other possible justifications for the release—including Washington's death, the quality of the tracks, and the "many differences between Dinah's approach and Aretha's"—Feather points to its soulfulness, "the element Dinah noticed after she had listened to the first four bars [of Franklin's performance] that evening in Detroit." For Feather, soul, "the indispensable depth of feeling for which no substitution is valid and no imitation will suffice," is the most significant quality that they share as artists, "the vital common denominator" that makes Washington irreplaceable (he insists "there will never be another Dinah") and animates "the unique and exciting presence of a 21-year-old girl named Aretha Franklin, with a future as big as her soul."

Feather's remarks concerning Franklin's grand future turned out to be prophetic, but not until Franklin left Columbia for Atlantic in 1966, where, under the stewardship of Jerry Wexler, she established herself as an exemplar of gospel-inspired secular singing and, it could be argued, as the best pop vocalist of the twentieth century. Despite the assistance of first-rate producers, arrangers, and musicians at Columbia, Franklin was, if not an out-and-out failure, a mystifying underachiever, incapable of approaching the commercial success that the studio's executives and her own perplexed advisors believed her talent merited and which R & B acts at Motown, Stax, Atlantic, and elsewhere were regularly experiencing. *Unforgettable* can be seen as her attempt to demonstrate her readiness, in the wake of the Queen's death and a decade after she had been bequeathed the role by Washington herself, to assume the mantle of "the next one," the most consequential link in the chain of black female vocalists that includes Bessie, Billie, Ella, Sarah, and Dinah.

Franklin's autobiography, *Aretha: From These Roots*, coauthored by noted R & B chronicler David Ritz, greatly assists our efforts to comprehend both the implications of influence as she understands and represents them and the anxieties that she felt when she was a singer unable to achieve her potential and after her establishment as the quintessential soul singer. Concerning itself not with communicating "the way [she'd] always felt about" Washington (which words attributed to her in the album's notes claim to be its raison d'être) but with transforming how critics, journalists, fans, family members, and artists she has herself influenced feel about *her*—despite and more important because of her regal achievements—Franklin's autobiography uses this album and other strategically selected moments from her life to reshape the legacy both of the struggling artist she had been and of the Queen of Soul, more than three decades into her reign, whose regal symbolic headwear observers have perceived as a veritable crown of thorns.

Suffering with the Blues?
Autobiography as Regal Contestation

One assessment of *From These Roots* characterizes it as a "light account of her life . . . so filtered it amounts to little more than a very controlled interview" (MrLucky).[4] While the reviewer sees its limited forthrightness as evidence that "she has no business writing a book or telling her story," the autobiography is nonetheless revelatory in its depictions of Franklin's feelings about the burdens she experiences as a consequence of her accomplishments. According to loved ones, music critics, and adoring fans, her cultural role as Queen of Soul necessarily positions her in a deep, dark, inescapably blue sea of personal suffering along with predecessors such as Smith, Holiday, and Washington, a notion of cosmic predestination she flatly rejects. As a consequence, her book is not a laborious act of memory and imagination, but a breezy summary of a sun-drenched life whose painful moments are referenced primarily because they offer opportunities for her to correct negative, embarrassing, or otherwise wrongheaded conceptions. Aware of the widely circulated views that her life has been inundated with and defined by trauma (for decades, books and articles have been littered with reports of her being abandoned by her mother and unlucky in love, and of her becoming, as a result, a painfully shy recluse imprisoned in her own misery) she uses *From These Roots* to argue that reports that her life is a tragic blues odyssey are highly exaggerated.

The autobiography offers a combative Franklin wrestling with people whose treatment of her or versions of her character she finds hurtful. It is laden with scenes of Franklin in conflict with young female peers; her beloved, but jealous and misguided, sisters; a famous unnamed performer at a major awards show; prominent younger singers whose styles she influenced, such as Natalie Cole, Luther Vandross, and Whitney Houston; well-established and emerging record producers; and even—as she informs us in the following passage—an unnamed person during her father's funeral: "I got so mad I gave one person (who shall remain unnamed) a shove, thinking, Don't you dare disrespect this service and my father and our last moments with him. Jesse Jackson stepped between us, I caught myself, and my respect for the church and what was at hand prevailed. Immediately thereafter we entered the sanctuary; my knees buckled, but I managed to stay standing and started down the aisle" (206). This combative spirit clouds Franklin's judgment, both at her beloved father's funeral and as she recollects the event for the reader; she seems unaware of the fact that, however troubling the "unnamed" person's act of disrespect may have been, since she does not identify it, she renders the reader incapable of assessing anything other than the inappropriate nature of her own actions. But more important than depicting herself as refined, sophisticated, or heartbroken is her desire to project herself as the mythic, combative, strong woman ubiquitous in the black cultural imagination. Indeed, it is her emphasis on her combativeness that I want to consider in light of Franklin's ascension to the status of the Queen of Soul following the death of the reigning deity, Dinah Washington. However else we might think of her tribute album, it was, at the very least, integral to her and her record company's efforts to construct a vehicle, after nearly five years of commercially unsuccessful and increasingly less impressive efforts, that would showcase her vocal gifts and establish her as the next great black female star.

Bloom's insistence that emerging artists establish their identities by attempting to outstrip the most luminous achievements of their precursors informs my efforts to investigate the relationship between the recently deceased Queen and the young and gifted Franklin, who was in grave danger of becoming a brief footnote at best in black musical history. Bloom's subject, of course, is canonical white male poetry, whose tradition-minded creators devise phrases, sentences, and verses to contend with both their indebtedness to their artistic fathers and the fact that "a poem is a response to a poem, as a poet is a response to a poet" (Bloom, *Map* 1). Clearly as compelled by the politics of succession as Bloom's poet—in an especially apt phrase, he references "the voice of the other . . . always speaking in one who has survived death"—Franklin's tribute features "response[s]" to songs associated with a forebear; it is an album whose purpose is, in part, to enable Columbia and the young singer "to capitalize on the sudden public interest in Dinah's work" caused by her death (Bego 61). In the process, Franklin strives not merely to step into footprints left by her idol, but, after her journey to—and through—her catalogue, to leave her own deeper, more permanent marks.

Whether we accept Bego's view that Franklin's life is uniquely emblematic of "the melancholy and heartfelt sound of the blues" or, for that matter, the suggestion of Mahalia Jackson that Reverend Franklin's daughter, like "anybody that sings the blues[,] is in a deep pit, yelling for help" (33), certainly we might recognize parallels between her consideration of an idol's blues, pop songs, and modes of performance and Washington's own efforts to perfect her craft by paying close attention to the subtle vocal style of her own predecessor, idol, and, later, friend, Billie Holiday. As I have suggested, Holiday's style had a major impact on the young Washington, a "mesmerized" fan who "returned night after night" to hear her sing at a popular lounge in Chicago,

> making mental notes on her stage demeanor as well as her phrasing. . . .
>
> Lady Day sang without extravagant gestures: She swayed her body slightly, snapped her fingers to the tempo, relied on her voice to hold the attention of the audience. Dinah was accustomed to more outright acting on stage and she began to tone down her own presentation, trying to see

if she, too, could hold an audience with the sheer power of her singing. She studied Holiday's singing style closely, too. According to Jimmy Cobb, to whom she later spoke often of her time playing at Garrick's upstairs from Billie Holiday, "She got so she could mimic Lady Day—she could really sound like her. Later, every now and then she would do that on the stage—not too often, but when something led up to it, and she felt good, she would do it." (Haskins 21)

Her origins as a church performer notwithstanding, Washington's recorded voice reflects much less the boisterous, rafters-shaking emotionality of gospel than the subtle, microphone-enhanced intimacies of nightclub, jazz, and torch singing most typically associated with figures such as Holiday. In Washington's case, the lines of stylistic descent are clearly traceable in her use of aspects of Holiday's "stage demeanor," "phrasing," and "singing style" in her own imaginative, seemingly refined artistic self-presentation.

While the future Queen of the Blues emulated Holiday, as a teenager Franklin "decided that the person after whom she most wanted to fashion herself was Dinah Washington"; indeed, Bego posits that "it wasn't just the blues in general that fascinated Aretha; it was the music of one particular blues singer: Dinah Washington" (33). Contending that she was "a very important catalyst in Aretha's life" and career (35), Bego cites musicians who, having witnessed her behavior during and especially after the older singer's performances in Detroit in the late 1950s and early 1960s, believed she "worshipped" Washington (36). Despite being herself a seasoned gospel performer who had interacted, in her home and elsewhere, with figures such as Mahalia Jackson, Martin Luther King Jr., and Sam Cooke, the young Franklin behaved "just like a groupie . . . pay[ing] homage" to and "mesmerized by her self-confident and flamboyant" idol, who "was exactly what Aretha longed to become—a magical songstress who seemed to be in total control of her personal life" (37).

Nearly a decade before commenting on Aretha's soulful performance in late 1963, Washington offers a similar appraisal that was overheard by Lloyd Jones, who was present when she confidently informed his brother Quincy, who produced albums for both the Queen of the Blues and, much later, Franklin, "Rev. C. L. Franklin has a twelve-year-old daughter up in Detroit named Aretha. She's the next one. You watch" (Jones 107). Unlike Patti Austin, whose father was a close friend of Washington's and who, in fact, became her "surrogate daughter, as well as her protégé" (Haskins 102), the shy Aretha never actively sought the attention of an artist who served as an enthusiastic mentor to young performers such as Austin, the Hines Brothers, and Little Esther Phillips (Haskins 86–87). In stark contrast to Austin's portrait of her intimate connection with Washington, whose support—which included helping her get a recording contract— was, she contends, "the reason that [she was] in the industry" (Haskins 176), Franklin depicts herself as physically removed and emotionally distanced from the older singer. The daughter of a mother who left Detroit when she was six and died four years later and of an exceptionally busy single father, as we will see, Franklin was, in Mahalia Jackson's view at least, desperate for mature female nurturance, which she received most consistently from her grandmother and gospel great Clara Ward, the close friend (and possible lover) of Franklin's father whom Aretha identifies as "my greatest influence" (Franklin and Ritz 154).

But while she acknowledges that she "would not have minded" having had Ward—whom she loved deeply—as a stepmother, Franklin appears vehemently opposed to the idea of Washington's serving as a substitute mother and artistic mentor. Note, for example, her depiction of the Queen's unwilling, even embarrassing, exit from her household: "Once I recall seeing the Queen of the Blues herself, Miss Dinah Washington, right below me." (Aretha was watching from the top of the staircase of her family's house.) "And what a surprise to watch, from my unseen vantage point, as she was being carried out of the house by Ted White, a man I would one day marry. To this day I don't know why White was carrying her out, though I suspect Dinah may have gotten overzealous" (43). Like so much else in *From These Roots*, this scene is so burdened by perspectival distance ("my unseen vantage point") and Franklin's lack of curiosity (her alleged failure subsequently to ask White about the incident) that it seems maddeningly evasive. But from my own interpretive "vantage point," the image of her future husband removing a probably inebriated and sexually aggressive Queen from the Franklin house is sufficiently rich compensation. At the very least, this passage leaves open the possibility that Washington is carried from the house for being "overzealous" with Franklin's dapper father, whom women "pursued . . . aggressively night and day, and in the front row [of his church] sitting rather high. One actually showed up at the house with a suitcase" (27). Certainly, the image is discrediting—the idea of the often married singer's possible pursuit of "Daddy" was so offensive to Franklin that, because of his part in thwarting the brazen older woman's advances, she offers her first husband, whom she depicts generally as a villainous leech, the role of hero here—as White's efforts, and her representations thereof, deny Washington an intimate place in her father's life and, by extension, her own.

Franklin's desire to exile Washington is also apparent in her discussion of the older singer's final removal, as it were, by death:

> Naturally I was stunned by the news of Dinah Washington's death. She was the Queen. When she died in 1963 under tragic circumstances, we were all stunned. It was suggested that I sing a tribute. I was honored to be asked. *Unforgettable*, after her big hit, was the name of the album, and Bob Mersey wrote ten beautiful charts for ten songs I had selected.
>
> As I sang, of course I thought about my brief personal association with Dinah in Detroit, those nights I heard about her walking the bar at the Flame Show Bar, people jammed in twenty deep and spilling out into the streets for blocks. I recalled catching a glimpse of her in Chicago, her hometown, as she sashayed across the parking lot on her way to the newly built Roberts Hotel; her short jacket was stylish and her hat broke beautifully. She was kind of sharp that night. Another time she came by my dressing room at the nightclub on the West Side of Detroit and commented that my shoes needed to be arranged in a more orderly fashion; many times I step out of things and leave them where they are until I return to pick them up. My unspoken response was, *What does she have to do with my dressing room or the arrangement of my shoes?* However, I was highly flattered that the Queen had stopped by to hear me sing. (95–96)

Absent here is anything approaching the heartfelt ruminations of the young singer who was an enthusiastic admirer of Washington's vocal skill and career accomplishments. She focuses not on her former idol's singing—she describes having "heard about," but not witnessing, her stage performances—but her mode of dress and her assumption of maternal prerogatives in response to a messy dressing room. Depicting Washington as a clothes horse who was also a skillful negotiator of the bar and the parking lot, but not as a great singer, Franklin denies the Queen the roles of daunting influence and surrogate maternal advisor.

Read figuratively, Washington's dressing room comment might be seen as an inquiry into whether the young Franklin, whose destiny she'd earlier prophesied, was indeed prepared for her coronation, was ready, in other words, to step into the role—into the neatly arranged shoes—of the black community's vocal Queen. Franklin clearly does not recognize such possible meanings in Washington's concern with her footwear, however, and her autobiography represents *Unforgettable* as something other than evidence of her great respect for a deceased idol. Indeed, the tribute album becomes, for the former "groupie," merely a vehicle, part of her own and Columbia's efforts "to package me more commercially" (96), not an occasion to confront what we could call an anxiety of succession.

According to her autobiography, the voice of Franklin's precursor is no more significant than those of the long list of contemporaries. Denying Washington the status of essential secular musical influence, *From These Roots* presents her as mourned by an unspecified "we," commemorated not because of any particular attachment on the younger singer's part to her music, but at the suggestion of a similarly unspecified "it." The long-established, much-fawned-upon Queen of Soul, Franklin denies Washington's influence even in her discussions of her tribute album, reimagining the musical landscape she enters as one with no dominant figure, no "Queen," but as a level plain ripe for conquest:

> As a nightclub performer, I am mindful of the pioneering women who preceded me, like Dinah Washington, Sarah Vaughan, Lena Horne, Ella Fitzgerald, Hazel Scott, Ruth Brown, Damita Woods, and Joyce Bryant. They were highly respected vocalists who understood the art of elegant presentation. . . .
>
> Other singers working in this vein impressed me. Nina Simone and Betty Carter were wonderful, with unique attitudes and strong personalities. I also loved Andy Bey. Andy and the Bey Sisters worked the Village a great deal during my early years in New York. . . . Andy never got the recognition he deserved. He and his singing sister were jazz originals and brilliant impressionists. So were Blossom Dearie and Peggy Lee. These ladies were hip; they knew how to entertain and stay true to their jazzy roots.
>
> I appreciated many pop vocalists. Rosemary Clooney was cool, and so was Doris Day. I always thought Doris was underrated as a vocalist. I also loved her lighthearted movies and have always wanted to do films in the vein of *Pillow Talk* and *Where Were You When the Lights Went Out?* That was Doris at her comedic best. Her son Terry Melcher was at Columbia during my stint here, and we briefly met. (87–88, 89–90)

While elsewhere in her autobiography she acknowledges Washington, generally, including in her curiously evasive remarks about her tribute album, Franklin's rambling recollections position her as part of a pack of "highly respected" and "pioneering" singers by whom she was "impressed" and of whom she was "mindful." She resists the notion that Washington was any more significant a point of stylistic reference than, say, the "cool" Clooney, despite or perhaps because of the fact that, for an emerging singer in particular, recording an album like *Unforgettable* confirms and directly bestows upon its subject and source a singularly influential and/or honorific place. Franklin's dubious depiction of an artistic field in which Washington's and Clooney's contributions are, for her, equivalent can be understood only if she has forgotten her former idol's impact or if we consider her tribute as, in fact, an act of "individuation" wherein "initial love" has become what Bloom calls "revisionary strife."

Over and over in *From These Roots*, Franklin manifests an abiding concern with artistic succession. She claims her mother, her father, his church's musical director, Reverend James Cleveland, and the legendary gospel performer Clara Ward, as inspiriting influences, while declaring that attempts by music critics to establish John Hammond, Jerry Wexler, Mahalia Jackson, and Washington as largely responsible for her discovery, success, gospel intonations, or secular style are simplistic or simply incorrect. Manifesting a keen desire to correct critical misperceptions of her career, she says, for example, that while she "held Mahalia in high esteem," "Clara Ward was [her] number-one idol and mentor," and that "in future years," "books would credit Hammond for discovering me, but it was Daddy who first realized my talent, and Daddy who first presented me to the public in gospel and prepared me for secular music with tender loving care" (62, 81). In addition, as I've suggested, she discusses at length her own influence on subsequent singers such as Cole, Houston, and Vandross, all of whom she positions as antagonists.

In the case of Luther Vandross, who produced two of her most popular albums of the 1980s, *Jump to It* (1982) and *Get It Right* (1983), and who admits that she had been an idol of his "from whom he had learned much about how to sing," Franklin became offended when "all of a sudden Luther wanted to tell [her] how to sing":

> His job was to produce and advise the artist about phrasing, diction, and melody, and to be adventurous and say certain things, but definitely not

say, "Sing it like this." I definitely didn't need him to tell me how it should be sung. Well, Mr. Vandross wanted to know who had produced my recent number one, and I felt he should be reminded that I had enjoyed at least twenty gold records before I or the world knew his name. I picked up my coat and walked out of the studio as he and I continued shouting at each other. (194–95)

Similarly, working with Whitney Houston on a duet became a contentious experience when the younger singer, who "intimated to *Jet* and *Ebony* that [Franklin] had inspired and influenced her," but with whom Franklin was "very badly mismatched in terms of maturity and experience and sensitivity," started to feel "unappreciated" by her "Aunt Ree." For her part, "Aunt Ree" declares that she "continue[s] to appreciate her and sincerely wish her the best" and invites the troubled younger singer to "come to [her] for support or advice anytime" (224). Placed alongside her abiding concern with the issue of influence, Franklin's depictions of her involvement in generational conflict as the Queen whose dominance of the field is greater than Washington's had been when she was herself an ephebe suggests that considering her tribute album as an act of revisionary strife may prove quite fruitful indeed.

"Our Lady of Mysterious Sorrows"

David Ritz's prefatory remarks in *From These Roots* emphasize the thoroughness of the four-year "process" of collaborating with the "careful and conscientious" Queen on her autobiography and, more important, Franklin's desire to correct the inaccurate accounts of her life and character that had circulated "for well over thirty years":

Journalists have often given us the impression of an Aretha they do not know. They've analyzed and mythologized, speculated and flat-out invented a character who bears little resemblance to the real Aretha, the Aretha sitting in the living room telling you about her father, her fond remembrances of Sam Cooke, her passion for roller skating, her days playing teenybop hops one night and sophisticated supper clubs the next, her feelings about other divas and other days when disco pulled the rug from under the soul stars and life was a challenge. . . .

In this book, which she has waited a lifetime to write, Aretha speaks for herself. (xi–xiii)

According to Franklin, the genesis both of widespread misrepresentations of her as a singer who lives the blues and of her subsequent wariness of the press was *Time*'s June 28, 1968, cover story about soul music. In a profile identifying her as its exemplar following the release of her first Atlantic album, *I Never Loved a Man the Way I Love You*, and featuring testimonies from figures such as Ray Charles, who proclaimed her "one of the greatest I've heard any time," and Janis Joplin, who called her "the best chick singer since Billie Holiday," Franklin—Lady Soul—is depicted as a deeply pained young woman. To support his claim that "her mother deserted the family when Aretha was six and died four years later, two shocks that deeply scarred the shy, withdrawn girl," the author, Christopher John Farley, cites the informed views of a family friend, Mahalia Jackson, the most celebrated gospel singer of the twentieth century, who notes that "after her mama died . . . , the whole family wanted for love."

The "deeply scarred," love-starved Aretha was raised primarily by the "barnstorming evangelist" father, Reverend C. L. Franklin, the charismatic pastor of Detroit's New Bethel Baptist Church. Describing him as "strapping stentorious charmer who has never let his spiritual calling inhibit his funloving ways," the article informs us that he was convicted in 1967 of income tax evasion, and that he encouraged his daughter to perform on his national gospel caravan tours, during which she was exposed to "post-performance parties among older troupers in hotel rooms, where the liquor and sex were both plentiful." As a consequence of these experiences, Franklin "remains cloaked in a brooding sadness, all the more achingly impenetrable because she rarely talks about it—except when she sings." The burdens about which she "rarely" speaks include her relationship with her then husband, Ted White, "a former dabbler in Detroit real estate and a street-corner wheeler-dealer," who "roughed her up in public at Atlanta's Regency Hyatt House Hotel."

If soul music is, according to the article, "suffused with the sensual, somewhat melancholy vibrations of the Negro idiom," the combination of Franklin's immense talent and inescapable "sadness" made her its poster child in the wake of the *Time* profile, after which analyses invariably referred to her as a melancholy blues woman. For example, in his autobiography, *The Rhythm and the Blues*, Jerry Wexler, who had a hand in virtually all of her seminal releases during the late 1960s and early 1970s, calls her "Our Lady of Mysterious Sorrows. Her eyes are incredible, luminous eyes covering inexplicable pain. Her depressions could be as deep as the dark sea. . . . [A]nguish surrounds Aretha as surely as the glory of her musical aura." Wexler continues, "As we worked together—over the next eight years we would do fourteen albums—there were times when she would call me late at night and express some of the sorrow in her soul, intimating problems at home" (212). After noting that "*Time*'s cover story branded her as a 'victim' and battered wife and forever reinforced her in-grained fear of interviews and publicity," Peter Guralnick speculates in *Sweet Soul Music* that, like Elvis Presley (whose life he would later explore in exquisite detail), Franklin, "'plagued with a feeling of insecurity' . . . , found solace only in withdrawal" (344, 347–48). And utilizing a similar thesis, Bego, who "confessed to her that it was [his] dream to collaborate with her someday on her autobiography," responded to Franklin's rebuff ("I'm not interested in doing that," she said, "I don't want to write a book") with a biography whose emphasis is her "inexplicable pain": "Jerry Wexler has stated that an underlying sadness surrounds Aretha's personal life. When I asked him to clarify his comment, he replied, 'Well, it wasn't ca-price or temperament, it was just sadness.' I set out to discover the cause of Aretha's sadness" (2, 3). Bego's efforts to verify the aforementioned commentators' hypotheses led him, for example, to describe her teenage pregnancies not as a result of unprotected sex with boys in her age group (as she later insists in her autobiography), but as part of "a pattern of vic-timization by the men in her life" whose "traumatic" effects were such that, "at the age of fifteen, Aretha Franklin had already earned the right to sing the blues" (32).

Seeking to counteract what must have felt like an almost unrelent-ing deluge of negative analyses of her life, an understandably defensive Franklin uses *From These Roots*—the type of work she told Bego more than a decade earlier she had no interest in collaborating on with him and which, according to Ritz, she had "waited a lifetime to write"—to con-struct a public image of herself as an empowered, joyous, down-to-earth woman. Looked at as discursive "wrestling" over how she is portrayed, as a text in which she feels compelled to do battle even with her beloved sisters Erma (whose public insistence that the Queen of Soul "was an introvert" she lambasts as "the biggest lie ever told about me") and the deceased Carolyn (whose expression of concern about her famous sister's ability to survive the 1984 death of their long-comatose father Franklin interprets as questioning her "faith and trust in God" and "strength of character" [233]), an otherwise shallow autobiography becomes a quite intriguing self-portrait.

Note, for example, her extensive commentary on Farley's article for *Time*:

> When I learned I was going to be put on the cover of *Time* magazine, I was excited and pleased. They were calling the story "The Sound of Soul" and saw me as a symbol of the soul explosion that had enthralled the nation. As it turned out, though, *Time* became the main source of the false and thoughtless lies about my mother abandoning her children, which Gladys Knight and Cissy Houston perpetuated in their memoirs. I don't understand why neither lady bothered to ask me whether the story was true before printing it, since, like all public figures, they themselves must have been the subject of incorrect press as well.
>
> The article also painted me as a woman trapped by the blues, like Bessie Smith and Billie Holiday. Nothing could be further from the truth. I am Aretha, upbeat, straight-ahead, and not to be worn out by men and left singing the blues. *Time* described alleged incidents between Ted White and myself, some of which were not reported accurately. Even worse, my own words were taken out of context and turned around to make the writer's point. Due to the stature of *Time*, the mistakes were picked up by countless writers in the years ahead and reported as a fact. For a long time I declined many interviews because I did not trust certain journalists. I didn't want my words taken out of context; I certainly didn't want a false picture of myself. In my professional growth and maturity, however, I have learned how to address such matters and have done many wonderful (and accurately reported) interviews. (123)

Franklin clearly does not object to being turned into a symbol; as she tells her readers, soon after the release of *I Never Loved a Man* and not long before the *Time* cover story appeared, she was "anointed . . . Queen of Soul" by "noted disc jockey, Pervis Spann." "He placed a beautifully bejeweled crown on my head, and I still cherish the memory of my silver-sequined gown. The only queens I had known of were Dinah Washington and Elizabeth I and II. To be considered worthy of the same title held by Dinah was an honor of the highest order" (118). But while she embraces her new title, Franklin resists the notion that, in addition to prodigious talent and popular acclaim, the "anointed" female exemplar of the blues tradition must experience, and persevere in the face of, levels of almost unimaginable pain that reportedly mar—while, at the same time, enable our mythologizing of—the lives of earlier members of black female vocal royalty. Historically, the blues queen's narrative evinces the depths of her implication in, and struggle to survive in the face of, the most debilitating of human heartaches; the painful experiences and early deaths of Smith, Holiday, and Franklin's most direct predecessor, Washington, are deemed not merely symbolic but evidence of a necessary correlation in the lives of black female royalty between pain and artistry.

The cultural significance of these female artists involves their capacity both to endure deeply troubled blues lives and to transform the resultant pain into great, highly emotional singing. In other words, these queens are represented as having been saddled with tragic circumstances (including, of course, no-count lovers) whose survival energizes their responses to love-gone-wrong lyrics, helping them hone vocal styles that, despite their differences, effectively convey their capacity to thrive—albeit, at times, just barely—in the face of almost unbearable burdens.[5] *From These Roots* grapples with the power of such suppositions to shape impressions of preeminent black female singers—including, ironically, Franklin's own views of her predecessors—even as it insists that they limit the capacity of critics and fans to develop a cogent understanding of the Queen of Soul's life. While she embraces the views of informed listeners that her talent is comparable to Holiday's (she quotes John Hammond, the producer of both Bessie Smith's last and Billie Holiday's first recordings, who "praised [her] as having the best voice he had heard since Holiday" [81]), she resists the notion that, like Lady Day, her ability to perform the blues is the result of her survival of its negative impact on her life. And despite having to contend with misrepresentations of her and of her mother's presence in her life that she chides contemporaries like Knight and Houston for believing and repeating publicly, she is nevertheless willing to accept on faith what may be the equally "false and thoughtless lies" that inform widely embraced characterizations of Smith and Holiday as women "trapped by the blues."

Franklin also insists that *Time* offers a "false picture" of, among other things, her relationship with White, while acknowledging that only "some" of the details of the reporting were not "accurate," and informs us that "my own words were taken out of context and turned around to make the writer's point." It appears that, in addition to the obvious pain this widely disseminated picture of her blues life caused her, the article's ability to shape public perceptions may have suggested to her that she could manipulate autobiographical facts in order to assert her own corrective point of view. For if *Time* got "some" of the details of troubles in her first marriage wrong, it got others right, and that combination of truth and falsity, along with its acknowledgment of both her talents and her blues-filled life, has come to determine her identity for music critics and fans alike. A contentious response to the continuing power of these views of her early life, many of which she knows to be either wholly false or only partially true, simultaneously to exalt and imprison her in and as a gloriously limited symbol, "the Queen of Soul," Franklin's autobiography can be said to constitute her own skewing of familiar "truths" in an effort to reshape her public image. *From These Roots* joins autobiographical self-scrutiny, which is always fundamentally incomplete and, hence, necessarily only partially truthful, and public relations, whose emphasis is the marketing of appealing aspects of the life of a celebrated person rather than its honest rendering.

Franklin's concerns with autobiographical truth and public relations are apparent, for example, in her discussions of White, in which her refusal to mask her disdain leads her to attempt literally to write him out of her musical legacy. Their relationship is presented as incontrovertible evidence of her youthful blindness, as the naive, love-starved single mother of two was initially able to have a relatively "peace[ful] relationship" with him despite the fact that "he was seeing young ladies other than myself." Later, perhaps to avoid the critical gaze of her preacher-father, whose disapproval of Franklin's boyfriend was reportedly quite intense, they "were married by a justice of the peace on the road somewhere in Ohio" after "White's spontaneous suggestion," though Franklin claims not to "recall why I was not married in New Bethel with Daddy presiding" (104).[6] Describing her singlemindedness, once she signs with Atlantic, Franklin characterizes herself, at that point a relatively new bride, as a "young woman . . . into music and music only," and her husband's contributions—he's listed as coauthor of such important songs as "Dr. Feelgood," "Think," and "Since You've Been Gone"—as consisting only of "a few of the lyrics here and there, but the majority of my songs came from my heart and soul and were created solely by me" (110).[7]

Indeed, whatever negative repercussions Franklin believes resulted from the *Time* article, it undoubtedly helped to cement her status as the Queen of Soul for mainstream audiences and, hence, to increase interest in her work significantly. And if her heightened wariness of the press was one consequence of the article's characterization of her as abused blues woman, another may be her representation of Mahalia Jackson, whose seemingly informed remarks about Franklin's life are featured prominently. Jackson is quoted in *Time* as saying that her mother's absence was particularly painful for the sensitive young Franklin: "I don't think she's happy. Somebody else is making her sing the blues"; Jackson adds that Aretha confessed to her, "I'm gonna make a gospel record . . . , and tell Jesus I cannot bear these burdens alone."

Notwithstanding Franklin's insistence that her "mentor," Clara Ward, "took gospel where gospel had never gone before, introducing the form to the world beyond the black church" (154), Jackson's numerous recordings and television appearances, along with her close public association with Martin Luther King Jr., established her, at the very least, as the preeminent gospel singer of the 1950s and 1960s. Given that stature, Jackson's comments, which lent credence to the article's depiction of Franklin as a woman suffering with the blues, were partly responsible for helping to shape public perception of the younger singer. But if, as the *Time* article reports, Jackson had been a close enough family friend to serve as Franklin's confidant, she is, at best, a limited presence in the autobiography. Indeed, in her most extensive appearance in *From These Roots* (Franklin's description of the aftermath of her participation in a gospel program sponsored by the gospel luminary), Jackson looms as an authoritative, insensitive figure whose behavior harms the barely teenaged novice:

> Even though Clara Ward was my number-one idol and mentor, I held Mahalia in high esteem. Mahalia was downhome and a devout Christian; she fondly told the story of wrestling alligators in her native New Orleans before she moved to Chicago. Mahalia had a depth of soul and a majesty about her. She was a pious woman and absolutely sincere; you felt how deeply she loved the Lord.
>
> When she praised my performance and thanked me for coming, I took it as the highest compliment. After the concert, though, one small matter still lingered in my mind: I hadn't been paid. That evening I didn't say anything to Mahalia. I was just too shy to ask her for money. I looked up to her

and found it hard to put my thoughts to words. This was my first time away from my dad, and I had no idea how to state my request. I was just hoping she'd hand me an envelope. I was all packed up and ready to head for the airport when I decided to call her. I really did want to get paid.

"Miss Jackson," I said.

"Yes, baby, what is it?"

"This is Aretha, and I just wanted to say that I'm leaving to go home."

"Well, that's fine, baby. Be sure and tell your daddy hello for me."

"I will."

"And . . . uh . . . Miss Jackson . . ."

"Yes?"

"I just wanted to say good-bye."

"Okay, Good-bye, Aretha, and thanks so much for coming."

Finally, I asked, "What do you want me to do, Miss Jackson?"

"What do I want you to do about what?" she asked. "Why, I want you to go home, baby. Everything is over."

"I mean about being paid."

"Okay, baby, I'll talk to your dad about it."

So I left Chicago with my heart broken. (63–64)

Jackson subsequently disappears from the text, despite her central role in crucial events about which Franklin writes or in which she was involved: King's funeral (which Franklin herself attended); the gospel singer's own funeral in 1972 (at which Franklin performed); and the live recording and commercial success of *Amazing Grace*, the gospel album she promised Jackson she would make to help her to release her "burden." Given Franklin's use of her autobiography to settle old scores, it is possible that, because of her role in the *Time* article that established Franklin's public image as blues sufferer, Jackson is denied a central place in the Queen's career narrative, and is represented (albeit in an intentionally amusing fashion) as an insensitive adult female who literally refuses to give the young singer her due and is, hence, not worthy of the "high esteem" in which Franklin had held her.

Later, Franklin is able to turn the tables, as it were, refusing, in quite dramatic fashion, to honor Jackson's contributions publicly. After signing a contract in early 1984 to star in the musical *Sing, Mahalia, Sing*, Franklin withdrew from a tailor-made part that, coming in the wake of her memorable cameo appearance in *The Blues Brothers*, she believed could have propelled her to a level of multimedia stardom on a par with Diana Ross and Barbra Streisand. The role, she admits, would have allowed her to "spread [her] wings" artistically by offering her a setting to display characteristics she had in common with her long-deceased family's friend: "religious convictions" and the ability to "stomp-down, flat-footed sing" (203). She also shared with Jackson a fear of flying, precipitated, in Franklin's case, by a terrifying experience while traveling from Atlanta in early 1983 on a two-engine prop airplane that "did a couple of those drastic drops" and had its passengers "bouncing all over the sky" (200). Not able to fly to New York from Detroit to begin rehearsals for her role, she set out by car. She writes that "after being on the road four or five hours, all I could see in front of me was highway. With another fourteen or fifteen hours to go, I didn't think I could make it. It didn't occur to me to break up the drive into two days. So we turned around and headed back. I had to pass on playing Mahalia" (203). Clearly, some dissembling is apparent here. Even figuring frequent rest stops into the equation, it is hard to imagine anyone needing eighteen to twenty hours to traverse the approximately 650 miles of highway between suburban Detroit and Manhattan, just as it seems unlikely that the thought of "break[ing] up the drive" didn't occur to Franklin or someone with whom she was traveling. Whatever else contributed to her refusal to honor her commitment to portray Jackson, which ultimately led to her having to pay the show's producers over $200,000 (Bego 300), her general combativeness, emphasis on settling scores, and sense of her own iconic stature may all have been factors in her decision ultimately not to play a part that called on her to embody, and help to solidify the legacy of, a precursor—as Diana Ross, struggling to establish herself as a solo artist after leaving the Supremes, did a decade earlier by playing Billie Holiday in *Lady Sings the Blues*—whose commentary about her maternal longings and romantic troubles helped permanently to define Franklin as a woman of deep, unyielding sorrow.

A few other examples of Franklin's discursive wrestling in her autobiography should suffice. Another figure who suffers in *From These Roots* for helping to shape the public image of the Queen of Soul as a symbol of victimization is her contemporary and former friend Gladys Knight. During her discussion of one of the most traumatic events in twentieth-century American history, the assassination of Martin Luther King Jr., Franklin chides Knight and the members of the Pips who, after finagling transportation on the airplane she had chartered to attend the funeral, failed "to say thank you for the free ride" (119). And in a strategic swerve following her praise of the Sweet Inspirations, who often sang background on her 1970s recordings, she identifies Knight for a second time (along with lead Inspiration Cissy Houston) as a perpetuator of false, painful rumors:

> When the Inspirations showed up, we knew there was gonna be some serious singing. Unfortunately, over the years Cissy and I didn't get to know each other out of the studio. But I have always regarded her as a friend, although I feel she is confused these days about certain things regarding my family and statements that she and Gladys Knight have made about me. (I realize that Gladys has been under an extreme pressure having to do with career disappointments. I truly am sympathetic and will pray for her.) (117)

These catty, patronizing remarks are obviously intended to wound Knight, one of the most successful and enduring vocalists to have emerged during the reign of Lady Soul, whom she elsewhere derides, as we have seen, for failing to check the veracity of the stories she's heard concerning maternal abandonment. Certainly Knight was well past her heyday as a chart contributor when *From These Roots* appeared, but so, too, was Franklin, who, except for the success of her hip hop-influenced release, *A Rose Is Still A Rose*, had not released a noteworthy album since 1986's *Who's Zooming Who?* And, clearly, Knight's "career" cannot be viewed as disappointing even if Franklin's transcendent work is the sole measure of success; indeed, their careers are parallel in terms of their length and record sales, if not critical acclaim.[8] I'm not concerned here with the question of their relative merits as artists, but with how Franklin's curt dismissal of Knight demonstrates the lengths to which she went to diminish or belittle those figures whom she believed either have tarnished her image or challenged her right—to use Bego's discussion of the reasons for a young Aretha's admiration of Washington—"to be in total control of [representations of] her personal life" (37), to determine the public nature and meanings of her own life.

Before I move back to the subject of Franklin's engagement of Dinah Washington, I want to examine a telling moment in which she participates in precisely the sort of potentially injurious rumor mongering for which she castigates Knight, Houston, and *Time*. Speaking of the sales of "Angel," written primarily by Franklin's sister, Carolyn, Franklin relates the opinions of unnamed friends that Wexler was furious because she'd replaced him with Quincy Jones as the producer of the 1973 album (*Hey Now Hey* [*The Other Side of the Sky*]) from which this achingly beautiful single was taken. According to Franklin's friend, Wexler sought, as a consequence of his anger, to undermine the single's capacity to become a million seller:

> Carolyn had written soaring melodies before, but none soared higher than "Angel." The song had wings. It combined loneliness and hope in a way that spoke directly to the heart. "Angel" sold in excess of 900,000 copies and was about to hit a million records when Jerry Wexler told me to make a decision to continue promoting "Angel" or record "Bridge over Troubled Water" right away. The label explained if we didn't record and release "Bridge" then, it would be too late. Well, I had no idea "Angel" was so close to a million records, and I felt that, regardless of "Bridge," it seemed to be a hit and would go all the way. But some people felt "Bridge" was deliberately intended to stop the sale of "Angel" before one million. Truthfully, I cannot comment one way or the other. "Bridge" hit as well, but I've always regretted that "Angel" wasn't given a longer life. Tension developed between Quincy [who produced the album on which "Angel" appeared] and Jerry Wexler. I'm afraid Q thought I could have been more supportive of him. I didn't realize what the problem was until long after it was over. (157)

Given her emphasis on the pain that the wide dissemination of half-truths and unsubstantiated rumors has caused her, Franklin's willingness to sling mud here is startling. Essentially, she intimates that her long-time producer sabotaged the potentially stratospheric success of "Angel" because he did not want a single that he did not himself produce for Franklin to achieve such a status.

Wexler, if you will recall, is a figure who labeled her "Our Lady of Mysterious Sorrows," a formulation that has become nearly as central a part of her "star story" as her soulful voice and soaring interpretive powers. As a result, his importance as a producer, record executive, and friend is glossed over in *From These Roots*. While she acknowledges his crucial role in her career—she described him as a "warm and personal" figure who "made me feel secure and comfortable," and praises him for recognizing, unlike the executives of Columbia, the importance of basing the music around her, "not only my feeling for the song but my piano playing and basic rhythm arrangement, my overall concept" (108)—she offers no hint of the personal connection Wexler claims they shared. Rather, she suggests that his refusal to credit her fully for her contributions limited her career significantly:

> As much as I appreciate the soulful studio environment in which Atlantic placed me and the sensitive musicians who played by my side, one point was deceptive and unfair: I was not listed as a co-producer. Wexler was the producer, and later [Tommy] Dowd and [Arif] Mardin were coproducers. Looking back, I see that I certainly fulfilled a coproducer's role. At the time I didn't realize the crucial significance of my function. And in the music business few people tell you anything, particularly if you don't ask. No one volunteers pertinent information. (111)

She portrays Wexler as a petty figure who robs her of money ("little did I know how much money was going back and forth across the table until my awakening"), a platinum single, and an official title ("a coproducer's role") that would have offered her additional financial recompense, further confirmation of her extensive contributions to her soulful sound, and opportunities to nurture emerging artists. (She goes on to say that "sometimes I wonder what would have happened if I had been a credited producer early on. I may well have had another career as a producer of other artists, soundtracks, commercials, and so on" [150].) While Wexler's autobiography speaks lovingly of her both as a person and an artist, and while he credits her for the fact that, despite "her reliance on unreliable men . . . , [she] actually broke the chain of songs of self-pity, those poignant but somewhat masochistic lyrics sung by her mythic soul sisters like Bessie, Dinah, and Billie" (215), as I have suggested, Wexler also confirms impressions of Franklin's personal life as that of a quintessential blues woman or "mythic soul sister." He speaks of her "inexplicable pain," "depression," and "anguish," and calls her both "Our Lady of Mysterious Sorrows" and, in less honorific terms, "a woman of impenetrable solitude" (212–13), characterizations that appear on pages that feature a stunning photograph of her clearly about to drown in her own tears, an image that provides powerful visual support for his contentions. In response, Franklin handles him as roughly as she does others of whose views of herself she disapproves. In this case, she casts racially charged aspersions (the white oppressor of black talent; the greedy Jewish businessman stealing from unsuspecting blacks) at a figure whom black record executives hung in effigy in the late-1960s to underscore their call for "black political power, black economic power, black management job, black owner-ship, [and] black-run labels," and who was told by a black industry insider that he had been marked for assassination (because of perceptions that he had stolen from the black artists with whom he had worked) during a 1968 convention he attended to accept an award "on Aretha's behalf" (Wexler 227).

Toward a Reading of *Unforgettable*: A Rationale

I will not discuss in detail all of the songs that comprise Franklin's tribute to Washington. Even if Nelson George is correct that her "voice commu-nicated so wide a range of emotion as to truly defy description" and that the body of her Atlantic output reveals "not one Aretha Franklin but a cast of hundreds of women: some sweet, some mad, some cool, some sad, some angry, and a great many playful and sexy" (105–6), the songs on *Unforgettable* that are most crucial to her efforts to develop a signature artistic voice are not those on which she adopts a mode of presentation "similar" to Washington's "moody expressiveness" (Bego 61) or the "vein of black popular music of the day" that is called "sophisticated cocktail swing" (*Rolling Stone Illustrated* 130). In my view, there is nothing par-ticularly distinctive about her versions of "Unforgettable" and "What A Diff'rence A Day Makes," and certainly nothing that will cause us nec-essarily either to recall them fondly or to forget performances of these classic songs by Washington or, for that matter, by Nat "King" Cole and Washington's protégé Esther Phillips, respectively. Like her covers of these songs from Washington's late period, Franklin's versions of "Don't Say You're Sorry Again," "This Bitter Earth," and "If I Should Lose You" are highly orchestrated period pieces that "vividly display," as Leonard Feather states, "Aretha's musical and emotional range," but do little to suggest the "fierce, gritty conviction" (George 105) that emanates from her more accomplished soul performances. (Still, I want to acknowledge that her rendition of "This Bitter Earth" is absolutely wonderful.) Since, as George (echoing Franklin and Wexler) understands, she became Lady Soul only when she began recording with a producer who "gave her voice the kind of complementary musical backing" that suited "her gospel-style piano" and singing, Franklin's skill at Washingtonesque shading is less relevant here than those occasions when she employed songs recorded by her predecessor as templates for the multifacted blues and spirited, gospel-inspired style that distinguish her from her idol. And finally, despite her own appreciation of what in the liner notes Feather calls its "remarkable technical achievement" and gospel atmospherics, I find little to recommend in "Soulville." Consequently, I concentrate on four songs, "Cold, Cold Heart," "Drinking Again," "Nobody Knows the Way I Feel This Morning," and "Evil Gal Blues," whose discussion will further illuminate the central concerns of this chapter: inheritance, individuated voice, and Franklin's struggle to establish her own regal sonic presence.

"Nobody Knows" "Evil Gal Blues"

One of Washington's earliest hits, "Evil Gal Blues" "dates all the way back to Dinah's very first record session, in 1943, when she was a 19-year-old band vocalist with Lionel Hampton," the esteemed jazz vibraphonist who wrote the song along with Feather. Emphasizing its continuing importance to Washington (the liner notes inform us that "it remained in her repertoire until she sang her final show" two decades later), Feather calls her fans' attention to Franklin's efforts to "give it a more contemporary feeling rhythmically and a more pronounced beat," and alludes to lyrical changes that the young singer's version introduces. Nevertheless, he insists that, despite these changes, "it's still the same old story of the girl who'll 'empty your pockets and fill you with misery.'" In choosing to cover this song whose protagonist is what Haskins calls—in describing both Washington and the Empress of the Blues, Bessie Smith—"rough hewn, [and] moody" (60), Franklin positions herself explicitly in a blues lineage about which Washington was ambivalent at a similar stage in her career precisely because of its putatively negative connotations and its connections to Smith herself.

Washington's tribute to Smith contains "Fine Fat Daddy," which she composed nearly a decade after the death of the Empress; it is a song with stylistic and thematic affinities to her predecessor's quintessential recordings but not, like the other tracks on *Dinah Sings Bessie Smith*, drawn from her catalogue. Although it was produced during a vastly different period in her career, "Evil Gal Blues" represents a similar sort of gesture of appreciation. Along with "Salty Papa Blues," it was Washington's first foray into the world of recorded music as a solo artist and is, in some respects, a prototypical blues tale of a lover seeking ways to endure the misery caused by her man's absence. In response to a suitor's expression of interest in her, the song's persona warns, "I'm an evil gal, don't you bother with me," characterizing herself as a "no good" woman, with "men to the left / Men to the right," "in the east" and "in the west," a woman who will "empty your pockets / And fill you with misery." Because of her "evil" ways, her failure to conform to mainstream notions of American womanhood as constitutionally chaste, unselfish, and monogamous, she recognizes that her own ideal mate is not the sort of conventional, marriage-minded man desirous of sweet reciprocity whose heart is easily broken, but a similarly "evil man."

Indeed, she admits to being "down in the dumps" because she has lost her man—the "man here in Harlem [who] / Always loves [her] the best"— to "Uncle Sam." Using popular nationalist iconography, the song compels us to compare romantic and military endeavors, and to consider her Harlem lover's "misery" as a black man in the segregated armed forces and a participant in World War II. The absence of her ideal man, the result of forces beyond their control and not, as in many other blues songs, of his inconstancy, embitters the persona so profoundly that she appears unable to find pleasure in the attention, sexual and otherwise, of her cadre of men. So even if she was, in a sense, "evil" before her Harlem lover's departure, the lyrics insist that her "misery" stems specifically from the loss of her lover. The song suggests that sexual promiscuity is a constant and is not motivated by her "best" man's absence, so the fact that Washington's "evil gal" fills her male suitors "with misery" is not as significant as her being "down in the dumps" despite her seemingly inexhaustible reserve of men.

Franklin's "Evil Gal" rewrites the verses of this song, while preserving its chorus and bridge that identify the persona as a no-nonsense woman who will "empty your pockets / and fill you with misery." Although she is as concerned as Washington's persona with the gifts potential lovers can offer her, Franklin's "gal" emphasizes her contrary nature rather than the vastness of her male stable. Instead of locating men spatially ("left," "right," "east," and "west"), as does Washington's character, Franklin's gal calls attention to her overt hostility ("If you say, 'hello baby,' / I'm going to give you the evil eye"), lack of faith in male perceptions ("If you tell me, 'good morning,' I'll tell you that's a lie"), and demands to be plied by these same poorly treated suitors with expensive food and wine ("I want caviar for breakfast / Champagne every night") in exchange for her apparently unpleasant company. In Franklin's version, there is no "best" man, no possible resolution of her moral decadence, no sociopolitical situation whose referencing expands our perceptions of the causes and consequences of her persona's behavior, and, most significantly, no circumstances whatsoever that can lead her to feel "down in the dumps." While she is as capable as Washington's persona of causing "misery," she feels none herself, and is motivated only by her hedonistic pursuits.

There are other notable dissimilarities between the two versions of "Evil Gal"—Washington's opens with an extended (over one minute long) instrumental blues prelude dominated by piano, acoustic bass, and drums, while Franklin's, whose nine-second introduction features a gospel-inspired piano performance, gets to the lyrical point much more quickly; Washington's voice assumes a blues tonality similar to Smith's, while Franklin's frame of vocal reference is clearly church testifying; and so on. But the major "difference" (to invoke Franklin's own comparative formulations of her performances of Washington's songs) between the two as narratives is that the cover offers us neither a personal or social context for the gal's pursuits nor a sense that she has experienced deep emotional attachment and the pain of its absence. In other words, in contrast to Washington's gal, for whom misery is something with which she fills others and by which she is herself filled, Franklin's persona, who appears immune to the contagion of romantic love and a sense of global struggle, is simply a shallow, materialistic, happy-go-lucky heartbreaker. Because of its communication of its persona's pain and racially inflected sacrifice, Washington's "Evil Gal Blues" seems a more mature response to life's vicissitudes than Franklin's overhauled, rhythmically appealing version, which represents a spoiled woman-child incapable of deep emotion. Reaching back in "Evil Gal Blues" to Washington's blues beginnings, Franklin recreates the song's persona as less mature and less attuned to world events, someone for whom attitudinal élan is character rather than a means of dealing with the primary thematic emphasis of the blues: the inevitability of the pain of human existence.

In comparison to Washington's world-weary, womanly gal, Franklin's cover presents a persona who is devoid of womanly pain and, hence, hard-earned, hard-edged swagger. Similarly, her version of "Nobody Knows the Way I Feel This Morning," while it does not evince the degree of lyrical revision of her "Evil Gal Blues," also suggests a person unprepared to convey the nuances of the complex blues narrative. Franklin's remake, which presents a woman who is "down in the dumps," like the subject in Washington's "Evil Gal Blues," demonstrates that here at least she is embodying a persona who is willing to confront the pain of love gone wrong. But if the sociopolitical context and the "evil man" who "loves me the best" of "Evil Gal" are mature, complex subjects that Franklin feels compelled in that song to evade, "Nobody Knows" presents her with an even more daunting challenge. Washington's majestic recording, which is over eight minutes long and features exquisite musical accompaniment, is an undeniable tour de force, the near-perfect vehicle for her weary, bent-but-unbroken, plainspoken style that seemed so intimate to fans "sitting behind closed doors, with whatever their problems were," that they believed that "'this gal just sings right to you'" (Haskins 64). Its languid swing and guitar and piano flourishes enhance her excursion through her "flustrated" persona's sometimes contradictory reactions to her lover's choice to "stay . . . out all night / Till morning."

The song characterizes her feelings as uncommunicable ("nobody knows the way I feel this morning"), and while it offers a sense of the despair she experiences and of the responses she considers (including prostituting herself, recognizing that she's so upset at the mere mention of "my daddy's name this morning" that she could "kill you quicker than an express train," and ultimately "leaving here on a southbound train," resolute in the knowledge that "nothing's gonna bring your sweet baby back here again"), both the lyrics and Washington's performance emphasize her reasoned restraint. Unlike, for example, the guilt-ridden, knife-wielding persona of Washington's cover of Bessie Smith's "Send Me to the 'Lectric Chair," whose lover's affair with "a travelling Jane" causes her to go "insane," the persona of "Nobody Knows" resists murderous urges, which—as the speaker of "'Lectric Chair" learns only when she appears before the judge—are ultimately self-destructive. And despite her use of her vocal trademarks, including her poignant delivery of her signature "ooohs," "Lords," and "yeahs," the lyrics emphasize both the ineffability of her feelings and the refusal of a woman at her wit's end to manifest her anger by compromising herself or through violence (though she does give some advice to "girls" whose men are also "stay[ing] out all night": "maul him on the head with your rolling pin"). Restraint is so central to her self-presentation that she resists even the catharsis of screaming, telling us, "I feel like I could scream, holler, and cry / But I'm too stout-hearted, I'd rather die." Surveying a variety of what she holds to be overly emotional and, hence, self-defeating possible reactions to her lover's indiscretions (killing him, selling herself, mauling him with a kitchen tool, screaming, killing him some more), her only productive response, she recognizes, is to pawn her valuables ("my rings, my gold watch, and chains")—gifts, presumably, from her man—in order to collect enough money to book passage on "a southbound train this morning."

The marriage of form, content, and performance in Washington's lengthy track is unassailable. The music's lazy sway, the lyrics' emphasis on restraint, and the singer's cool resignation and refusal to "scream" or otherwise display her anger, either through her actions or by means of her voice, combine to make "Nobody Knows the Way I Feel This Morning" a quintessential expression of her artistry, which, according to Linda Dahl, results from her capacity to "mold a tune with ferocious ease" by toning down her "Wagnerian pipes" and the "latent power in the voice" in order to make "an indelible impression" by "conveying gradations of feeling." Franklin's interpretation of this song displays characteristic aspects of her emerging, overcome-by-the-spirit style quite effectively, but is marked by a musical and especially vocal desperation that is fundamentally at odds with its lyrical imperatives. Franklin's is, in truth, an almost awe-inspiring performance, the equal, in its go-for-broke emotionality, of "Think" and "Spirit in the Dark." However, it reflects such dissonance between form and content that she appears either to have failed to grasp the lyrics' meaning or, more likely, felt Washington's "tone[d] down," subtly phrased original was so majestic and, hence, so threatening to her as would-be Queen, that she sought literally to blast it from our cultural memories with "the sheer power" of her rafters-shaking voice (Haskins 21).

Franklin's version begins with a dizzying organ refrain, the swiftness and harshness of whose notes create an air of chaotic tension that prepares us for the increased tempo and the singer's prodigious wailing. While, as I've suggested, the lyrics insist on the mysteriousness and uncommunicability of the speaker's emotions, Franklin's brash, voluminous performance manifests anger so effectively that it leaves listeners with a great deal of doubt about whether she is actually capable of repressing her murderous impulses. Clearly, she seems to want to kill her lover, and her voice suggests that she may be on the verge of doing so, placing the lyrics' emphasis on the complexity of her feelings and on her internal struggle at odds with the song's performance. Indeed, the wailing, insistent organs and the sheer power of Franklin's voice create an atmosphere seemingly more appropriate to convey the angst of the "insane" persona of "Send Me to the 'Lectric Chair" than the restraint insisted upon by the lyrics of "Nobody Knows." Her protestations notwithstanding, we know exactly how her persona feels—she's angry as hell, and unwilling to endure any more heartache—so that when Franklin exclaims, "I feel like screaming" and "I feel like I could scream and cry," using seemingly every ounce of her energy, she appears unaware of the fact that her artistic choice conflicts with the lines she is delivering. The most generous interpretation I can offer of Franklin's reading is that, in contrast to Washington, she is representing a woman whose capacity for self-control is not as great as her desire for revenge, and whose anger overwhelms her good sense. As a consequence, in her version, the insistence in the lyrics that the character displays vocal and physical restraint loses out to the desire for full-throated assault.

Franklin offers a riveting display of vocal power, a representation of rage whose source could very well be her inability to match or improve upon, within the context of the lyrics' self-imposed limits, her idol's performance. As I have suggested, Washington's song is one of the clearest manifestations we have of her "mastery of the subtle vocal twists and turns" she learned from listening to "Holiday's smallish, keening voice [that] could cut like hot mustard" (liner notes, *Wishing on a Star*). While songs such as "Unforgettable" and "What A Diff'rence A Day Makes" demonstrate her capacity for such vocal subtleties, however resonant such records remain for many, because of their relative simplicity and lack of negative emotions, they do not inspire from her the sort of transcendent performance she offers in "Nobody Knows." In Linda Dahl's estimation, Washington's supremacy as a singer results from her incorporation of, and movement beyond, the stylistic implications of Holiday's legacy; Dahl insists, "For all her unquestionable musicality and emotional range—or perhaps because of it, there's simply too much latent power in the voice—Dinah Washington never communicated the essential *fragility* that lies at the core of Billie Holiday's singing." Washington's contribution to the tradition of black female performance was that, despite her hesitance to expose the "power" of her voice in ways that we associate with the great blues singers who preceded her and soul singers who followed her, her style, a "curious alchemy" of Smith and Holiday, enabled her to "mold a tune with ferocious ease" without conveying, as did Lady Day, "brittle, breathtaking vulnerability. She was very much in the Bessie Smith spirit—a woman broken but unbowed, a woman still *in charge*."

Whether or not we embrace Dahl's formulations fully (and clearly they ignore, for instance, Smith's often subtle use of "intonation and inflection," and her capacity to "convincingly convey . . . many moods on record" [Leland 336]), they help us to identify both characteristic qualities of singers in the regal line that Franklin was destined to join—Smith, Holiday, and Washington—and how aspects of the styles of each were incorporated (with marked and meaningful difference) into that of her successor. The "in charge" Smith, whom Angela Davis considers "the first real 'superstar' in African-American popular culture" (141) and whose big blues sound was especially compelling to Holiday (along with "Louis Armstrong's feeling"), employed what Dahl terms a "full-throttle" style whose most direct antecedents were the folk shouts of rural black southerners. While admiring Smith, Dahl notes, the "swing-oriented" Holiday sought to convey not bold, blueswomanly resilience, but a "brittle, breathtaking vulnerability." The style of her successor, Washington, combines Smith's oppositional spirit and Holiday's vulnerability, albeit constructed in a manner that downplays gospel stylings she learned during childhood. These formulations suggest that the logical next phase of black woman's singing is one in which a superbly talented performer as capable as Holiday of displaying "breathtaking vulnerability" and as skilled as Washington at rendering vocal nuance that did not necessarily devolve into victimization was able, in addition, to utilize both big blues sounds associated with Smith and the spirited fervor, emotional frenzy, and melismatic riffs of gospel stars such as Mahalia Jackson and Clara Ward in secular settings as effectively as such male artists as Ray Charles and Solomon Burke.

Franklin's emergence as "the next one," then, was predicated on her learning to combine these disparate styles, certainly, but more important, on her ability to move seamlessly between them as the lyrical occasion and sonic atmosphere demanded. As we have seen, Nelson George describes her Atlantic recordings as appearing to be the work of "hundreds of women" because "Franklin's voice communicated so wide a range of emotion." In my discussions of "Evil Gal Blues" and "Nobody Knows the Way I Feel This Morning," I have sought to demonstrate that Franklin strategically evades some of the artistic demands of these songs in the catalogue of her idol, especially the subtle evocation of emotional complexity that is perhaps the cornerstone of the seemingly effortless style of Washington. But if Franklin fails to distinguish herself fully in her approach to these songs or, for that matter, in the more pop-oriented, supper club material she covers such as "Unforgettable," "Somewhere Over the Rainbow," "For All We Know," and "What A Diff'rence A Day Makes," she certainly justifies the faith of Washington and others in her potential to become a singular artist in her remakes of "Cold, Cold Heart" and "Drinking Again." While, in my estimation, she handles other songs during her Columbia years with similar, wide-ranging, alchemical skill (including "Skylark," "Today I Sing the Blues," and "All Night Long"), her performances of "Cold, Cold Heart" and "Drinking Again" present her as capable, in ways that no singer before her had been, of articulating both the power and the brittle vulnerability, both the soul possession and heartbroken dispossession, that distinguishes the black female vocal tradition.

Freeing Your "Cold, Cold Heart"
from the "Dilution" of Country and the Blues

If Washington's "Evil Gal Blues" and "Nobody Knows the Way I Feel This Morning" explore the emotional nuances of the lyrics much more effectively than Franklin's covers, the young singer's interpretations of "Cold, Cold Heart" and "Drinking Again" are vastly superior to Washington's. In fact, they are, in my view, as accomplished as the greatest of her more celebrated, more commercially successful, Atlantic performances precisely because, like acclaimed songs such as "I Never Loved a Man (the Way I Love You)," "Dr. Feelgood," "Angel," "Ain't No Way," and "Until You Come Back to Me (That's What I'm Gonna Do)," they are mesmerizing manifestations of her singular versatility.

Like "I'm So Lonesome I Could Cry," which I will explore in some detail in my chapter on Al Green, "Cold, Cold Heart" was composed and originally recorded by Hank Williams. A chart-topping country hit during the second half of 1951, the song moved decisively beyond his relatively small, overwhelmingly white, rural, southern market when a struggling artist named Tony Bennett recorded it in May of that year for Columbia. Part of country's initial incursion into the American mainstream that included "Chattanoogie Shoe Shine Boy" and "The Tennessee Waltz," Bennett's cover "jumped to the top of the pop charts, and every record label had to have at least one cover version; both the Fontane Sisters and Perry Como did it for RCA, Louis Armstrong and Eileen Wilson for Decca, Tony Fontane and Dinah Washington for Mercury" (Escott 142, 143). As the summary of Williams's biographer, Colin Escott, indicates, Washington's version of "Cold, Cold Heart" was one of a number of recordings available to Franklin, who was nine when it peaked at number three on the R & B charts at the end of 1951. If Washington's version, featuring a curious admixture of jazz solos, intrusive strings, corny and colorless background vocals, and strained efforts by the singer at overly proper enunciation and uncharacteristic "big sounds," was the primary inspiration for Franklin, she went to great lengths to signal her awareness of the downhome flavor of Williams's original and its almost operatic interpretation by Bennett, whose rendition, like Washington's, obscures the song's hillybilly genesis.[9]

"Tickled" by the appearance of his composition at the top of the *Billboard* pop chart and prone to respond with "his shiteating grin" when he listened to it on the jukebox, Williams clearly profited financially from the "mainstreaming" of his style of music, exemplified by the fact that "Decca Records . . . estimated that 50 percent of its sales derived from country music, and even Columbia Records estimated that 40 percent of its gross came from country" (Escott 144). Still he remained

> suspicious of the trend, seeing it as a dilution of his music. "These pop bands," he told an interviewer in Charleston, South Carolina, "will play our hillbilly songs when they cain't eat any other way," and when he saw the trade advertisement for Bennett's "Cold, Cold Heart," it must have confirmed his darkest suspicions. The ad headline was "Popcorn! A Top Corn Tune Gone Pop." Tony Bennett was caricatured in a policeman's uniform holding up traffic while a witless hillbilly leads a pig and a mule across a busy city street. (145)

Escott insists that "the success of hillbilly songs refashioned for the pop market considered alongside the rush to record pop cover versions of rhythm 'n' blues songs a couple of years later meant that the music of the black and white underclasses was entering the pop mainstream through the back door" (144). The caricature he cites exemplifies how energetically this hybridized, gluttonish "rush" of bucolic, animalistic sensibilities was policed to avoid offending white, middle-class, urban tastes.

In choosing "Cold, Cold Heart" as part of the mainstream "rush" to the music of the dispossessed, Bennett and his producer, Mitch Miller, selected a song in which Williams appears nearly as wedded to Standard English practices as Tin Pan Alley's aggressively assimilationist Jewish lyricists. Indeed, while Williams uses "ain't" and pronounces "memory" as "mem'ry," he also produces lines reliant both on formal diction ("Another love before my time," "In anger unkind words are said that make the teardrops start") and on an iambic meter nearly as relentless as that of an Elizabethan sonnet. Rendering its lyrics suitable to a pop audience was much less of a challenge than, say, the "good ol' boy" phrasing of "Hey, Good Lookin'" or, for that matter, "Long Gone Lonesome Blues" might have proved. What mainstreaming "Cold, Cold Heart" required, besides getting Bennett to listen not to the "scratchy fiddle and everything . . . cowboy" about the original, but to its "particularly poetic" lyrics (Escott 145), was the erasure of the country sounds of the source material and placement of the words in a musical setting that would encourage (or at least allow) pop audiences to attend to their beautiful simplicity.

Williams's original is a mid-tempo tune that features, along with the singer's exaggerated twang, simple electric guitar accompaniment (and brief soloing in the song's beginning and break) and soft drumming. Rather than melismatically color syllables, words, and phrases in order to communicate the pathos of the narrative, which centers on the frustrations of a man unable to connect emotionally with his self-protective lover (who is still haunted by the "mem'ry" of her "lonesome past" filled with pain she suffered at the hands of a no-good man), Williams moves through the lyrics using a mournful, exhausted tone that abates only when he employs hillbilly pronunciations of words such as "thing," "can't," "your," and "heart." The relentlessness of his pace and his refusal to allow either his musicians or himself to dwell extensively on the painful situation they are portraying enable him to get through four verses, each containing four lengthy lines and complicated, even perplexing, situations, in just over two and a half minutes. (In her cover, Franklin uses only the first two verses, while Washington's, Bennett's, and Norah Jones's versions all cut the song's third verse.) The matter-of-fact nature of the performance, its refusal to dwell on or appear to recognize the depths of the lyrics' attendant pathos, seems to place aspects of the sound of Williams's original at odds with the "particularly poetic" words he uses to describe an emotionally crippling situation. Its sonic elements—danceable beat, simple instrumentation, good ol' boy, twangy delivery—divert attention away from or disguise well-crafted lines and compelling sentiments (manifestations of what David Brackett considers the "poeticizing innovations of Williams' lyrics" [88]) to which inexperienced listeners can attend only if, like Bennett, we filter out those sounds that suggest it is a generic hill-billy heartbreak song.

In his discussion of Williams's status as archetypal country performer, Brackett contends that "it is unlikely that the vast majority of his audience ever considered the 'lyrics' in isolation from the 'music'" (89). However, as I have indicated, such "isolation" was required to render what were, for Bennett and Miller, the commendable aspects of his song—its lyrics as opposed to its music—suitable for mainstream consumption. Bennett's version replaces country sounds with what the future jazz and pop stalwart himself calls "citified . . . strings and a big Percy Faith background," an expropriation that, for "the first time," made it possible for "a country song" to go "all over the world" (quoted in Brackett 89). Listening to Bennett's "citified" cover, featuring genteel rhythms, overwhelming strings, and the singer's dramatic, aristocratic phrasing, the combination of which is more likely to evoke in contemporary listeners images of a languid, white-tuxedoed Fred Astaire dancing alone in a spectacularly appointed marble parlor than of flannel-shirted, seemingly mismatched bucolic lovers pondering their relationship just before or during a Saturday night hoedown, one wonders if the song that went "all over the world" was, in fact, still "a country song" at all. Despite their origins and connections to the standard bearer of country authenticity, once the already poeticized lyrics of "Cold, Cold Heart" are given the classic American popular song treatment, they become not merely diluted, but, like a West African mask decorating the home of a bourgeois, urban, white northern American couple, almost wholly usurped, expropriated material whose cultural resonance and meanings are utterly transformed.

Once the lyrics were extirpated from their country origins, then, the song became a different "thing" altogether, or at least not precisely the same complicated "thing" that Williams had written. It might be more accurate to say that what "Cold, Cold Heart" became after Bennett's version gained mainstream popularity was a song with "different," even competing versions, "countrified" and "citified," whose lyrics seem curiously more at odds with mainstream expectations concerning country music than with the middlebrow "classic" genre to which Bennett's version obviously aspired. Given that versions of "Cold, Cold Heart" by the likes of Washington and Armstrong respond to and are inspired by the popular cover, reconnecting the citified song to its origins required a willingness on the part of subsequent performers to isolate its expropriated lyrics from the orchestrated American classicism in which Miller and Bennett had enveloped them and return them to something approximating their original cultural milieu.

If, more than half a century ago, Bennett's rendition of "Cold, Cold Heart" was more widely known than Williams's, the subsequent monumentalizing of the hillbilly singer (along with, no doubt, the concommitant demise of the type of highly orchestrated musical forms into which Miller and Bennett poured its lyrics) has served to reverse the fortunes of these recordings. No hint of Bennett's version can be detected, for example, in the renditions by Norah Jones and Lucinda Williams that appear on their respective albums *Come Away with Me* (2002) and *Timeless* (2001), the latter of which is a tribute to Hank Williams featuring such luminaries as Bob Dylan, Tom Petty, Emmylou Harris, Keith Richards, and Johnny Cash. Jones's beautiful track, whose dominant features—the light, swinging twang of her voice, her jazz-influenced piano playing, and an acoustic bass—commingle jazz and country, employs a softer sound than Williams's original, which her anguished voice and a lilting, midtempo beat locate as her primary referent. Similarly, while the tempo of Lucinda Williams's instrumentally sparse remake is appreciably slower, its essential elements—her unmistakably country pronunciations and tones, the guitar's somber, twanging chords, the equally mournful violin that approximates a hillbilly fiddle—recall the regional and sonic origins of Hank's version and register the inescapability of the heartache described in lyrics on their way to becoming, if not already deemed, "timeless" precisely because of their connections to the genre's transcendent star.

Unlike these recent, honorific covers of a canonical song penned and originally performed by a man who has become a musical deity, and despite the shared resources upon which country and the blues draw, Washington's 1951 rendition of "Cold, Cold Heart" is much more closely allied with Bennett's version than with Williams's original. In fact, it positions Washington as a vocalist within a big band or "sophisticated cocktail swing" setting, many of whose dominant features—an emotionally detached female singer whose voice manifests a touch of swing and decades of practicing the intricacies of proper English language usage, a dash of sophisticated jazz instrumentation, chippy, syncopated brass interludes, colorless, intrusive background vocal accompaniment that is either mildly amusing and maddeningly unlistenable to contemporary audiences—militate against its being a truly persuasive performance of Williams's composition. If Hugh Gregory is correct that Washington's "malleab[ility]," "her ability to cover pop tunes, rock out on the steamiest R & B numbers, and to swing on the most complex jazz arrangement[,] made her suspect" to diehard black musical fans and critics and is why she "remains underrated" (136), allowing herself, as she does on "Cold, Cold Heart," to be trapped within such a pallid musical environment may have signaled for some a lack of artistic integrity on her part. And though she sings harder and louder than usual, obviously trying to punctuate the lyrics rather than dwell artfully on their meanings and sounds, the volume lends to her performance a degree of urgency, and perhaps deep-felt frustration and even anger, but does not produce a generally sensitive interpretation of Williams's words. More than anything else, it seems that Washington is offering a rather pat, good-natured pop performance, trotting out her most dramatic and precise Bette Davis-influenced enunciation rather than seeking to convey the grand pathos the lyrics describe. Despite its relative popularity—only "What a Diff'rence a Day Makes," "This Bitter Earth," and her great duet with Brook Benton, "Baby (You've Got What It Takes)" spent more time on the R & B chart—her rendition of "Cold, Cold Heart" lacks the emotional depth and overall aesthetic appeal of her most accomplished work. And at several moments in the song, such as whenever the intrusive background singers are audible or when Washington exaggerates the genteelness of Williams's phrases, her version seems nearly as committed as Bennett's to accentuating its bourgeois lyrical features and suppressing its lower-class origins despite its employment of jazz musical elements that had already been absorbed into mainstream musical culture.

Given the concerted efforts of both Bennett and Washington to encase the song's beautiful lyrics in bourgeois sounds, what is noteworthy about Franklin's cover of "Cold, Cold Heart," produced more than ten years after its country, R & B, and pop successes, is its referencing of its original sonic atmosphere and of the constellation of musical resources that country music and the blues share. Part of what makes Franklin's rendition—offered nominally as a tribute to her black female idol—so compelling is that while Washington was satisfied to emulate, and at times exaggerate aspects of, Bennett's citified cover, her successor immerses the lyrics again in the constitutive southern, country sounds that Brackett and many others, including Williams himself, insist are greatly informed by the blues. And if the road between country music and the blues was already well traveled by R & B artists by the early 1960s, a phenomenon perhaps best exemplified by Solomon Burke's great single "Just Out of Reach (Of My Two Empty Arms)" (1961), and Ray Charles's classic album *Modern Sounds in Country and Western Music* (1962), what marks Franklin's efforts here as truly significant is their implicit commentary on the aesthetic costs of mainstream appropriation for artists who emerge from marginalized groups. If Bennett's and Washington's pop covers served to justify Williams's fears about the erasure of the regional and generic specificity of his composition, by reaching back beyond these "dilutions" to the song's origins, Franklin's offers a soulful interpretation that evokes—but does not seek to replicate—the sonic field the lyrics originally occupied. Put somewhat differently, Franklin's "Cold, Cold Heart" does not sound like Williams's, but it identifies its original country sounds as essential to the song's effective presentation. Without out claiming for her an immunity to temptations that are also evident in Washington's body of work—critics frequently cite Franklin's affinity for lame Broadway show tunes and her sometimes colossally bad musical taste—the musical textures of her "Cold, Cold Heart," including her deep soul singing, bluesy accompaniment, and movingly dissonant use of identifiably country sounds, position her very "different" interpretation as what, following Ralph Ellison's views of his own complicated participation in an emerging black literature, we might see as implicit "criticism" of Washington's pop rendition.[10]

While listeners might associate other songs on this tribute album with artists besides the Queen of the Blues—for example, "Unforgettable" remains, for me, Nat "King" Cole's—none of Franklin's performances gestures so self-consciously beyond Washington and toward other renditions as her remake of Williams's composition, enabling her to transform "Cold, Cold Heart" into a perfect showcase for her nascent mastery of the nuances of R & B performance. Relying heavily on her spirited, pained wailing and her more quiet, yet equally effective, sighs and moans, gospel-influenced interplay between organ and piano, and dramatic flurries and rhythmic punctuations offered by the drum, the future Queen's version eliminates background vocals altogether and replaces the synchronized pop wind instrumental interludes and the somber, jazzy tenor saxophone soloing of Washington's version with a harmonica (played by her ensemble's tenor saxophonist, Buddy Lucas) that offers unmistakable country resonances.

Washington's dedication to bourgeois language practices leads her, for example, to replace the contraction in the phrase "for things I didn't do" with "did not" and generally to utilize a mode of pronunciation that makes her persona seem altogether too pretentious, dignified, and/or self-satisfied to be deeply immersed in the "sad and blue" feelings she professes. Her performance would be unquestionably effective if her goal was to communicate the emotional distance of the "shackled" addressee, but it fails to convey the painful condition the persona articulates. Conversely, Franklin's soulful version displays emphatically the wrenching pain embodied in the lyrics that Washington's pop affectations serve to mute. Unlike her precursor, who seems unwilling to delve deeply into the emotional drama, Franklin's spirited performance of lines such as "I tried so hard, my dear to show / That you're my ev'ry dream" corresponds with the lyrical sentiments and evinces that effort and its painful consequences. The dominant features of Washington's pop rendition of "Cold, Cold Heart"—the lead and background vocals, the orchestrated wind instrument interludes—seem so thoroughly contaminated by bourgeois artifice that Paul Quinichette's impressive sax solos carry almost the full responsibility of conveying the song's emotions. In effect, his solos wrestle with the rest of Washington's "diluted" recording, striving to communicate the spirit of the blues that is evident in soul music, of course, but also in Williams's "sad and blue," "alone and forsaken" country tunes. As Washington's rendition demonstrates, his lyrics alone are not enough to ensure the communication of that "tragic" blues "spirit," but when they are placed in appropriate settings—Lucinda Williams's dirge-like tribute, Norah Jones's jazz-country hybrid, and Franklin's gospel-inspired, secular soul—they can be made to articulate the resilience for which the roots music of that region is renowned.

The country harmonica that punctuates key moments in Franklin's cover of the song serves as a sonic guide, a conduit, if you will, between Williams's hillbilly poetics and Franklin's heartfelt, deep soul performance. Her rendition implicitly critiques and moves beyond Washington's "dilution" of the song's emotional registers, executing a stylistic

return to the South, the site and source of "authentic" black musical artistry. Wrestling "Cold, Cold Heart" from Washington by reclaiming the
South as the song's essential setting, Franklin's gesture is as symbolically
resonant as her much discussed subsequent literal and artistic journey to
the heart of Dixie to record "I Never Loved A Man (The Way That I Loved
You)." And if other tracks in her Columbia catalogue showcase her gifts
as effectively as "Cold, Cold Heart"—"Maybe I'm a Fool," "Muddy Water,"
"Today I Sing the Blues," "Skylark," and another *Unforgettable* tune, "This
Bitter Earth"—her rendition of Williams's "diluted" song graphically
highlights the symbolic journey she had to undergo to forge her signature
style. Comparing her time at Columbia and Atlantic in *From These Roots*
Franklin emphasizes negative aspects of her experiences with her first
major record company.[11] But whatever benefits Atlantic's "TLC" and "camaraderie" provided her, "Cold, Cold Heart" is proof that, at least three
years before her first release for that company, her status as the "new
queen" (Bego 50) was virtually assured, in part, by her demonstrated recognition of the aesthetic costs of the compromises made by her precursor
to gain "commercial success."

In Waiting No More: "Drinking Again" in Regal Style

Like "Nobody Knows the Way I Feel This Morning," which features Washington's characteristic casual, bluesy swing, a cool but heartfelt declaration of the pain of her lover's absence, and the soulful accompaniment of
talented jazz musicians who work hard to keep the pop elements—the
sappy strings and synchronized wind instrumental refrains—from overwhelming their efforts, "Drinking Again" is a type of song that convinced
"hundreds of thousands" of listeners that she was "the queen of them
all" (Haskins 64). Given the power of this track, part of her first set of
recordings for Roulette Records, which Washington joined in 1962 after
fifteen years at Mercury because its owner, Morris Levy, a former owner
of the New York's famed Birdland and a longtime friend, had "promised
her mainstream exposure" (Haskins 171), Franklin's desire to cover it on
Unforgettable is understandable. But unlike her desperate, over-the-top assault on "Nobody Knows," she approaches "Drinking Again" with a combination of grit and vulnerability, of gospel excess and "cocktail swing"
subtlety that produces perhaps her most transcendent Columbia record-

ing and helps to establish new possibilities for the black female voice in the realm of American secular song.

In *The Gospel Sound*, Tony Heibult argues that "most of her biggest hits remind one of other gospel singers" (302) such as Clara Ward, Mavis Staples, and Mahalia Jackson, suggesting that Franklin—who admits in her autobiography that, during the 1970s, she "got a big kick out of emulating Diana Ross doing 'Ain't No Mountain High Enough,' Gladys Knight's 'Midnight Train to Georgia,' Mavis Staples's 'Let's Do It Again'"—created herself artistically by incorporating what she calls "the vocal idiosyncrasies" (148) of powerful black female vocalists into her own stylistic repertoire. If Heilbult's argument (bolstered by his subject's own acknowledgment of the appeal of vocal mimicry) is plausible, Franklin's performance of "Drinking Again" might be recognized as a tapestry of identifiable characteristics of black female singers who were popular after Washington's reign began: the assertive, almost masculine tones of the great rock 'n' rollers Ruth Brown and Laverne Baker; the long-suffering sweetness of popular girl groups like the Shirelles and the Marvellettes; the nuanced thoughtfulness of Dionne Warwick and Nancy Wilson (and Washington); and the spirited, frenzied gospel rapture of Ward and Jackson. A template for her future success, Franklin's rendition displays her ability, like no singer before her (and, perhaps, since), to bring together all of these vocal qualities.

Franklin begins "Drinking Again" before her musical accompaniment, holding for several seconds the contraction, "I'm," an impressive a capella moment that asserts both her presence and, we later learn, her essential isolation. Accompanied most prominently by a muted trumpet's sorrowful notes, she follows this moment with a simple declaration of her motivation for this act of self-assertion—"drinking again / Thinking of when you loved me"—that shows her proud announcement of her psychological and sonic presence to be essentially a form of dissemblance. But if Franklin begins on a note of vocal aggressiveness that portends an over-the-top performance, like her approach to "Nobody Knows the Way I Feel This Morning," her voice subsequently softens to complement what is, for the next minute and a half, a bluesy, Washingtonesque performance that emphasizes nuanced punctuation of the lyrics' deep, seemingly inescapable sadness. The song focuses on the persona's efforts to dull her pain in the face of romantic loss with the company of "total strangers," the possibility of self-deprecating humor, and an impotent cocktail of memory, smoke, alcohol ("a bottle of Seagram's"), and unfulfilled desire ("wishing that you were here").

In a much cited formulation, Ralph Ellison characterizes the blues as a "chronicle of personal catastrophe expressed lyrically" that is motivated by "an impulse to . . . finger its jagged grain, and to transcend it . . . by squeezing from it a near-tragic, near-comic lyricism" (*Shadow and Act*, 91). The conclusion of Franklin's performance of both willful self-assertion and the unconsolable nature of her persona's pain compels those listeners for whom the great black intellectual's formulations seem generally persuasive to wonder whether her "squeezing" confirms the form's emphasis on resolution and transcendence or evinces, in this case at least, their utter impossibility. Following her initial assertion of her pain-filled presence and her description of her place in the bar alongside other "broken heart[ed]" "jokers," the volume and despair of Franklin's performance increase as the persona comes to terms with the futility of her efforts to forget and replace her absent lover and of trying on unsteady legs "to make it on home"—the formerly joyous, love-filled domicile they shared before he left her, the clear antithesis of the smoky space of hesitant, insincere, alcohol-induced laughter in which she has sought solace. Her performance moves from prideful self-assertion, to fully elaborated manifestations of wizened restraint, to despair so great that it is expressed only as near hysterical ejaculations of incomplete thoughts she cannot make conform to the rules of either Standard English or a recognizable black vernacular ("with nothing but a memory / Memory, turn it back and it just, one more time, really").

Rather than resisting the song's "impulse," as she does in her rejection of the calls for vocal restraint of "Nobody Knows," Franklin builds "Drinking Again" to a crescendo that sagely utilizes its lyrical imperatives and musical environment in order to display, in the words of the great Laverne Baker song, a black woman's "soul on fire." According to Feather's liner notes, "Drinking Again" "was taped . . . with the studio dimmed to create the mood for Aretha." Franklin's interpretation of that "mood" or what Bego calls an "'after midnight' feeling" (62) ultimately moves beyond Washington's nuanced restraint in favor of a passionate demonstration of heartbreak whose almost inarticulate yearnings constitute another facet of the "spirit in the dark" she sings about in such a transcendent manner in her classic Atlantic performance. If the moving, grooving spirit in the Atlantic recording is the inseparability of sexual and religious ecstacy, in "Drinking Again" it is expressed as unconsolable pain, despite its blueswoman's late-night efforts to find some comfort—perhaps sexual, and certainly boozy, "comic" succor in the company of "total strangers"—in the wake of romantic "catastrophe." What Franklin introduces into the realm of black secular song is not gospel fervor or blues assertiveness, not introspective nuance and emotional restraint, all of which could be found individually in the recordings of black female and male singers who preceded her, but a capacity, as in her regal interpretation of "Drinking Again," to express and justify their simultaneous presence, to "communicate . . . so wide a range of emotion as to truly defy description" (George 105).

"What They Hear and What I Feel When I Sing It
Can Be Very, Very Different"

In the middle of a lengthy downturn in Franklin's pop fortunes—between 1975, the year after "Until You Come Back to Me" rose to number three, and 1985, when "Freeway of Love" earned the same chart position, none of her singles cracked the *Billboard* Top Twenty—the pop/jazz duo Steely Dan released "Hey Nineteen," an ode to lost youth that makes reference to Franklin's past glories and reached the *Billboard* Pop and R & B Top Ten in 1981. The song's focus is a middle-aged former "dandy of Gamma Chi" striving to understand his journey "from Boston . . . to Scarsdale," an affluent New York suburb, whose anxiety is heightened by his recognition of his place in the generational divide. Irrefutable evidence that he has aged significantly is the failure of the titular addressee, a girl who reminds him of "young and willing" coeds he knew "way back in Sixty-seven," to recognize the singer they are listening to as "'Retha Franklin . . . , The Queen of Soul." Wanting no further confirmation of the "hard times befallen / The soul survivors"—a group in which he includes both himself and the deposed Queen, whose emergence in 1967 was a major event in his youth—he tells her, "We can't dance together / No we can't talk at all."

This song of "growing old" rejects rock 'n' roll's idealized forbidden fruit, the stock figure of the nubile, inexperienced, unspoiled, and sweet young girl—examples of which include Chuck Berry's "Sweet Little Sixteen," Sam Cooke's "Only Sixteen," Ringo Starr's "You're Sixteen" and, to cite a less popular example, Al Green's "Sweet Sixteen"—because its speaker recognizes that she can do nothing for him but confirm the "waste" made of members of his generation by what the poet John Keats identifies, in his "Ode to the Grecian Urn," as "slow Time." However "slow," Time's effects are powerful enough to diminish the speaker's sex drive, the appeal of young girls, and the popularity of the Queen of Soul, whose "heard melodies" are beyond the limited knowledge base of the addressee of "Hey Nineteen." Steely Dan's last major pop single, concerned primarily not with Franklin but with what ignorance of her massive contribution signifies for younger generations, shares with the tribute album as a form the dual purpose of staving off our collective forgetting of its honored subject and of recontextualizing her achievements. And if, largely on the strength of the smooth, funky rhythms and Franklin references, "Hey Nineteen" and *Gaucho*, the album on which it appeared, secured for Donald Fagen and Walter Becker the only significant attention they ever received from R & B audiences, their appeal for such audiences was, in part, a function of the fact that the track sees soul as a valuable (and, it would appear from the addressee's lack of knowledge, potentially transformative) cultural entity whose preservation is essential.

Nelson George has argued that the period upon which "Hey Nineteen" reflects witnessed "the death of rhythm & blues," as black singers sought to present themselves as "universal," "pop" performers whose music transcended racial boundaries (169), rather than to communicate black specificity and difference. Thus, the demise of soul—the "high point in R & B music," of which Franklin was the dominant figure and which reflected and inspired "both social change and artistic creativity" (xii)—signaled the "assimilationist triumphs" of Great Society programs, the beginnings of what George considers truly damaging class divisions within the black community and the diminution of black popular music as an "adult" art form (181). But if efforts to erase black difference reflected and/or motivated the musical decline to which, in their own ways, both "Hey Nineteen" and *The Death of Rhythm & Blues* allude, an earlier song in which Franklin also figured prominently, Dyke and the Blazers' anthemic "We Got More Soul" (1969), represents the Queen as central to an era of black racial pride. This song praises "sisters and . . . brothers" for possessing "more soul" in key areas of self-presentation—"talk," "walk," "dance," and song—than, presumably, whites. A valuable cultural commodity, "soul" is best manifested, according to the song, in the musical "thing" of Franklin, Ray Charles, and James Brown (whose signature style the Blazers clearly strive to replicate).

And if not all of the figures "We Got More Soul" mentions remain at the forefront of our notions of soul aesthetics—the three others it praises are Johnnie Taylor, Pearl Bailey, and Nancy Wilson—Brown, Charles, and Franklin are firmly ensconced because of the perceived racial authenticity of their best work. In Franklin's case, soulfulness is a function of her ability to "deliver a wailing, begging, brooding stew of emotions that seemed to carry more truth, more low-down funkiness, and more strength than the loudest of the shouting male singers—Otis Redding, James Brown, and Wilson Pickett." And because, as funk theorist Rickey Vincent suggests, songs such as "Respect," "Natural Woman," and "Think" were received as racial "anthems" that "brought a new era of meaningful music with a groove to America" (*Funk* 123), Franklin's reign as the Queen of Soul was burdened with the weight of sociopolitical significance that none of her predecessors had to bear and which, in truth, does not always stand up to serious scrutiny. Making liberal use of two of her "anthems," for example, Bego suggests that Franklin "had become an inspiring symbol of black equality. With her own sense of pride and her dignified stance, she represented the new black woman of the late 1960s. In her own way she embodied the social and cultural change that was taking place in the country, merely by being herself without pretense. Respected by black *and* white America, she was the 'natural woman' that she sang about" (108).

Like Mark Anthony Neal, I believe that "the notion of Aretha being the 'voice' of the black liberation movement has been overstated" (50), but it apparently served the undeniably deep needs of groups of people at the time and subsequently. If Otis Redding felt that he lost his song "Respect," to "that girl," Franklin herself recognizes that she "lost" it both to nationalist and to feminist listeners who hear and continue to hear it as infused with anthemic racial and gendered meanings she insists she did not intend. While acknowledging the rights of her listeners (including, as she tells Gerri Hirshey, "Vietnam vets [who] . . . come up to me and tell me how much my music meant to them over there" [242]) to "their personal interpretation" of songs such as "Respect," which was adopted as "a 'new national anthem,' a bold affirmation of what the black struggle was all about" (362), Franklin resists efforts to claim a necessary connection between their feelings and the pain they "found . . . in my music." Indeed, she argues that "what they hear and what I feel when I sing it can be very, very different. Sometimes I wish I could make them understand that" (Hirshey 242), a failure that led her, as Brian Ward argues specifically about "Respect," to deny "steadfastly . . . that she had any such agenda when she sang it" (362). Of course, listeners' capacity to view songs as representations of our own situations and reflections of our own needs explains much of their power for and over us, and certainly blacks' nationalist needs in the late 1960s and early 1970s led them to invest "Respect" with liberationist powers, just as those needs led Franklin subsequently to cover "Young, Gifted, and Black," "Bridge Over Troubled Waters," and "Spanish Harlem," songs that offered the types of themes that the times and her listeners demanded from her and, indeed, virtually all prominent black performers.

These discussions of the meanings of Franklin's songs suggest that even if most listeners lack the skill to produce versions of her songs that will be widely disseminated and to wrestle overtly with her interpretations, they do reshape or take "away" from her those records that they find especially important. Their goals, in this regard, are not dissimilar from a young Aretha Franklin's respectful assault on Washington's material which, in the case of "Evil Gal Blues," can lead even to lyrical transformation: to invest them with meanings that may "happen . . . to be similar or different" from those which she intended but, more important, reflect our sense of "the way they felt best." Certainly, the totality of such a record—her singing, the lyrics, the pace and effectiveness of her musical accompaniment, etc.—impacts listeners' notions of the "best" interpretation, but it interacts, in sometimes mysterious ways, with their selective (if not consciously or strategically chosen) experiences to form their individualized sense of what it says and, hence, is. Unlike, for example, the songs that reference her soulful art or the spate of covers of Franklin's songs that appeared during the 1990s, from En Vogue's remake of "Something He Can Feel" to Mikki Howard's and Basia's of "Until You Come Back to Me," listeners' interpretations of her work generally do not become public. But their investment in her, her songs, and interpretations of her life and her career can be, at times, as important to their experiences as were Franklin's interpretations of Washington and, hence, of the artist she herself could become.

Franklin's pre-Atlantic secular work is generally dismissed in rich studies such as Guralnick's *Sweet Soul Music* and Hirshey's *Nowhere to*

Run as "restrictive pop songs, stylized jazz, or petrified show tunes" (Hirshey 238). Drawing upon Harold Bloom's theories of contentious artistic self-making, I've tried to demonstrate that one of Franklin's pre-Atlantic albums can be more productively understood as part of the process of her artistic self-creation, in which we can see her as "the true ephebe," "the potentially strong" singer at the beginning of her "quests for [artistic] fire," in whose "first voices" we can detect "what is most central in the precursors' voices." If Bego's biography is motivated by an urge to explore Wexler's notions of the source of Franklin's pain, this chapter constitutes my attempt to discover terms upon which to verify another of her former producer's claims: that her Columbia material was often "superb" (Wexler 203). Despite the decades-long efforts of Columbia's marketing department, including the two-disc compilation appropriately entitled *The Queen in Waiting* (2002), her recordings before the 1967 release of *I Never Loved A Man the Way I Love You* continue to be viewed as raiments draped over her during a failed apprenticeship which, in Hirshey's terms, never "quite fit" her (238).

If Nelson George is correct that her Atlantic records display a stirring multiplicity of selves; if Robert Christgau, seeking to construct logical connections between Franklin's "lifetime of psychological hardship" and the sometimes "unsure" "sense of self" she manifested in her recordings, is persuasive in his assertion that her work is often transcendent precisely because of its "signs of struggle" (*Growing Up* 103), evaluators of her career must themselves resist the urge to offer facile, uninformed dismissals of her early work and explore, among other things, "signs of struggle" in releases such as *Unforgettable*. Documenting the young singer's efforts to construct herself specifically in response to Washington's artistic legacy, her tribute album can best be seen not as the harbinger of Franklin's development of a signature style, but, rather, as evidence of the limitations of doing so.

However we assess the "more soul" which Franklin is said to possess, and whatever interpretation we feel compelled to reduce her to because of our own needs and desires, listeners seem destined to fail to account adequately for the contradictions and vastness of her musical catalogue and personae, as when "people don't realize" what Wexler calls "her articulation and her lyric intelligence [because] . . . they just see her as a belter, a soul screamer" (Bego 59). But whatever else it is, soul—which "became as much of a trend as it did because of Aretha Franklin" (Hirshey 241) and whose expansive possibilities its future Queen first began fully to realize in her production of "similar or different" interpretations of songs associated with her idol Dinah Washington—is the manifestation of both the capacity to "scream and cry" and of the possession of a sufficient cultural and "musical intellect" (*Growing Up*, 103) to know when not to.

The meaning and value of music are not located in the materials of music themselves [but] within the contradictory discourses through which people make sense of and assign value to music. —**John Shepherd**, "Music, Culture, and Interdisciplinarity"

A life in harmony with nature, the love of truth and of virtue, will purge the eyes to understand her text. By degrees we may come to know the primitive sense of the permanent objects of nature, so that the world shall be to us an open book, and every form significant of its hidden life and final cause. —**Ralph Waldo Emerson**, "Nature," *The Selected Writings*

He [Al Green] had the confidence in his own genius to see himself as an artist, not an entertainer providing a . . . fantasy. —**David Jackson**, "Al Green Changes Hearts and Minds"

"something like wholeness"

Al Green's *Call Me* and the Struggle

for Thematic Integrity

In the introduction, I spoke about recent manifestations of Al Green's self-referential impulses, his uses, in the later phases of his career, of fragments of his well-known songs as links between his classic hits and his more contemporary efforts. Those impulses did not simply emerge in the context of various late-career attempts to recapture a mass audience, but were on display as early as 1973 when, during the fadeout of the middle track from *Call Me*, "Your Love Is Like The Morning

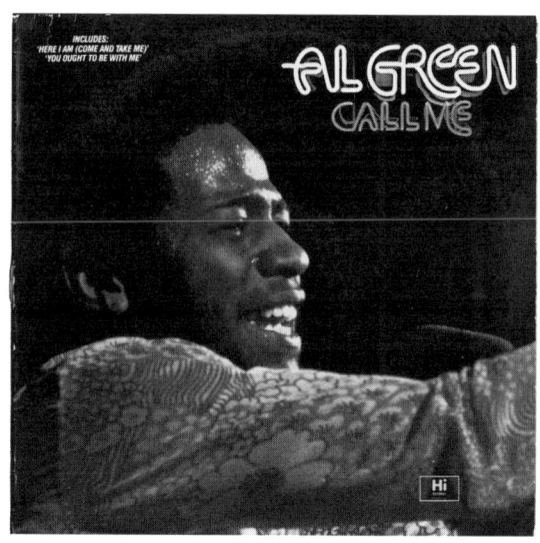

Al Green's most critically acclaimed album synthesizes "calls" to and from a variety of sources: hesitant, departed, and cruel lovers (including those featured in well-known country songs), oppressed blacks, nature, and, finally, a forgiving God.

Sun," he sings the titles of "Tired of Being Alone," "Let's Stay Together," and "I'm Still in Love with You," all of which appeared on and, in the case of the last two, were the titles songs of earlier albums. Drawing on a variety of sources, including Green's 2000 autobiography, this chapter considers this and other intertextual gestures, including his covers of well-known songs, as interpretive keys to discerning some of the meanings of his career more generally and, in particular, of *Call Me*, which is often spoken of as not only his best album, but one of the finest of the rock era.

   The high regard in which the album is held is in part a function of its evaluators' sense that, musically and thematically, *Call Me* "moves in one sinuous body" (Christgau, *Rock Albums of the '70s* 159), displaying an integrative quality that distinguishes it from the great majority of pop albums, which generally offer a hodgepodge of unrelated songs, themes, and narrative situations and persona. My analysis of this album seeks to contextualize its lyrics, both those Green had a hand in writing and versions of well-known country tunes ("I'm So Lonesome I Could Cry" and "Funny How Time Slips Away") that he places alongside, and in a variety of ways incorporates into, the body of his own compositions that explore romantic and, ultimately, religious yearning. The thematic links and imagistic repetitions that appear in the lyrics allow listeners to consider the album as more than an arbitrary compendium of narratives. I

explore whether and how the aesthetic ideals that Green claims motivate his art, including his desire to produce an album that is a coherent,
thematically unified structure, are actualized in *Call Me*. In other words,
I seek to make imaginative sense of the language generally and of the
discursive repetitions in particular that mark this collection of musical
tracks. These repetitions—images of the morning sun, of heartbroken
characters confronting former lovers who are involved with other men,
and of distraught figures seeking sexual and spiritual satisfaction—constitute the means by which Green attempts to create an album that is an
integrated artistic statement.

"Sin and Salvation Trying to Sing the Same Song"

According to Peter Shapiro, author of Rough Guide's *Soul: 100 Essential
CDs*, Al Green's fifth solo album, *Call Me*, is his "masterpiece. A sad, painful, but ultimately uplifting exploration of loss, it displays the most gen-
erous view of love and sex ever voiced by a male singer" (68). Featuring
three of his most popular singles (the title track, "You Ought to Be with
Me," and "Here I Am [Come and Take Me]"), his definitive remake of the
Willie Nelson composition "Funny How Time Slips Away," and the soul-
stirring spiritual "Jesus Is Waiting," this album appears on both VH1's and
Rolling Stone's lists of the greatest albums of the rock era, and *R & B: The
Essential Album Guide* calls it a "one-album slice of how wonderful Green
can be" (242).

Perhaps his most perceptive interpreter, Robert Christgau, argues in
Rock Albums of the '70s that "no other album documents Green's genius
for the daring nuance so thrillingly" (159). Christgau's appreciation of his
talents is even more evident in his essay "Pop Songs to God," where,
after acknowledging that "all aesthetic judgments are open to perpetual
debate," he offers the bold assertion that "Al Green isn't just the last soul
man; except for James Brown, he's the greatest. And except for Aretha
Franklin, he's also the most gifted singer ever to work the turf. In fact,
he may conceivably be the finest vocalist rock and roll has ever known"
(*Growing Up* 462).

Clearly, a critical consensus has emerged, which, if not necessarily
echoing Christgau's view of Green's preeminence, suggests that his "vul-
nerably sensual vocal delivery" (Fruter 240), "his unbridled joy and soul-

ful instincts" (Graff et al. 240), his creation of a seductive stage presence "that earned him a huge female following" (Werner 180), his mastery—under the tutelage of producer Willie Mitchell—of "the technology of recording" and his capacity to work effectively with the propulsive musical accompaniment provided by Mitchell's Hi Rhythm Section, helped to produce a music "of layered elegance" (Guralnick, *Sweet Soul Music* 305, 306) that places him at the forefront of musical artistry during what music critic Nelson George calls "the period of soul's most majestic performances" (157).

In the characterizations that emerge, time and time again, in music buyer guides and scholarly assessments of Green's music, he is represented as a troubled figure "wrestling with two very different kinds of joy," sexual and spiritual, and who, as a result, "symbolises the secular/ sacred divide that gives soul music its emotional power" (Shapiro 67). Certainly, the *Rolling Stone Encyclopedia* is correct to suggest that Green's trademark "wildly improvisational, ecstatic cries and moans came directly from gospel music" (George-Warren and Romanowski 391). It is also the case that before he abandoned R & B in favor of gospel music in the late 1970s, Green did occasionally investigate sacred themes either directly (for example, "God Is Standing By," "My God Is Real," and "Jesus Is Waiting") or in love song lyrics suffused with subtle religious symbolism ("Take Me to the River," "Living for You," "L-O-V-E"). And in comments made long after his commercial heyday, his return to gospel music, and his call to the ministry, Green encourages us to reimagine tracks such as "Tired of Being Alone" and "You Ought to Be with Me" in extraromantic terms, insisting, for example, in *Take Me to the River*, his 2000 autobiography, that "when you listen to Al Green's greatest hits, that's exactly what you're hearing—sin and salvation trying to sing the same song" (4). Indeed, after his spiritual reawakening in 1973, he began to insist that listeners who recognize nothing even slightly religious in the lyrics of songs like "I'm Still in Love with You" accept a claim he made in a 1989 interview: "My spiritual beliefs were as much a part of the records I made in the 1970s as they are a part of what I'm doing now" (Bayles 273).

Since at least the late 1970s, scholars have recognized that autobiography is a mode of storytelling in which the meanings and motivations for the selection of historical events are shaped to fit their narrators' perspectives and ideological needs. For example, according to James Olney, it is through "the act of writing . . . that the self and the life, complexly intertwined and entangled, take on a certain form, assume a particular shape and image" (22). One moment in *Take Me to the River* in particular exemplifies Green's awareness of the fact that the autobiographer strives to make the specific events he chooses to highlight fit his discursive needs. He speaks of the "The sight of my daddy, staring straight ahead, tears rolling down his cheek and falling onto the open Bible in his hand," which, "even now, I can hear . . . plopping on the page" as a childhood experience that supports his contention that "My whole life has had a soundtrack to it, and the clearest scenes in my memory always have songs playing behind them" (12). But in the following paragraph, he asserts,

> Of course, memory is an unreliable sort of thing. There's no way tears on a page could have carried over tambourines banging and voices rising higher and higher until the people jumped clear out of their seats, shouting and signifying. Or maybe it's just that you hear things differently when you're a child. To my mind, there wasn't much difference between those folks carousing in the roadhouse [whom his guilt-ridden father occasionally joins to "listen . . . to down-and-dirty blues throbbing through the warm Southern night"] and the ones raising the roof at the revival [at which the family gospel group appeared]. (12–13)

Here, Green collapses, exaggerates, misperceives, and misremembers events in order to highlight two crucial issues that the autobiography subsequently investigates: his father's sorrowful, guilt-ridden life, whose mistakes Green strives mightily to avoid, and his father's and, more important, the singer's own formative struggles to reconcile—and act on his recognition of—the fundamental differences between "the roadhouse" and "the revival," between the blues and gospel as forms of soulful expression, between the lures of sin and the soul-cleansing possibilities of salvation. If the essential unreliability of memory means that it can be strategically utilized, autobiography can be defined in part as the written by-product of the struggle to interpret past events in ways that satisfy both the genre's and the writer's need for coherence. As an adult who is a soul icon and a minister, the autobiographer remembers his father's tears as amplified because such amplification justifies Green's insistence on the centrality of his father's unresolved religious and economic angst both to the events he chooses to represent and to the unifying narrative arch he creates to give his own life thematic meaning.

In addition, *Take Me to the River*, his most thoughtful assessment of the place of his "spiritual beliefs" in his popular music, suggests Green's awareness of a manifest gap between personal experience, lyrical content, and musical performance, between, that is to say, the enabling events that shape the singer's life and the emotionally charged stories that he creates and/or embellishes in his performances. Speaking, for example, of his haunting rendition on *Let's Stay Together* of the Bee Gees' song "How Can You Mend a Broken Heart," which, as discussed in the introduction, he insists he "owned," Green—at a point in his life when he was wary of "the distraction of another person, the responsibility for someone else's happiness, or the accountability that comes from being committed"—"could imagine how a man might feel, pleading for the love of one good woman," but he adds, "As far as firsthand experience went, I was just guessing" (271, 273). Similarly, he is able to simulate religious fervor, as he claims in his discussion of "Jesus Is Waiting," the final cut on *Call Me*, which he describes as "a song [he] had written without even really knowing why" (288): "'I've been a fool,' I sang in 'Jesus is Waiting,' 'disregarding your love . . . .' I sang those lyrics with feeling, even with conviction, but it was a fervor that I could only remember once knowing. I could recite the words of repentance, the formula for forgiveness, and the attitude of saving grace. But behind that knowledge was spiritual ignorance" (289).

In an autobiography purporting to deconstruct the mythology surrounding "the Last of the Great Soul Men" (3), Green insists that, before he was born again in Christ, he was able to fake religious salvation in his performance of "Jesus Is Waiting" just as effectively as he stepped into the role of the heartbroken, "sadder-but-wiser penitent." Green's admission that he can infuse religious and romantic narratives with inauthentic emotion forces us to confront the potential paradox implicit in our interactions with what Simon Frith, who insists that devoted pop music listeners "assume that we can hear someone's life in their voice," speaks of as "the performing body": "at the core of our understanding of . . . language must be the knowledge that even the most direct form of human expression—the unmediated articulation of fear, anger, ecstasy, and so on—can always be faked" (185–86, 217). According to Frith, however, it is not just the singer whose role involves interpretation, but also the listener's: "If all songs are narratives, if they work as mini-musicals, then their plots are a matter of interpretation both by performers attaching them to their own star stories *and* by listeners, putting ourselves in the picture, or, rather, placing their emotions—or expressions of emotion—in our own stories, whether directly . . . or, more commonly, indirectly, laying the performance over our memories of situations and relationships" (211).

If we acknowledge that emotions can "be faked," and that the singer sings and the listener hears *interpretations* of the words of "mini-musicals" over whose meanings there can be—and often is—debate, we are on much safer ground if we consider Green's lyrical and autobiographical narratives *as performances*, as enactments of his "star story" rather than as necessarily accurate depictions of what he experienced and how he felt during the composition or recording of lyrics about love, God, or another subject. Even if he is able when he listens to "Jesus Is Waiting" as a ministerial autobiographer with a complex history and discernible agenda to "clearly hear what was only a still small voice" of Jesus waiting for his renunciation of a hedonistic pop star's life during which he "had carnal relations with more women than I can remember or confess" (275), others are free to view the song as a sincere manifestation of deep religious feeling or—either because we are unmoved by his performance or know, for example, of Green's fornicating ways at the time—as spiritually bereft and, hence, artistically unsuccessful. Similarly, although he characterizes his greatest hits as narratives in which you can hear "sin and salvation trying to sing the same song" (4), we can question the claim's veracity, reject it outright, and continue to regard songs like "Let's Stay Together" and "Here I Am (Come and Take Me)" as solely and simply about romantic love and loss.

Take Me to the River is a record of the iconic seventies performer's efforts to confront the essential autobiographical challenge, which, as I have suggested, is to connect disparate personal events in one's life so that what emerges is a thematically coherent and formally cohesive narrative self. In part, Green pursues such goals by associating his individual struggles with familiar American narratives generally—he speaks with no small degree of irony of his life as one in which "the rags turn into riches, the rainbow ends in a pot of gold, and everybody lives happily ever after" (263)—and with defining moments in Afro-American history such as slavery, sharecropping, migration, and the civil rights movement. In his estimation, blacks during the historical periods in which these events took place were forced to confront a prevailing tension between earthy and heavenly concerns that helped to determine the trajectory of social and spiritual negotiations between (and often within) members of the race. This tension was especially pronounced for blacks during the twentieth century who possessed marketable vocal skills:

> Black people in America have always been torn between walking with Jesus and wandering in the world, clear back to the times of slavery when we either cried out in captivity by singing the blues or held out for a better hope by singing spirituals. The church and the roadhouse have always been two stops on our long road to liberation, and we've been walking the line for hundreds of years. It's only natural that some of us lose our balance once in a while. That struggle is part of what makes us great as a people . . . and part of what makes our music so powerful. (6)

Green confirms perspectives offered in *Fire in My Bones*, an engaging study of spiritual transcendence in black gospel music, where Glen Hinson speaks of the "special responsibility" confronting those who are blessed with "the power of the gift of song," precisely "because that power comes with no constraints. Any gifted singer can stir the emotions. Toward any purpose. For evil or for good. For deception or for truth. For the soul's condemnation or the soul's redemption. Just as with prayer, the Lord grants the gift but doesn't dictate its use. That decision rests wholly with the gift's receiver" (211–12). Recognizing that "all of the great soul singers learned their best licks in the church choir loft," Green emphasizes the difficulty such singers experienced when confronted with religious prohibitions against performing the blues and, later, R & B and rock 'n' roll, the dominant secular forms that derived stylistically from black church musical practices. Green insists that talented black vocalists who are aware of "the gift's affective power" but who do not believe that it must always be used to, in Hinson's words, "steer reflection toward worship" (212), are forced to confront an often debilitating dilemma. According to Green, "No one can tell you the pain of having the choice between lifting up your voice to God or taking a bow for your third encore. That's something you have to experience for yourself. Like Sam Cooke. Like Marvin Gaye. Like Al Green" (6).

Green says of general religious struggles to accommodate the urgent demands of both the spirit and the flesh: "I know that our struggle is not against flesh and blood, but against prinicipalities [*sic*] and powers and that it's a struggle that goes on every day in the depths of my soul. God is not done with Al Green, the good, the bad, and the one in-between. God has promised that, one day, He will do for Al Green what Al Green can't do for himself: heal the divided soul and make him whole" (8). Green's words echo and invite us to consider the spiritual dimensions of W. E. B. Du Bois's theory of double-consciousness, the twentieth century's pre-eminent formulation of the constitutive struggles for Afro-American identity. Du Bois argues that blacks' experience of America has forced upon them a divided sense of self or "twoness,—an American, a Negro; two souls, two thoughts, two unreconciled strivings, two warring ideals in one dark body" (45), whose unity, dependent, as it is, on a wholesale reformation of the nation's racial politics, policies, and practices, is virtually unimaginable. In speaking of his own "divided soul," Green appears to echo Du Bois and to reference the title of an earlier examination of the life of an important R & B singer, David Ritz's acclaimed biography of Marvin Gaye. Green concedes that his own "divided soul" and self, susceptible in perpetuity to Satanic "principalities and powers," cannot be made "whole" without divine intervention. Further, given his place at the end of the line of soul men that includes Gaye and Sam Cooke, both of whom experienced violent, sin-stained deaths, and Green's own infamous encounter with a deranged, pistol-packing, married female fan who burned him with a pot of boiling grits months after the release of *Call Me*, his quest to heal his divided soul takes on special narrative significance.

This struggle for "wholeness," his effort to bring incongruent and competing aspects of his personality and being into harmony, links the aesthetic challenges he faced as an author of his life story with those he confronts as a writer-producer-performer of long-playing records who aspires to be more than simply a singer of popular R & B hits. I want to pursue possible connections between Green's quest for personal wholeness, his performance as a self-conscious autobiographer striving to bring together disparate events of his life into some sort of narrative unity, and his vision of his recordings as coherent structures ("I think of my albums like a book, you open it at the first track and that'll be the opening theme of my album"). That quest for thematic unity may also be seen as a function of Green's desire to imbue his R & B albums with formal aesthetics that govern gospel performance, in whose groups' sets, according to Hinson,

> no song stands alone. Nor do the words that precede or follow it. Instead, songs and commentary flow together, creating a whole only when heard

as a set. Each part of the set—every song, every introduction, every testimony—offers itself as a frame for creative elaboration; each part invites
the crafting of its own unique trajectory. At the same time, the set itself
emerges as a frame; its loose structure also invites a singular and situation-
specific realization. . . . Within this overarching frame, the individual
parts—though not themselves subject to the set's logic—nonetheless contribute to its ultimate realization. (280)

Like Green, I am striving to forge persuasive connections between his
experiences and his songs; as a listener blessed the interpretive freedom
Frith claims for all engaged members of the popular music audience,
and as a scholar with a long-standing fascination with artistic quests to
construct what Hinson calls "overarching frames," I'm searching for ways
to bring together seemingly disparate aspects of his creations and performances.

Echoing Frith's formulations, John Shepherd and Peter Wicke emphasize the listener's role in determining meaning in ways that are useful
for my purposes here. In the following passage, they explain that "we
do not 'receive' a 'message's' meaning . . . but rather construct meaning.
. . . Music, therefore, does not simply convey the intended 'message' of
the composer to the listener. However, in its physical or material, which
is to say symbolic form, music nonetheless carries a trace of intended
meaning" (19). They then quote Jean-Jacques Nattiez, upon whose analysis they draw extensively: "The symbolic form is embodied physically and
materially in the form of a trace accessible to the five senses. We employ
the word *trace* because . . . the esthetic process (if it is in part determined
by the trace) is heavily dependent upon the lived experience of the 'receiver.'" Keeping in mind these notions of the interpreter's contingent
freedom to "construct meaning" within certain limits, I examine material—including Green's autobiography—that leads me to identify the
repetition of phrases, images, and song titles in *Call Me* as the feature
that yields "traces of intended meaning."

Certainly, such an analysis must include an investigation of how
Green's efforts to resolve the inherent tensions between elements of his
divided soul might be said to manifest itself in parts of the album including but not limited to its final song, "Jesus Is Waiting." In dealing with
that issue, I will need to offer a plausible response to a question about
the relationship between this gospel song and the rest of the album that

Green himself poses and admits he has never been able to answer adequately: "If I had fallen so far away from the love of God, how is it that I could see my way clear to write and sing a song like 'Jesus is Waiting' on a [sic] album that was supposed to be about nothing more than flirtation and romance and the hot passions that spring up between a man and a woman?" (290).

Matching Words and Feelings:
Writing Nature and Black Country Boy Aesthetics

I realize that the previous section may appear to confirm critical perspectives that insist that Green's most popular work primarily reflects his struggles with purported incompatibilities between the pleasures and pain of religious testifying and romantic pleading (or, for that matter, the difficulty of achieving their successful resolution). If I am to challenge such ubiquitous perspectives as I have promised, before I explore *Call Me*, I need first to discuss, in some detail, Green's representations in *Take Me to the River* of the circumstances surrounding his composition of his first significant hit, "Tired of Being Alone."

After what he characterizes as the fluky success of the single "Back Up Train," which he recorded in 1967 with his group, Al Greene and the Soul Mates, and the commercial failure in 1970 of his first solo album, *Green Is Blues*, he struggled to establish himself as a solo artist, striving to find vehicles and a vocal style that would propel him beyond the mediocrity of his first two albums. "Convinced that black artists could tap into the white rock & roll bonanza" (Green 249), his producer, Willie Mitchell, encouraged the novice singer, whom he'd promised to make a star in eighteen months, to tackle material such as the Beatles' "Get Back" and "I Want to Hold Your Hand" and the Doors' "Light My Fire." As Green explains, such ill-fitting songs, which left him "trying to cram in little bits of emotion before hurrying off to the next verse before the band left me behind" (249), made him long to demonstrate "what I was actually about as a singer instead of just showing off my abilities as a human jukebox" (250).[1] Precisely what he was "about" was, at that point, still in process, but as his description of the origins of his first fully self-penned vehicle attests, his own initial authorial contribution to the Al Green phenomenon was the result of his capacity to marshal some of the most inspiriting aspects of long-cherished perceptions of himself and of the natural world. As he describes his musical apprenticeship under Mitchell, a significant part of the process entailed his learning to transform himself artistically so that he could produce the sorts of sounds his mentor believed would represent his most artistically and commercially viable style. That style, which Mitchell called "silky on top [the sonic space inhabited by the singer, and], rough on the bottom [where the Hi Rhythm Section dwelled]," encouraged Green to give up a mode of singing that he describes as "loud and gritty and full of my mannish ways" in favor of one that is marked by the "slow," "silky," "soft, tender, [and] vulnerable" cadences of a "little boy" (238, 39).

While his stylistic transformation to boyish vulnerability was not fully completed until his third album, *Let's Stay Together*, from the beginning of his association with Mitchell, Green's sense of his own artistic maturation was tied not only to perfecting a specific sort of vocal delivery, but also to his becoming a songwriter. He tells his readers—as he frequently told his producer—"I wanted to write and record my own songs" (246). Emerging at a moment when many of the most celebrated acts had begun to exert greater control over their recordings, Green believed that if he was going to be able to achieve the sort of vocal vulnerability Mitchell promised would make him a star, he would have to showcase that style in performances of vehicles of his own self-fashioning.

According to *Rock Facts*, an official publication of the Rock and Roll Hall of Fame (into which Green was inducted in 1995), the singer-songwriter phenomenon of the 1960s and 1970s is a largely "middle-class, college-educated" (and white) development personified by such figures as Bob Dylan and Neil Young, whose songs' "naked emotion and soul-searching introspection" were influenced by "the integrity and outspoken nature" of "the work of two rural artists: Hank Williams and Woody Guthrie" (Henke). If Green, a black high school dropout from the deep South, is generally denied admission to the exclusive rock 'n' roll singer-songwriter fraternity—though one consumer guide does laud him for his "vast creativity as a composer" (Pruter 241), and he was inducted into the Songwriters Hall of Fame in June 2004—he embraces aspects of its ethos, evinced on *Call Me* in part by his becoming a masterful interpreter of narratives authored by white southerners that deal with what Williams calls "lovesick blues." Indeed, Green's account of his primary inspiration when he was writing "Tired of Being Alone"—access to the natural world of the sort he regularly experienced as a child in Jacknash, Arkansas, before dire economic conditions forced his family to migrate north—suggests that the southern origins he shares with Williams are precisely what helped to awaken and shape his vocal aspirations in the first place.[2]

Despite his aspirations to become a full-fledged singer-songwriter attempting to reach the highest artistic standards of his age and genre, it is difficult to imagine that each of Green's popular albums was conceived or can convincingly be investigated as containing a series of thematically intersecting narratives. In fact, like virtually every other pop album, most of them seem to be collections of songs with no discernible thematic connection. Still, after his first two albums, Green, striving for his own version of musical sophistication and rock artistry, exerts greater control over which songs appear on his popular albums; beginning with *Let's Stay Together*, he authors or coauthors the great majority of his songs, and he starts getting coproducer credits on his fourth album, *I'm Still in Love with You* (1972). In the wake of, among other critically acclaimed albums, the Beatles' *Sergeant Pepper's Lonely Hearts Club Band* (1967), which Martha Bayles describes as a technologically sophisticated "montage of diverse sounds that sustains the illusion of coherence and depth" that helped "transform . . . rock into 'an art form'" (221), the notion of the pop musician as artist achieves a level of legitimacy that continues to color our responses to older singers and our reception of emerging ones.

But as the authors of the breezy but informative study *Precious and Few: Pop Music in the Early '70s* attest, in the estimation of many, the label "singer-songwriter," coined in response to self-consciously literate, introspective white solo acts such as Dylan, Joni Mitchell, and James Taylor, did not apply to the seemingly banal, unlettered, unself-reflective, and wholly conventional romantic songs of a performer such as Green: "A singer-songwriter was more than just someone who sang his or her own songs (otherwise everyone from Paul Anka to Al Green would fit the bill); a singer-songwriter wrote and sang songs that were serious, soul-searching, and really about something" (Breithaupt and Breithaupt 80). Green's discussion of writing "Tired of Being Alone," however, challenges views that his work wasn't sufficiently "soul-searching" or the result of intense scrutiny. Indeed, in part because that discussion demonstrates that he shares with the preeminent American intellectual Ralph Waldo Emerson, author of classic essays such as "Self-Reliance" and "Nature," an abiding interest in connections between human emotions and elements of the external world, we can explore other aspects of the "something" that Green is "really about."

Green describes being alone in a rural Michigan hotel room between concert dates, "walking over to the window" at dawn, and "looking out across the empty highway to the frozen fields on the other side."

> As I watched while the sun slowly seeped into the dark sky, like milk being poured into a bowl, I felt myself standing in the middle of some great empty place, as if the universe and everything in it had been cleared away in a circle from all around me. It was a lonely, solitary sensation, but the strange thing was, I didn't feel the ache of a man left to himself. It was more a peaceful feeling, a kind of soothing sensation, as if I was far away from every human sorrow and strife.
>
> I could see the trees and farmhouses start to take shape out of the shadows as the sky brightened and the stars faded at the horizon. Somewhere, far away, I heard a rooster crow and a dog bark in answer. I could still hear the melody of that dream song in my brain and, in that moment, like poets and songwriters through the ages, I tried to match words to my feelings. (252–53)

Here, Green represents himself as the quintessential "lonely, solitary" artist inspired both by emotion and by nature, whose majesty and inscrutability can only be approached through a form of symbolic substitution ("I tried to match words to my feelings") of which poetic metaphor— "the sun slowly seeped into the dark sky, like milk being poured into a bowl"—has served traditionally as the most distinguished manifestation. While this passage is important because it undermines contentions about omnipresent manifestations of his religious dilemma in his popular songs, it is followed by Green's gesturing toward a sort of religious piety—his insistence that he's "watching God's creation unfold in all its perfection" (253)—a largely perfunctory effort that is certainly secondary, at least in terms of what it contributes to our understanding of the paradoxical nature of his formulation, to his insistence on the transience of the pain of absence and his ability to transcend it. Ultimately, Green insists, his efforts to "match words to . . . feelings" that become "Tired of Being Alone" are not the result of the pain of loneliness and solitude that he experienced initially, as his mood briefly reflects the feelings traditionally evoked in the works of "poets and songwriters" in response to the empty highways and frozen fields that he witnesses. Instead, he begins to write only after he is overcome by a "peaceful feeling" and "soothing sensation" that result from and/or in his recognizing that he is "far away from every human sorrow and strife," feelings that correspond with the image of brightened skies and what he interprets as the life-affirming exchange he overhears between a rooster and a dog that confirm his beliefs about the transitory nature of his isolation.

After insisting that the first major hit he composed was the result of his efforts to match words to his feelings, Green then suggests that it is purely the byproduct of inspiration—he "wrote down the words just as they came to [him], listening hard to make sure [he] got them all right"—leaving the reader to determine which of these competing views of creativity is more plausible. What he does not leave in doubt, however, are the personal goals and emotional conditions that motivate him. The lyrics of loneliness do not emerge as a direct reflection of how he feels; instead, he informs us, he writes of loneliness after the angst it produces has passed and in anticipation of its inevitable return, when, in other words, the internal mood that serves as an emotional equivalent of the empty and frozen highways he witnesses has been transplanted by brightening skies and a resultant sense of "perfect peace" that overcomes him. "Tired of Being Alone," then, is the product of feelings inspired by a desolate rural scene that sunlight routinely reshapes, and from his realization that, however inspiring he finds witnessing a morning "so pure, so beautiful that [he] wanted it never to end," "with no one to share it, sooner or later [he'd] grow tired of being alone, tired of being on [his] own." In his autobiography, then, Green constructs "Tired of Being Alone" as a song of what was and what may be, rather than as an effort to match mood and language or to put directly into words how he feels at the time of the song's composition.

Green's poeticized formulations of connections between what he observes and what he feels call to mind Emerson's notion of a "radical," divinely ordained "correspondence between visible things and human thoughts" (202). While I will later use the classic essay "Nature" to illuminate aspects of Green's descriptions of the place of nature in his art, I cite Emerson here primarily because his formulations help me to highlight the fact that the lyrics of "Tired of Being Alone" are curiously devoid of references to the external world that allegedly inspires them. Certainly, the lyrics manifest what we might see as a consistent and effective compositional style, deriving largely from their aggressive use of internal rhymes and near-rhymes that echo the lines' concluding sounds, where the urgency of his appeals to his absent lover is most pronounced. Note, for example, the following: "I guess you *know* that I love you *so* / Even *though* you don't want me no *mo.*'"

Simon Frith has argued that unlike poems, which "'score' the performance or reading of the verse in the words themselves, words that are chosen in part because of the way they lead us on, metrically and rhythmically, by their arrangement on the page," song lyrics "are 'scored' by the music itself" (181). In Frith's view, "Good lyrics by definition . . . lack the elements that make for good lyric poetry. Take them out of their performed context, and they either seem to have no musical qualities at all, or else to have such obvious ones as to be silly. . . . The best pop songs . . . are those that can be heard as a struggle between verbal and musical rhetoric, between the singer and the song" (182). If we accept Frith's views on such matters, the effectiveness of a song such as "Tired of Being Alone" is not primarily a function of lyrical sophistication at all, but of sonic qualities. Those qualities include Green's uncharacteristic (for his hit songs) utilization of an interplay between "mannish" and vulnerable boy styles, the propulsive horns and insistent drumming that replicate his rhythmic use of simple rhymes and near-rhymes, and the modulation of tempo that affords Green the opportunity both to emphasize and to abandon the rigid rhyme and sound scheme of the verses and other pop song conventions. (One such convention that the song ignores at times is narrative consistency, as evinced by the fact that, early in the song, Green's persona insists that the object of his affection didn't "go for saying that" she loves him, while, in the seemingly improvised coda or fade out, he exclaims, "Sometimes I wonder if you love me like you say you do.")

But given the link Green himself makes between this song's composition and poetic attempts to "match words to . . . feeling," we cannot help noting that while he is able to describe the sense of angst and longing he had felt and expected to feel again, he fails to incorporate into such lyrical musings his provocative insights into connections between nature and human states of feeling that constitute, in Emerson's view, the crucial feature of the intellect's efforts to "search . . . out the absolute order of things as they stand in the mind of God" (199). However effectively "Tired of Being Alone" connects its propulsive rhythms and internal rhyme schemes to its lyrical affirmation of the searing pain of loneliness, however successfully Green swoops and soars, shouts and whispers, begs and pleads, roughs up and sweetens his voice, it is difficult for me, after encountering his autobiographical discussion of its composition, not to wonder why the song represses what Emerson calls "the presence of a higher [force], namely, of [nature,] the spiritual element [that] is essential to its perfection" (198).

Throughout *Take Me to the River*, Green insists that his urge to sing resulted from his desire to produce sounds that replicated those that emanated from nature or, at the very least, the rural, southern roads he traveled as a boy. In the first chapter, Green suggests that his vocal gift is a product not of devotional imitation of human models ("Elvis or Otis, Jackie Wilson or Wilson Pickett"), whose styles his own is thought at times to resemble, but of inspired attention to—and, ultimately, recreation of—the "language" or sounds of nature:

> If you really want to know what my earliest influences were, you'd have to go back to the rain on the window, the wind in the corn crop, or the water lapping on the banks of the river. That is music to my ears.
>
> I can still remember childhood days when I'd wake up early to the birds singing in the trees and throw open the window just to catch their whistles and chirps. It made no difference to me that it was the dead of winter or that my brothers were yelling at me from the bed we shared to shut the window and stop acting a fool. They just didn't hear what I heard. And it would be a long time before I understood in my mind what I always knew was true in my heart—God speaks through His creation and the language he uses is music to those with ears to hear. (11–12)

Green, who insists that music, the sounds that emanate from God's "creation," is a divine language, assures his readers that his primary recollection of his artistic apprenticeship involves neither his covert nocturnal attempts to "pick up [on the radio] those hot and heavy sounds out of Memphis, the forbidden fruit my mama said would rob me of my soul" nor, when he was a teenager whose family had migrated from Jacknash, Arkansas, to Grand Rapids, Michigan, "singing five sets a night with Jr. Walker and the All Stars back behind me like a runaway freight train." Instead, what he remembers most and was most deeply inspired by was "just walking along by myself down a country road, singing a song with no words, just 'sha-la-la,' and making up the melody as I went along" (13).

Certainly, Green does not wildly romanticize his sharecropping past, which taught him that "poverty has a way of robbing a child of his identity and self-worth, making him nothing more than just another mouth to feed" (13). Still, in his pastoral recollections he fondly represents aspects of his southern history, particularly his sense of being profoundly connected to nature and to God, the sources of his artistic inspiration. The North, to which his family migrated in a last-gasp effort to save his parents' marriage, unraveling as a consequence of economic pressures typically faced by sharecropper families, his father's subsequent heavy drinking, and his mother's fundamentalist disapproval thereof, was a barren landscape for young Al, not a promised land of improved opportunity. Further, the move was jarring to his burgeoning creative sensibilities because, in Grand Rapids, he had to "struggle" to "keep connected to the things that had made my young life worth living. Cut off from the glory of the natural world, lost in the shuffle of our uprooted family, feeling as forlorn and lonely as I could ever remember, I began to turn inward, losing some of the spontaneous joy that had always made the world seem bright in my eyes, and with it, that childlike innocence that trusted and believed the best in everyone" (61). His father's quest for economic self-sufficiency in the North was no more successful than those of "many [who] had traveled that same road before us . . . [about whose "bitterness and broken dreams"] you can read . . . in history books" (56). For "little Al," however, the move caused a premature termination of his childhood, and "the change was almost too much to bear. Where was the sound of singing birds? Where was the warm caressing wind blowing up from the Gulf of Mexico? Where was the tender, patient murmur of Mama's voice, singing about how Jesus loved the little children as she rocked me to sleep?" (62). Reading these formulations, I cannot help but recall the fact that the states of feeling described in "Tired of Being Alone" are themselves disconnected from their natural analogues, and I want to ask of that song, "Where are the trees and farmhouses? Where are the rooster's crow and the dog's bark?"

Both an American rags-to-riches tale and the story of a creative child's desire to become an artist, *Take Me to the River* revolves around Green's efforts to recover "the sound of singing birds" and something approximating "the tender, patient murmur of Mama's voice," to which his family's migration robbed him of easy, comforting, life-affirming access. Wanting to prove that he was different than his "bitter and bent" father, who had "been beaten down so long and robbed of his own dreams and ambitions that he just stopped believing it could happen for anyone else, either"

(110), Green actively pursued success as a pop singer in part to defy him. Indeed, Green resented his father, whom he believed was "trying [to] rob me of my very life and soul. For me, music was what made every day worth living, what put the glow at the horizon of the future, where everywhere else I looked all I could see was folks held captive in an endless cycle of poverty" (90). His father's abandonment of the South's natural music and attempted theft of young Al's dream of a musical career recall, for me, Janie's description of her grandmother in Zora Neale Hurston's canonical southern novel *Their Eyes Were Watching God*. As someone whose painful life as a slave left her with, at best, a limited capacity to envision a liberated, joyful life for her offspring, Nanny thwarts her granddaughter's desire to embark on a "great journey to the horizons in search of people; it was important to all the world that she should find them and they find her." Like Janie, a "born orator" silenced by a loved one whose oppressive influence she must actively reject because Nanny "had taken the biggest thing God ever made, the horizon . . . , and pinched it into such a little bit of a thing that she could tie it about her granddaughter's neck tight enough to choke her" (85), young Al must learn figuratively to pursue the horizon's glow, and literally to incorporate it and other natural elements into the body of his musical narratives.

The dialectical thinking that inspires his fundamentalist mother and spiritually "betwixt and between" father to perceive sacred and secular urgings as occupying separate, noncontiguous realms is evident in Green's strategic depictions of the North and South as what literary critic Robert Stepto argues are traditional Afro-Americanist formulations of distinct areas of "symbolic geography" (66). According to Stepto, canonical black narratives, including autobiographies such as *Narrative of the Life of Frederick Douglass* and *Black Boy* and first-person novels such as *Autobiography of an Ex-Coloured Man* and *Invisible Man* that present themselves as the memoirs of fictional characters, are linked because, as reflections of a culture, they are "bound historically and linguistically to a shared pregeneric myth"—"the quest for freedom and literacy"—which "eventually shape[s] the forms that comprise a given culture's literary canon" (xvi, xv). Given the nature of blacks' American origins, that "shared . . . myth" posits slavery (and subsequent forms of institutionalized oppression) as its informing structural device, making a "perilous assertion of mobility [typically from southern to northern environs] after the assault of bondage" (67) an essential dimension of such texts.

In his representations of the North and South, Green appears acutely aware not of these literary texts necessarily, but certainly of what Stepto terms Afro-American "canonical stories" (xv). However, he adds his own twist to such stories, positing that economic lack, rather than an intransigent racism, mars his experience of the pre–civil rights South, the site of his artistic inspiration and maternal nurturance. In his representation, both music and comfort are unavailable in the barren North, where "the sounds of those streets, grinding and rattling twenty four hours a day, was [*sic*] a harsh and high-pitched caterwauling that jangled my nerves and set my teeth on edge" (66). His personal freedom and artistic development—both of which are integral to his achievement of psychic wholeness—depend, to invoke Stepto again, on a literal and/or figurative ascent from and (re)immersion in the nurturance and more easily accessible divine natural presence that the symbolic geography of the South represents.

Already we have seen how nature inspires (but is not included in the narrative of) "Tired of Being Alone," a reformulation that requires him to invest the North, which he had previously depicted as totally bereft, with southern possibilities. Green further illuminates his vision of nature in the South in his description of his search for a house in Memphis following the success of "Let's Stay Together."

> And the funny thing was, once I started imagining what such a place might be, what came to me was the home I'd left behind just over the river in Arkansas so long ago. That's not to say I wanted to find myself a shotgun shack on a sharecropper's lot. No, what appealed to me was the calm, serene beauty of God's creation. I wanted to be close to nature, someplace where the birds were singing sweetly and the scent of pine needles floated on the evening air like perfume, someplace where I could get away and get in touch, lose myself and find myself. (283)

Earlier in the autobiography, Green, who emphasizes the longing he felt as a boy to replicate nature's sounds, discusses the felt sense of loss that resulted from practicing the gospel songs in the repertoire of his older brothers' singing group:

> Instead of just walking along through the woods, singing whatever nonsense notes and words that popped into my head, I'd bear down on the songs I'd heard my brothers rehearsing. And sure enough, I improved. My

technique got better, I could hold a note and stay in tune and remember all the words to all the verses. But looking back on that time, I get the feeling I was giving up something too, trading the spontaneous joy of singing like the birds in the trees, just for the simple joy of it, and trying to fit myself into a structure that sometimes seemed lifeless and dreary in comparison. (27)

As he moves away from boyish southern vulnerability and the source of natural song and toward socially prescribed modes of singing and being—including the macho posture he adopted in order to protect himself in the urban North—Green stops singing like "the birds in the trees" and starts to replicate the "man-and-a-half" styles of the most acclaimed and successful male soul singers of the mid-1960s, including Otis Redding and Wilson Pickett. Ultimately, Mitchell is able to convince Green to stop "trying to hit those Jackie Wilson high notes or rattle the rafters with an Otis-brand soul growl," helping him to recognize the aesthetic and commercial benefits of adopting a softer, "jazz vocal style with those mellow chords and progression laid lightly over a sandpaper-and-grits R & B rhythm section. . . . Singing softer, listening to myself, really understanding the words and feelings and melodic changes—these were all techniques that brought out the real soul in my music . . . and the real music in my soul" (239).

This style offered him "a pure pleasure that I seemed to come by naturally, issuing forth from the deepest part of myself" (239), reminding him of the type of singing he used to do as a southern child. As he characterizes it, his singing during his most popular period reflected "a soft, tender, vulnerable side of [himself] that could only express itself through singing, like a little boy crying for his mama or a grown man weak for the love of a woman. To sing like that, you've got to let something inside of you loose, give up your pride and power, and let that surrendering feeling well up inside until it overwhelms you and uses your voice to cry out with a need that can't be filled" (239). *Take Me to the River* sets up a telling contrast between Green's biological and professional male progenitors in which—not surprisingly—music is the central component. Green's description of Mitchell contrasts sharply with that of his father, who robbed him of nature, childhood innocence, and secular music. Mitchell, Green says, "gave me the freedom to be a little boy again, to go back and relive a part of my life that had taken another direction when we'd pulled up stakes and moved to Grand Rapids" (240). Despite his appreciation of the obstacles his father faced, Green insists that his father's choice to move his family to the North took away the sensitive son's access to nature and song: "[I] blamed my daddy for what we didn't have and what we couldn't get" and saw him a figure over whom "failure . . . seemed to hang . . . like a dark cloud" (103).

Also, his father's refusal to allow secular music to be played at an audible level in his house denied him not only that music's possibly compensatory pleasures, but, I believe, access to information that might have helped him to confront successfully some of the most disastrous aspects of possessing a divided soul, including an unhealthy view of women. A few pages before he describes his father's throwing him out of his Grand Rapids house as a teenager for playing Jackie Wilson's "A Woman, A Lover, A Friend" too loudly, he discusses the persistence of what we must see—even if Green does not appear to—as an immature male perception of women:

> For me, the female form had always been a haven of comfort and safety. As a boy, I knew I could always hide in the warm embrace of my mama, my grandma, or any one of those aunts who treated me like their own son. But when that boy began to become a man and those feelings of security and protection began to get mixed up with the desire to prove my masculinity, I wasn't sure which way to turn. Part of me was aching to make my move, to relieve that intolerable itch between my legs. The other part just wanted to lay my head against a warm breast and have my head stroked until I drifted off to sweet sleep. (86)

An adolescent Green is confounded by a "strange mix of motives" where women—whom he considers either maternal figures or sexual objects— were concerned. Having begun his discussion of his expulsion by crediting his soul man forebear, Jackie Wilson, whose record he was playing too loudly for his father's comfort, with giving him "the chance to take charge of [his] life and try it on [his] own" (85), Green then names the specific song, thereby providing knowledgeable readers the opportunity to understand the flaws in his father's blanket condemnation of rock 'n' roll. Certainly, it is at least ironic that Wilson's song addresses, in the most inoffensive way imaginable, the precise issues about which, earlier in the chapter, young Al was admittedly confused and his father, situated painfully "betwixt and between" sin and salvation, cannot comfortably speak.

"A Woman, A Lover, A Friend" tells the story of a man searching not for an idealized, "make believe" "saint," not for a casual sexual partner or a self-sacrificing maternal figure, but for a supportive, affectionate female who "doesn't mind giving so that she may receive." In fact, Wilson's song rejects the precise dialectical formulations of women as either nurturers or sexual objects that Green cannot himself move beyond even after he becomes a popular "soul-singing ladies' man" who had numerous trysts with female fans because, he comes to believe, he was attempting to find "a substitute for a mother's love" (49). Instead of contributing necessarily to his soul's eternal damnation, as his mother suggests secular music inevitably would, this particular pop song contains insights about healthy romantic relations that Green desperately needed and that neither his mother—who appears to be little more to him than a comforting symbolic breast—nor his angst-ridden father can provide. Sexuality and spirituality remain mutually exclusive for Green, who is denied, and banished for seeking, alternative models by his father whom he "blamed . . . for what [they] didn't have and what [they] couldn't get."

Consequently, Green's perceptions of females appear stagnant; even after his religious rebirth, he never seems to move far beyond an adolescent view of them either as objectified sexual itch scratchers or as unproblematic sites of maternal comfort. In a startling formulation, he describes the many female fans with whom he has had "carnal relations" as "bodies and voices . . . blended together long ago, one lonely form all blurred and transparent, like a restless ghost that wanders through my memory" (275–76). The relationship that he depicts most fully is his first, with a prostitute named Juanita, with whom he lived soon after his father threw him out of the house. He goes to great lengths to legitimize and normalize this union:

> Across the years, . . . our relationship took on every kind of variation you could imagine: from mother and son, to father and daughter, to pimp and whore. At any given time, I was her lover, her "pretty little boy," and her confessor. In the same way, she would play the role of the daughter, the breadwinner, or the hardworking mother who only wanted to have her feet rubbed at the end of a busy day. You could say our relationship was complicated, but to us, it was simple. We were everything to each other. (130)

From my perspective, theirs was a terribly flawed relationship, though Green himself seems unaware of its fundamental problems. Generally, he depicts himself and Juanita in hierarchical relationship to each other, and even his sense that "what we saw in each other was a kind of idealized beauty" signals their inability to view each other as human beings rather than as symbols. Because of such thinking, his notion of "everything" positions Juanita not as "a woman, a lover, [and] a friend" as in the Jackie Wilson record whose healthy formulations of romantic love his father silenced, but, unsurprisingly, in terms of the mother/whore dialectic that confounds him throughout the narrative. As a result, he strategically juxtaposes Juanita and the "saint[ly] religious leader of Mother Bates's House of Prayer," from whom he "learned more of what true faith is all about" (76) than he did from his mother, and who'd "be sitting in a pool of golden light" while young Al, a featured performer in her revival circuit, watched her "praying and ministering for hours after each meeting" (77). According to Green: "In my mind, Juanita will always occupy a place in my life directly opposite from, but equally important to, Mother Bates. They are like two magnetic poles, forces that kept me in balance between them, the one calling me to the purity of the faith, the other to the pleasures of the flesh. I make no judgment, nor do I cast any condemnation. As Mother Bates was born to her work, so was Juanita" (127).

The only other significant relationship with a woman he details is with the seventies R & B artist Laura Lee, whom he considers a "gift" from God and describes—in terms that the sentiments of Wilson's song—as "a true friend and boon companion, someone I could trust and who called on me to be trustworthy, maybe the most selfless and loyal person who ever cross the path of my life" (277). Unlike Juanita, about whose beauty "there was no question"—endowed, as she was, with a "high yellow complexion that set off her dark almond eyes and jet-black hair, straightened and swept up off her forehead *as if* she were a lady of true style and sophistication"— "Laura was not a beautiful woman as some folks count beauty, but she had another kind of comeliness, an inner light that illuminated her face and shone forth in a smile as radiant and *warm as the morning sun*" (127, 278, emphasis added). Green met Lee, with whom he "shared a bill on some Southeastern dates shortly after the release of *Let's Stay Together*," at the height of his despondency over the death of his cousin Little Junior Parker, whose hit "Driving Wheel" he covered on his previous album, *Al Green Gets Next to You*, whose intriguing version of "Funny How Time Slips Away" he seems to have learned quite a bit from, and to whom he later dedicates "Take Me to the River" in the song's spoken introduction. Unlike the tension he experienced during his sexually charged meetings with other women at the height of his popularity, who "forget their natural feminine shyness and Christian modesty and just come right out and tell me how they feel . . . and what they want to do about it" (274)—these women, then, act like the prostitute Juanita, who tells Green during their first encounter, "You certainly are a pretty young thing" (129)—Green's mind is placed "at ease" by Laura Lee's chaste response to his own "sharp second look" (278).

He describes his relationship with Lee, who also went from singing in the church to seeking success as an R & B artist, as "different—and maybe stronger—than any romance": "We were soul mates, birds of a feather, two halves of one whole. There was something pure about our love as it grew over the years that followed, something that remained as innocent and authentic as that moment when she first offered her hand in friendship" (280). The fact that Green views his close, mutually supportive connection with Lee as something other than romance rather than potentially—as the Jackie Wilson song suggests—its truest expression, may be explained in a variety of ways.[3] His notion of romance might simply be a response to the troubled relationships he'd witnessed, including that of his parents. At the very least, however, there is ample evidence to suggest that his perception stems from and contributes to his inability to see comfort and sexuality as being conjoined in or possible with one person.

However we conceive of its sources, clearly Green remains cognitively stuck in dialectical thinking about relationships, even in connection with his "soul mate," who is represented in terms of what we will see is a central metaphor of *Call Me* ("warm as the morning sun"). His problems are further demonstrated by the fact that he insists that Lee's (minor) "star story," best evinced by such R & B "female liberation" songs as "Wedlock Is a Padlock" and "Women's Love Rights," which Green characterizes as "proud-and-loud declarations of independence" (279), was just "a lot of pretending" (279–80). (In the liner notes to the Hot Wax release of her greatest hits, the deep-voiced, bluesy singer herself insists, "The women's lib thing—that's not really me at all," but goes on to say, "One partner in a romance should never dominate the other.") According to Green, she was just his sort of woman because, like him, she understood the difference between who she was and what she performs: "Now, understand, I personally didn't go for the upfront and outspoken type of woman. I liked my girlfriends meek, mild, and obedient. But in spite of her strutting and bragging, it seemed to me that Laura could never quite get away from who she really was—a daughter of the church, gifted in song for the glory of God" (280). In stating his preference for the sort of docile, pliable woman he suggests fundamentalist churches encourage its female members to become, Green speaks of Lee's liberated women themes and "soul sister style" of singing not as expressions of her true being and beliefs, but simply as performances. However "gifted in song" she may be, what makes her an appropriate soul mate for Green is her ability to remain "meek, mild, and obedient," despite her professional act and the changing attitudes about gendered inequity into which that act taps and from which it profits.

Acting Out Soul: Singers, Songwriters,
and a "Multiplicity of Authorial Voices"

Like many R & B releases of the 1960s and 1970s in particular, Green's songs of love, happiness, and, soul-shattering loneliness confirm the veracity of Leroi Jones's claim that "any historical (or emotional) line of ascent in Black music leads us inevitably to religion, i.e., spirit worship" (181–82). But when applied to his popular period specifically, and, I will argue, to *Call Me* in particular, attempts to locate a "secular-sacred divide" or, for that matter, their productive synthesis, in his songs generally reflect the sort of revisionism that Green himself encourages and in which he actively participates. Knowledge of his eventual (albeit temporary) repudiation of secular music in favor of gospel music and the pulpit of his Memphis church, the Full Gospel Tabernacle, motivates critics looking for an overarching interpretation of the meanings of his music to view it as reflecting a traditional twentieth-century dilemma for vocalists trained in black churches who feel called upon to explore the pleasures and vicissitudes of romantic love rather than human struggles to achieve spiritual salvation. Over and over, one line from Green's last commercially successful solo release "Belle"—"It's you that I want, but it's Him that I need"—is cited as evidence of Green's efforts to resolve his dialectical concerns once he has been born again in Christ after *Call Me*'s release. These concerns are then grafted upon and seen as an animating force in his entire popular oeuvre.

Green's acknowledgment of his capacity to perform states of being he is not experiencing or has not experienced should give pause to those who insist that there necessarily exists a one-to-one correspondence between events in his life and his composition or renderings of musical narratives into which he inserts himself vocally. Indeed, this acknowledgment confirms David Brackett's perspectives in *Interpreting Popular Music* on the

> distinct disadvantages [inherent in] . . . this way of conceptualizing the relationship between singer and song. Even for singer-songwriters it is questionable whether the song only expresses the autobiographical details of their lives. . . . [T]here exists the possibility that a song and a recording may present a range of affect that exceeds the composer/performer's intentions: listeners may interpret a song in a way that has little to do with what the performer "felt" when he or she recorded or wrote it. At still another level, the notion of a strict identity between lived experience and a song's meaning eliminates the effect of the song as a musical performance: the musical codes and the manner in which the song is performed may either contradict or reinforce the content in the lyrics, adding new layers of nuance by "acting out," inflecting, and contextualizing them. There is thus the possibility—even in a performance by a solo singer-songwriter in which singer, instrumentalist, arranger, and composer are one and the same person—of a multiplicity of authorial voices in the musical text. (15)

Brackett's assertion that we see "song as a musical performance" instead of as an unmediated expression of "lived experience" encourages us to explore multiple aspects of the singer's "star story," including but certainly not limited to the insistence on the part of Green himself and his critics that his popular songs be seen primarily in terms of his struggles to heal the sacred-secular divide. If analyses of his work continue merely to reiterate such assessments, future investigators will have nothing new or illuminating to say about perhaps the most accomplished R & B artist to emerge during the era of the singer-songwriter and, with the possible exception of Luther Vandross, the genre's most skillful interpreter of others' songs. They will find themselves lacking persuasive ways of assessing Green's work, may ignore the singer's important and sometimes fascinating lyrical contributions to his artistic success, and may fail to recognize—as did the R & B artists Smokey Robinson and Jeffrey Osborne, who assessed *Call Me* for VH1's celebration of the one hundred greatest albums of the rock 'n' roll era—that if that album's songs encourage listeners to fall in love, these listeners are not closely attending to the album's consistent depiction of romantic love as almost unmitigated anguish.

My own analysis of *Call Me* manifests my notion of Green as a reflective singer-songwriter and a gifted interpreter who is fascinated with the possibilities of spiritual and narrative wholeness, and who insists that each of his albums can be read as a series of self-contained but nonetheless thematically related songs. This album, featuring what, from a variety of perspectives, we could call "a multiplicity of authorial voices," might be characterized as thematically consistent (or, perhaps, even repetitive) and highly allusive. These allusions include the use of the phrase "the morning sun" (which, as we have seen, he employs in his autobiography to refer to Laura Lee) in two of the album's songs, the "overlooked classic," "Have You Been Making Out O.K," and "Your Love Is Like the Morning Sun," whose fadeout consists of Green singing the titles of three of his earlier hits, "I'm So Tired of Being Alone," "I'm Still in Love with You," and "Let's Stay Together."

What we make of these allusions will ultimately determine what we see as the connections between Green's compositions and the songs he covers, between the album's hits and its other tracks, between songs that were "supposed to be about nothing more than flirtation and romance and the hot passions that spring up between a man and a woman" and the album's gospel finale, "Jesus Is Waiting." I engage Green's album as a structure, as a suite or "set" of unified sounds, images, and themes (to invoke Glenn Hinson's gospel terminology), not unlike many of the most critically lauded albums of the rock 'n' roll era, including *What's Going On*, that, for the first time, made the production of long-playing art a tangible (if not easily achievable) goal for the most ambitious of black singer-songwriters. But because he "was always marketed as a singles artist" (Christgau, "Growing Up" 465), albeit one whose desire to produce thematically unified albums apparently led him to resent and resist that characterization, I must briefly take up again, this time in more detail, investigations in seventies pop music criticism of the differences between singles and albums as forms through which artistry is best manifested.

"Distill an Essence, Seize a Moment":
Singles, Albums, and the "Age of the Artist"

In his introduction to *The Heart of Rock and Soul: The 1001 Greatest Singles Ever Made*, Dave Marsh argues that, "after 1970, . . . the story [of rock and roll] has always been told in terms of albums" because, in the estimation of many influential critics, they "are pop music's most effective vehicle for expressing complexity of style and personality" (ix–x). Marsh suggests that this dominant critical practice assumes that self-contained musical production — "writing, performing, and producing" — is the height of pop artistry largely because "so much criticism revolves around implications of intention," which makes it "extraordinarily useful to have writer and performer (and perhaps producer as well) wrapped up in one person" (xiii). Chiding his colleagues for overestimating the musical value of progressive rock albums, Marsh's project is to demonstrate the singles-oriented artistry manifest in the genres of rhythm and blues and country, whose "two to six minutes of music . . . distill an essence, seize a moment, sum up a movement, galvanize an audience" (xiv–xv) in ways that long-form progressive rockers in particular, and albums in general, are by and large incapable of doing.

Marsh's assessment helps to illuminate the presuppositions of pop music criticism at the precise moment when at least some of its participants were inclined for the first time to consider rock 'n' roll at its best not merely as commerce, but as art. By the early 1970s, the Presley–early Motown–Phil Spector model of the vocally and/or instrumentally gifted but lyrically and technologically unskilled singer or group (who had to be supplied with words, sentiment, studio time, musicians, production, and, hence, his or her "sound" by a record company) was replaced by that of the self-determined, technically proficient singer-songwriter who partly or fully controls the writing and/or selection of his material and, hence, the means of musical production. Such singers were more likely to consider the album as something other than a pastiche or grab bag of songs discovered, collected, or composed by the company's paid staff. Notwithstanding Marsh's perspectives on a singles-driven black music's generally successful evasion of what he doubtlessly views as the neofolk singer-songwriter's and the progressive rock musician's long-play pretensions, certainly a number of R & B artists were susceptible to the lures of thematic weightiness and formal stretching out.

The near universal praise heaped upon Marvin Gaye's *What's Going On*, for example, is a reflection of the success of thematic, formal, and musical risks he was able to take largely because he seized control over the direction of his career from the Motown machine generally and, in particular, from Berry Gordy, his brother-in-law and professional patriarch, with whom he battled frequently. In the wake of the death of his good friend and singing partner Tammi Terrell, and his disenchantment with his nation's domestic policies and international agenda, if Gaye was to prove that he was a serious artist who could do more than sing (and occasionally coauthor) love songs, he had to write, produce, and make stylistic decisions that ran counter to the wishes of his patriarch and Motown's Quality Control department, which "picked and scheduled the releases [of recorded music as album cuts and singles] at the company's weekly product evaluation meetings" (Edmonds 27). Several years before this seminal album's release, that department refused to put out Gaye's version of "Heard It through the Grapevine"—which Marsh considers the best single in history—largely because it didn't sound like the most popular hits of the period or like the singer's own earlier work. Gaye responded by breaking "the Motown mold," producing in *What's Going On* what Martha Bayles calls "his own version of the art rock album, conceived as a whole greater than the sum of its parts," and which moves off of the beaten track of romantic love and "venture[s] into forbidden territory: poverty, pollution, the Vietnam War, and the 'generation gap'" (230).

In Gaye's own estimation, his use of a higher register and jazz-like cadence—which he continued to employ in all of his subsequent recordings—signaled that he'd "finally learned how to sing" because he'd "taught himself to 'relax, just relax'" (Marsh 24). Whatever else we can say about this album, its abandonment of the subject of romantic love in favor of spiritual and political themes, its consistent mid-tempo groove, its offering of several tracks whose nearly identical instrumentation and background singing link them sonically with one another, and its coda (which repeats the opening and title track's refrain, "Mother, mother, everybody thinks we're wrong / but who are they to judge us / Simply because we wear our hair long") all signal that Gaye strove to create a coherent work of art. Its efforts to forge aural and thematic connections between tracks rather than to replicate a typical Motown or pop, love song–laden album composed of fragmented parts—potential or actual hits and obviously less marketable "filler"—are palpable.

Using Marsh's formulation here, we could say that Gaye strives to create "thirty to fifty" minutes of music that can, like great singles such as "Grapevine," "distill an essence, seize a moment, sum up a movement, galvanize an audience." Gaye brings together sound, theme, and form, producing a unified work whose striking coherence and musical power led Motown's most fabled writer and producer, Smokey Robinson, to call it "the single greatest record ever made by anyone" (quoted in Ritz, "Marvin's Miracle," 13). And though *What's Going On* did not introduce political commentary into R & B (the period from 1964 to 1969 witnessed the release of many poignant message songs, including Sam Cooke's "A Change Is Gonna Come," Wonder's "A Place in the Sun" and his version of Bob Dylan's "Blowin' in the Wind," and the Impressions' series of Curtis Mayfield-composed tracks, "Keep On Pushing," "We're a Winner," "This Is My Country," and "Choice of Colors"), it extended the artistic boundaries of such commentary, encouraging such maverick soul singers as Green, who recognizes connections between his career and Gaye's, to enter into "the age of the artist."

If a pinnacle of popular musical achievement since 1970 is the formally and thematically unified LP, pop aesthetics are out of step with modernist and postmodernist sensibilities. Unified by what has been widely recognized as a hermeneutics of suspicion, its creative practitioners and theoreticians challenge what they term tyrannical formulations of artistic wholeness and insist, instead, on recognition of the fictiveness and contested nature of human constructs. The art that is seen by such intellectuals as most responsive to contemporary social conditions is fundamentally suspicious of unifying gestures, manifesting a crafty self-awareness of its own gaps and a seriously playful sense of the formal, ideological, and social conventions that governed its construction.

According to Terrence Hawkes,

> Structure can be observed in an arrangement of entities which embodies the fundamental ideas of wholeness, transformation, and self-regulation. By wholeness is meant the sense of internal coherence. The arrangement of entities will be complete in itself and not something that is simply formed of otherwise independent elements. Its constituent parts will conform to

a set of intrinsic laws which determine its nature and theirs. These laws confer parts within the structure overall properties larger than those each individually possesses outside it. Thus a structure is quite different from an aggregate: its constituent parts have no genuinely independent existence outside the structure in the same form they have within it. (Quoted in Shepherd and Wicke 23)

To use the notions of structure provided in this account, the pop album is overwhelmingly an "aggregate" of disconnected stories, "of otherwise independent elements." Unless the music or the singer goes out of the way to circumvent the form's conventions, its "intrinsic laws" require that the listener expect no connections among an album's songs, which are linked only by measured silence that serves, in fact, to caution the listener against imagining that its tracks constitute a unified narrative. Green's desire to create thematically unified albums, then, runs contrary both to the traditions of his industry and to general and expert perceptions of his artistic output.

"The Structure of the Sequence":
On Morning Suns and Allusive Lyrical Closure

With regard to issues of structure, the most analytically rich moment on *Call Me* occurs at the end—just before and during the fade—of "Your Love Is Like the Morning Sun," the midpoint of this nine-song album. After lamenting his lover's absence by invoking, among other conventional pop song metaphors, bright days, love-filled air, and gray skies, Green sings (as noted earlier) the titles of his three definitive hits: "I'm tired of being alone / I'm still in love with you / Let's stay together, together." Given Green's comparison of his own work to the efforts of "poets and songwriters through the ages . . . to match words to . . . feelings," it is useful here to examine this song's allusive conclusion in the context of formulations offered by Barbara Herrnstein Smith in *Poetic Closure: A Study of How Poems End*, which seeks "to explore the general dynamics of the relation between structure and closure in poetry" (ix).

According to Herrnstein Smith, "Poetic structure is, in a sense, an inference which we draw from the evidence of a series of events," "a hypothesis whose probability is tested as we move from line to line and ad-

justed in response to what we find there" (13). What she terms "strong closure" occurs when "we can perceive these events as related to one another
by some principle of organization or design that implies the existence of a
definite termination point. Under these circumstances, the occurrence of
the terminal event is a confirmation of expectations that have been established by the structure of the sequence, and is usually distinctly grati-
fying" (2). Conversely, "weak poetic closure" results when, for example,
"the structural forces of continuation are not arrested or overcome, when
a conclusion is not determined by any thematic principles," and "when
the last allusions are to beginnings or to unstable events" (210).

"Your Love Is Like the Morning Sun" references and ultimately resists
the notion that, in Emerson's formulation, "every natural fact is a symbol
of some spiritual fact. Every appearance in nature corresponds to some
state of the mind, and that state of the mind can only be described by
presenting that natural appearance as its picture" (200). Romantic heartbreak shakes Green's persona of a belief in such correspondence; if, in
its title, the song begins with a classic metaphorical formulation, a is
like b—"your love is like the morning sun"—we move, gradually, through
lines that suggest the opposite, that a is not or at least no longer like b,
and ultimately to an instance of apparently "weak poetic closure" where
Emersonian correspondence is abandoned altogether in favor of allusions
to earlier Green song titles and musical narratives.

In the song's first verse, the bitter persona appears to be the antithesis
of Emerson's "transparent eyeball . . . , the lover of uncontained and immortal beauty" (193); though he recognizes the accuracy of received beliefs that the morning sun is a "picture" of love, he asserts, because of his
heartbreak, "I don't care." The chorus emphasizes the lack of correspondence between nature and human states of mind: "Love is the morning
sun, shining so brightly / It's me that's missing your love." Later, he observes an "appearance in nature" that does, indeed, match his own mental
state—"All the skies are gray, messing up my day"—and insists that his
lover's departure leads to further disruptions of the natural order. Interestingly, a hint of masculine anxiety creeps into Emerson's suggestion
that, in its truest form, loving nature is a strenuous activity; he insists
that "the high and divine beauty which can be loved without effeminacy,
is that which is found in combination with the human will" (198). Similarly, Green's persona, who is able to coordinate neither his "will" nor his
love with traditional formulations of nature's beauty, feels compelled to

act in ways that contradict his notions of appropriate gendered behavior. Instead of enjoying a love like the morning sun, he is reduced to "throwing up my hands, not being a man / Don't you know that's not going to pay."

Having exhausted the explanatory possibilities of metaphors that connect images of nature and human states of being, the persona pursues other associations, in particular, connections between his tale of woe and earlier Green hits. However else we might describe this curious—though not unprecedented—lyrical gesture, these allusions encourage the attentive listener to consider thematic connections between "Morning Sun" and these songs, whose words Green forces to fit the melodic contexts in which they resurface. Generally, fadeouts and, as I have suggested, the pregnant silences that follow them create closure with respect to the concluding song and anticipation of the next. Green's allusions, however, expand the song's narrative range, encouraging us, certainly, to recall the hits he references—which, in fact, may never be far from the minds of people aware of his "star story"—and to consider connections between them and this metaphor-laden song. In addition, it compels us, I believe, to ponder the possible implications of other moments of repetition on this album, including, as I will discuss below, the use of the morning sun in the lyrics of the second track, "Have You Been Making Out O.K." and the fact that like the preceding song, "I'm So Lonesome I Could Cry," "Morning Sun" connects the persona's loneliness to elements of the external world. In addition to compelling us to recall what has come before in Green's career, these allusions may have the effect of preparing us to consider connections we have already encountered and those we experience as the album continues to play.

We can perhaps best investigate Green's lyrical allusions here by means of a form of intertextual analysis, which, as I discuss in the introduction, is a mode of literary and cultural investigation centering on the reader's efforts to discover what an interpretable event means by attempting to examine the presence of other texts. R & B is filled with examples of singers explicitly referencing the work of fabled singers and, when they have achieved such a status themselves, their own earlier songs. Two of the hit singles of sixties soul legend Solomon Burke, "Can't Nobody Love You" and "The Price," offer telling examples. In the former, Burke quotes compliments offered in songs by two of his contemporaries, Sam Cooke and Ray Charles, to female addressees they seek to impress. Interestingly, he seems to suggest he, Cooke, and Charles are singing to and about the same sweet woman:

> Now listen, Sam called you cake and ice cream
> Hell, he called you cherry pie
> Ray Charles called you his sunshine
> But you're the apple of my eye.

Similarly, "The Price" folds fragments and themes of three of Burke's own definitive hits, "I'm Hanging Up My Heart for You," "If You Need Me," and "You're Good for Me," into a single text, collapsing narratives composed by three different sets of writers in order to give the illusion that they are, in effect, chapters in a musical book that documents phases of a single relationship. "The Price," coauthored by Burke himself, begins with the following spoken introduction:

> After I hung up my heart for you darling,
> And I said if you need me, all you have to do is call me,
> I stood up and I told the whole wide world that you were good for me,
>   baby

In contrast to these examples, the hits Green invokes were all written either solely or partly by him, yet they seem different from one another in terms of the positions of their persona vis-à-vis the objects of their desire: the first, "I'm Tired of Being Alone," is a lusty, tearful plea for the return of a departed lover who can end his stark isolation; the second (though chronologically the third), "I'm Still in Love with You," a celebration of a lengthy, "really real" love whose future promise the song's persona sees reflected in "that look in [the] eye" of his lover; and the third, "Let's Stay Together," the song most closely identified with Green, acknowledges the "good or bad/happy or sad" aspects of romantic love whose inevitable periods of flux he pleads with his lover to endure.

All three of these songs, however, manifest a keen awareness of the potential impermanence of romance: while "Alone" clearly references post-breakup difficulties, Green's persona in "Let's Stay Together"—whose lyrics evince, according to liner notes provided by Robert Gordon, "a complexity of emotions" connected to the fact that "the couple decided to break up" despite the fact that they still love each other—implores his lover not to be like "people who break to make up." The persona of "I'm Still In Love with You" never loses sight of the potential hurt to which emotional vulnerability exposes the open-eyed lover, who is well aware of the fact that his satisfaction with being "wrapped up in your love" could easily transform itself into the state of being "wrapped" in unfulfilled "dreams" of the dearly departed in "Tired of Being Alone." What ties these songs together, then, besides Green's vocals and the Hi Rhythm Section, is their similar efforts to escape, contain, or control the potential pain being in love can bring, and the desire of the various persona to ward off this pain by pleading either for the return of the dissatisfied lovers or for them to stay despite their inevitable dissatisfaction.

Like "Tired of Being Alone," "Morning Sun" is an evocation of loss and a plea for reconciliation. Interestingly, however, it is a narrative that strategically utilizes figurative language to delay the listener's recognition of that informing romantic loss. That gesture's strategic nature is signaled by the differences between the song's title and the lyrics concerning the object of figuration. Almost all pop hits take their titles directly from frequently repeated lines of their choruses. Note, for example, the *Billboard* Top Ten chart for April 14, 1973, the only week in which *Call Me*'s title track cracked the upper echelon of that long-standing industry record of sales and radio play. Including Green's hit, nine of the ten songs (in descending order, Vicki Lawrence's "The Night the Lights Went Out in Georgia," Gladys Knight and the Pips' "Neither One of Us (Wants to Be the First to Say Goodbye)," Dawn's "Tie a Yellow Ribbon Round the Ole Oak Tree," The Four Tops' "Ain't No Woman (Like the One I've Got)," the Carpenters' "Sing," War's "The Cisco Kid," the Stylistics' "Break Up To Make Up," and Roberta Flack's "Killing Me Softly With His Song") reflect this general designative pattern. (The song that doesn't, Anne Murray's "Danny's Song"—written by John Denver and originally entitled "Annie's Song"—is, however, dedicated to its subject.)

Hence, the seemingly slight differences between the title of Green's track and the song lyrics that inspire it are, in fact, quite significant. In the title, the love of the addressee is compared favorably to the soothing solar warmth. In the song's chorus, however, the line that inspires the title, "Love is the morning sun," suggests that it is "love" in a more general sense, not the specific affection of the addressee, that "is"—rather than "is like"—"the morning sun." In this densely figurative song, which ends by invoking and virtually demanding that the listener connect it to famous titles from Green's corpus of work that are, of course, a large part of the "star story" that compels him or her to purchase *Call Me* in the first place, the lyrics themselves resist actualizing its own title's association of the (absent) addressee's and "the morning sun."

The intertextual resonances of "Your Love Is Like the Morning Sun" mark it as a song that brings together—attempts to make whole—key elements of Green's star story. So, if Green strives in *Call Me* to create a musical book with thematically interconnected tracks, this deceptive, otherwise easily forgotten track—it is neither one of the album's three golden singles nor one of its popular quiet storm classics, neither one of the two definitive remakes of country classics nor its striking religious climax—is obviously an essential analytical starting point. Read in light of *Take Me to the River*, it offers—in contrast to "Tired of Being Alone," which Green's perceptions of the external world inspire emotionally but not lyrically—one of his most successful attempts to wed his preeminent subject, the pains of romantic love, to nature, which he purports is his art's source and ultimate object.

The synthetic designs of "Your Love Is Like the Morning Sun" are further evinced in its metaphoric echoes of the album's second track, "Have You Been Making Out O.K." As is the case in "Morning Sun," the use of natural images and atmospheric allusions to illuminate the pain of romantic heartbreak is featured in "O.K.," which contains the album's first solar reference. "O.K." details a male persona's visit with a former lover during which he pleads with her to return to him despite the fact that she is involved with another man. Insisting, in the first verse, that he has undergone a significant attitudinal transformation ("I don't wanna change you now"), he suggests that he is concerned primarily or solely with her welfare ("I want to know how you've been making out / How've you been"), and pointedly asks, "Would you rather be here with him / Or would you reconsider and come running back to me," and "Can you make it on your own?"

The song's particular use of elements of nature hints strongly that his efforts are doomed. The sun enters the lyrics in a question, tied explicitly to Green's formulation of wholeness as the ultimate sign of spiritual and romantic achievement ("Did the morning sun warm your soul / Did he make you happy, did he make you whole?"). His inquiry concerning her emotional and psychic health is answered in the next verse, which, in contrasting how well the former lovers have fared since their breakup ("Hey girl, since you been over here / My life has been cloudy and days been awful dim / But you're looking well"), echoes a reference to nature in "Your Love Is Like the Morning Sun" ("All the skies are gray / Messing up my day"). Apparently, the addressee has indeed found a satisfying relationship that has helped to make her "whole," one in which, unlike their flawed union—troubled by his efforts to force her to change to fit his perceptions of what she should be—outside ("the morning sun," her appearance) and inside ("your soul"), male and female, nature and humanity, seem unified and in harmony with one another. Driven to visit her by the "cloudy," "awful dim" quality of his own life since her departure, he asks her to return to him despite witnessing her newfound joy firsthand.

But if "Morning Sun" connects itself or can be connected to songs that appeared both before and, in one instance, on *Call Me*, its most important intertext may be "I'm So Lonesome I Could Cry." If the dialectical perspectives and formulations of the singer's aesthetic origins and singer-songwriter ideals that structure *Take Me to the River* are any indication, Green's quest involves discovering how to sing and write songs that manifest both his southern nature and the nature of his vision of the South. His discussion of composing "Tired of Being Alone" outlines the beginnings of that endeavor, as we have seen, but the lyrics themselves fail to connect the song's theme of romantic loss to the elements of the external world that help to generate and explain them. Generally speaking, Green's hit singles—including the three referenced in "Morning Sun" and the three that appear on *Call Me* ("Call Me [Come Back Home]," "Here I Am [Come and Take Me]," and "You Ought to Be with Me")— hardly utilize nature at all, and none of them with anything approaching its centrality in "Morning Sun" and "Have You Been Making Out O.K." Aimed at a mass audience, much of it lacking an informed southern and/or rural perspective and, hence, according to his formulation, ill-equipped to comprehend his musings about nature, Green's hit songs of romantic longing do not endeavor to make these links. And while critics generally see a sacred-secular divide as the primary dialectic in Green's work, I want to posit that in *Call Me*, that divide is subsumed by and into Green's efforts to write about romantic loss as a vulnerable country boy whose muse is nature. In his first extended effort to write "naturally," to reference a little-cited moment in "Belle," to bring the theme of romantic loss together with formulations of nature as inspiration and site of metaphoric plentitude, Green turns to Hank Williams, one of country music's most influential lyricists.

In his discussion of *Call Me* in *Take Me to the River*, Green reports, "I took on country music for the first time with a rendition of Hank Williams's 'I'm So Lonesome I Could Cry' and Willie Nelson's 'Funny How Time Slips Away' (287). Apparently, he either forgets or strategically ignores the fact that, as he states a few paragraphs earlier, his previous album, *I'm Still In Love with You*, features "a six-and-a-half minute version of Kris Kristofferson's 'For the Good Times'" that "totally summed up the cool and understated feel of the album" (286). (Granted, it is possible that Green no longer believes that "For the Good Times" sufficiently reflects a country aesthetic, but he refers to it explicitly as a "country and western song . . . , from the fields of Nashville, Tennessee," in *Live . . . Tokyo*.) In an important sense, however, he is correct, if by "took on" he means fully confront the artistic and thematic implications of those songs as they relate to the album's other tracks and to his general project as a singer-songwriter. Green's "For the Good Times" is, in my estimation, one of his finest recordings, but it stands as an excellent track on an album—littered with great songs—which lacks an overarching thematic center. When the lyrically majestic "For the Good Times" follows an uninspired cover of Roy Orbison's comparatively trite "Oh Pretty Woman," it is impossible to recognize any significant connection between them, thematically or otherwise, except that they represent "good" and "bad" examples of Green's performances of white-authored songs. On *Call Me*, by contrast, Williams's song offers a resonant model of vulnerable southern male lyricism that appears to inspire two songs that convincingly conflate nature and romantic loss, while Nelson's song—whose narrative line Green appropriates in "Have You Been Making Out O.K." and whose notions of ex-lovers being forced to "pay" at the end of their relationship is echoed in "Morning Sun"—leads him thematically from the soul-shattering heartbreak of romantic loss to the physical, emotional, and spiritual comforts of religious love.

As I discussed in the preceding chapter, Williams is widely considered the prime progenitor of country music, the rock upon which that popular musical form is built. In part, his place in country music is a function of his ability to render what David Brackett calls "the 'feminine' sentiments of vulnerability and romantic loss" (95) in narratives whose imagery, self-reflexivity, and stylized delivery audiences from the 1940s to the present viewed as authentic articulations of specific forms of regional and class ontology. (In that regard, Williams shares attributes with Green, whose artistic persona Christgau describes as "modest, even fragile," "brashly

feminine and seductively woman-friendly" [*Growing Up* 462–63, 464].)
Leaving aside the question of the socially constructed nature of the
notions of identity to which these formulations allude and the fact that, as
southern forms, "blues, rhythm and blues, and country have long shared
a mutual pool of resources" (Brackett 98), Williams's status as the source
of country music lyricism makes his catalogue a logical place for Green,
the hesitant "jukebox" who became "a supernatural cover artist" (*Growing
Up* 465), to explore, given his investment in the South as the site of musical and spiritual inspiration.

As Colin Escott relates in his biography of Williams, "I'm So Lonesome
I Could Cry" was "originally intended to be spoken, not sung," partly because Williams "was concerned that some of the lines might sound self-
consciously artsy and alienate his audience" (15). An example of "lyric
poetry," as Jennifer Lawler calls it in *Songs of Life: The Meaning of Country
Music*, this song, which "through metaphor and imagery, . . . expresses
an abstract idea, that of loneliness," is distinguished from other classic
Williams songs of heartbreak such as "Cold, Cold Heart" and "Homesick
Blues" by its lack of narrative line and heavy reliance on densely figurative language. According to Lawler, the song contains "images [that] illuminate the emotional state of the narrator, but there is no real narrative
voice, since there is little narrative, merely imagery and metaphor" (19).
If these country music experts are correct, "I'm So Lonesome I Could
Cry," the song which Williams "would often cite as his personal favorite"
(15) and which Lawler calls the first example in the genre of "lyric poetry"
that eventually becomes the form in which "country music poetry is most
original," offers a sophisticated example of how to render an interior state
(a sense of loss) metaphorically by connecting it to elements of the natural world and the products of human ingenuity (whippoorwills, trains,
robins, etc).

As I have indicated, according to Green's assessment of his performances during his popular period, he sought, in a voice that approximated
the natural sounds he'd imitated as a boy, to sing "that surrendering feeling," to expose "a soft, tender, vulnerable side of myself" that sounded
"like a little boy crying out for his mama or a grown man weak for the love
of a woman" who was tormented by "a need that can't be filled" (240).
"I'm So Lonesome I Could Cry" offered him a vehicle through which he
could reconnect to and express such sentiments, as well a model of song-

writing possibilities and materials that greatly assisted his efforts to "play around with the musical formula that was serving us so well" (287).

Perhaps because he was worried whether people would understand what he was trying to say, Williams invests "I'm So Lonesome I Could Cry" with readymade explanations of the meanings of the metaphors he utilizes. In fact, as Lawler argues, the lyrics seem to offer not a story per se, but the speaker's identification of elements of the external world whose reported qualities match his own sense of unabated loneliness. Hence, the whippoorwill is identified as both "lonesome" and "too blue to fly," the "midnight train" is "whining," the moon "hides its face and cr[ies]" "behind a cloud," and the "weep[ing]" of the robin "when leaves begin to die" "means he's lost the will to live."

Certainly, as we would expect in any provocative case of intertextuality, there are telling differences between Green's and Williams's angst-filled songs of nature. For example, while both "Lonesome" and "Morning Sun" urge listeners to use specific senses to connect nature and human pain, the privileged mode of perception in Williams's song is aural (we are instructed to "hear" the whippoorwill's "sound," the train's "whining," the "weep" of the robin, and even "the silence of a falling star"), while Green's song emphasizes the visual ("Look at the morning sun"). Indeed, "Lonesome" maintains such confidence in both the universality of such angst, which is as inevitable a part of the life cycle as the season when "leaves begin to die," and the synchronicity between nature and its persona's state of mind that, unlike most popular songs, it need not have a narrative—one that explains the specific conditions of the lover's departure—appended to it.

"Morning Sun" offers a similarly sparse narrative, especially when compared to "Have You Been Making Out O.K.," but perhaps because it questions the accuracy or applicability of universal notions of nature's meanings, it seems uneasy with its minimalist storytelling base, and is compelled, consequently, to attach itself to more conventional musical narratives. In choosing as its narrative *terra firma* three earlier, infinitely less poetic hits, and connecting itself thematically and metaphorically to "Morning Sun" and, as we will see, to Nelson's "Funny How Time Slips Away," the central track of *Call Me* hints at a larger intra- and intertextual practice that enables us to experience the entire album as a formally integrated structure, as thematically interconnected chapters of a book.

"To Bind Up All the Different Parts of Al Green":
Connecting *Call Me*'s Individual Parts

Take Me to the River was written in part to challenge the perceptions of fans, masters of ceremony, and others that the singer is "a man . . . who needs no introduction" because "everything you needed to know about Al Green could be heard on a greatest hits collection" (2). Green appears to resent efforts to reduce him and his artistry to such songs, whose post–*Call Me* examples—including "Sha-La-La (Make Me Happy)," "Oh Me, Oh My (Dreams in My Arms)," and "Full of Fire" —he sees not as fine recordings, but merely as the lucrative fruits of "punching the clock in a music factory," of "locking down the hits" by "cranking out the formula" (306). Certainly, his dissatisfaction stems in part both from his increased religious fervor, which caused him at times to "break out in a long and heartfelt passage of Scripture" during concert performances of songs like "Let's Stay Together" (305), and his growing disinterest in "the world of [pop] music, [where] there *was* nothing left to prove" (326). Demystifying the process of creating hit songs at a point in his life when he sought "to bind up all the different parts of Al Green back into something like wholeness" (324), he considers even one of the best of his singles released after *Call Me*, "Sha-La-La (Make Me Happy)," as merely a "pleasing . . . piece of pop candy" (306) and the worst, "Full of Fire," as evidence of the fact that, during the disco era, "all that it took to top the charts was to crank yourself to 120 beats a minute, . . . [which] any fool with a drum machine could [do]" (326).

In addition, he directs our attention to little-known album cuts such as "I'd Fly Away," "Glory, Glory," and "Home Again" not because of their musical quality, but because they contain "echoes of my newly established faith" (302). Such gestures suggest that Green, who aspires to produce thematically unified albums, wants his readers and listeners to consider connections between his hits and the rest of the tracks on his long-playing records. And if, as he insists, "the good that's in [him] and the bad that's in [him] can't live peaceably side by side," if "the Al Green who sings 'You Ought to Be with Me' wants nothing to do with the one who sings 'Jesus is Waiting'" (2), the sort of personal and formal wholeness to which he aspires necessitates that neither he nor his audience privilege the good or popular over the bad or unpopular, and that both Green and the listener develop ways of effecting and assessing their meaningful coexistence.

Call Me contains three million-selling singles, "You Ought to Be with Me," "Call Me (Come Back Home)," and "Here I Am (Come and Take Me)," each of which expresses a speaker's desire for a more emotionally fulfilling relationship with an addressee despite the problems that threaten the possible union. In "Call Me," for instance, the speaker and his addressee prepare to part after having spent a "beautiful time . . . together," which can be no more than temporary because he "act[ed] . . . foolishly" at some point. Granting her freedom to pursue other relationships, he invites her to return "home" if she becomes sad or if "somebody's doin' you wrong." Similarly, the speaker in "Here I Am" shares beautiful times with his addressee, but the sporadic nature of their encounters leaves him heartbroken and "begging . . . every day" for "a love that I cannot have" from a woman who goes looking for affection or for ways to fulfill herself sexually at the dark end of dangerous streets. Finally, "You Ought to Be with Me" records its speaker's efforts to enter into a relationship with an addressee who appears to want merely to be friends, in part because she calculates the possible success of this union in terms of the opinions and actions of others, and in part because of her interest in "some other guy." These songs all discuss or contain the speaker's belief in the possibility of transcendent romantic love, his frustration because the addressee is unwillingness to commit, the threat of a romantic rival, and the virtual certainty that the speaker's desires for emotional intimacy will not be fulfilled.

In terms of the romantic situations they examine, then, the hit songs are similar to the ballads already discussed, but, unlike them, these up tempo, top 40–friendly tracks do not generally employ "pictures" of nature to illuminate human states of being. (One of the few exceptions is found in "Here I Am," whose still hopeful speaker's use of a common pop song romantic metaphor—"I know it's you and me baby / That makes the world go 'round"—is exposed immediately as little more than naive, lovestruck drivel.) Beyond its use of rhymes and near-rhymes at the ends of lines of these hit songs, Green's language is colloquial rather than poetic, and gives the impression of being "nearly a transcription of his individual 'voice,' . . . a possible utterance, . . . what [he] . . . might say" (*Poetic Closure* 16). Like "Tired of Being Alone," these hit songs embody Green's primary theme—boyish vulnerability in the face of a romantic "need that can't be filled"—but do not achieve Green's synthetic ideal because, in Emerson's words, they fail to investigate "analogies between man's life and the seasons" and, hence, lack spiritually transcendent "grandeur or pathos" that "throw[s] . . . light upon the mystery of humanity" (Emerson 202, 199).

"Meaningful Sequences": Country Versions, Gospel Compositions, and Other Acts of "Connotative Reference"

As we have seen, Green suggests that "Jesus Is Waiting" seems out of place on *Call Me*, an album whose subject is "the hot passions that spring up between a man and a woman." Green strategically overstates his case here, since others of his popular albums, focused primarily on the same "hot passions," contain gospel songs like "God Is Standing By" and "My God Is Real." Considering this willingness to record gospel songs and his failure in earlier and subsequent popular albums to participate in the late 1960s–early 1970s R & B embrace of social commentary, "Jesus Is Waiting" appears less out of place on *Call Me* than "Stand Up," which he says provided him with "a chance to reflect [his] feelings about all the social and political upheaval that was going on at the time" (287). While it is effectively rendered by Green and his musicians, "Stand Up" offers little more lyrically than a string of rapidly voiced clichés about brotherhood, hard work, and social uplift ("Keep your step, don't fall down on your face / And let someone take your place / It's you, I know you can do it / Tell me that there's nothing to it"), betraying, along with his failure to include similar social commentary on his other popular albums and his limited discussion of such issues in his autobiography, Green's minimal engagement as a writer in the subject. In fact, as an example of the "utopian pop" that Don and Jeff Breithaupt identify as a major trend in early 1970s music, "Stand Up" seems utterly derivative lyrically, piling trite phrase upon trite phrase in such rapid-fire succession that the words, when they are intelligible, register more as parody than as heartfelt engagement in social commentary. In other words, it shines very little light on the mysteries of the human condition, for if Green's concern was indeed "all the social and political upheaval" that marked the early 1970s as a veritable "ball of confusion" (to reference the Temptations' song whose list of ills is too long to recount here), self-reliance and brotherly love are, at best, laughably simplistic responses. In the context of *Call Me*, "Stand Up" suggests that personal and spiritual fulfillment ultimately requires explorations of realms in addition to or beyond the romantic, but that all "utopian pop" can offer is, at best, false hope.

In order to best demonstrate the plausibility of my points about Green's artistic and thematic concerns, I have explored the songs that make up *Call Me* out of sequence. But having identified "Stand Up," the third song on the album, as a track that explores—and, I believe, effectively under-cuts interpretations of it as offering anything other than a false—resolu-tion, I want to conclude with a discussion of *Call Me*'s final three songs, "Funny How Time Slips Away," "You Ought to Be with Me," and "Jesus Is Waiting." In particular, I'm interested in investigating the relationship of these songs both to others on the album and to Green's general quest for thematic and formal wholeness.

As I have already asserted, the narrative line of Green's composition, "Have You Been Making Out O.K.," is virtually identical to that of Willie Nelson's "Funny How Time Slips Away." In both, the speaker—still smart-ing from the painful dissolution of a relationship—visits his former lover, who has taken up with another man. If "Morning Sun" engages thematic and lyrical aspects of Williams's classic "I'm So Lonesome," albeit with a telling difference relating to Green's rejection of a one-to-one correspon-dence between scenes of nature and states of human feeling, "Making Out O.K." introduces into the storyline of Nelson's much-covered song a sense of remorse and self-recrimination about behavior that contributed to the relationship's demise. Both "Making Out" and "Funny" emphasize their speakers' use of conventional greetings and inquiries about the psy-chic and physical health of players in the dramas. But while Green's com-position seems focused primarily on its addressee's well-being, Nelson's lyrics, in which he restates his addressee's question about his health and expresses concern about the man who's replaced him in her affections ("How's your new love, I hope he's doing fine"), manifest the speaker's refusal to voice even the slightest bit of interest in his ex-love's welfare. Instead of the bitterness expressed in "Funny," in whose imagined world news has reached the speaker that his ex-love has offered the same assur-ances to her new mate about the permanence of her affection that she'd offered him ("I heard you told him you were going to love him 'til the end of time / That's the same thing that you told me"), the speaker in "Making Out O.K." is remorseful, and hoping against hope for the opportunity to demonstrate that he's learned from his mistakes and can now be a better mate.

Green's typical persona in his romantic songs is that of an anxious, vulnerable, boyish supplicant begging not to be hurt, but "Funny" forces him to express not only bitterness, but a desire for retribution; he repeats, over and over again, "Remember what I told you, in time you're gonna pay." If "Making Out O.K." rewrites "Funny," it does so by divesting Nelson's romantic situation of its vengeful bitterness. In a telling moment in Green's appropriation of "Funny," where, to use the literary theorist Mikhail Bakhtin's formulation, he "populates it with his own intention, his own accent, . . . adapting it to his own semantic and expressive intention" (293–94), the singer seeks similarly to, if not to tame down the base passions that mark Nelson's lyrics, then at least to invest them with what is, for him, a characteristic vulnerability. Just before he departs, the persona says, "I guess I'll see you somewhere around / You don't know, you can't know / When I'll be back in town." At the end of this line, Green's voice enters as background accompaniment, declaring, in opposition to the bitter, vengeful narrative line, "maybe tomorrow." But if that declaration introduces elements of doubt into Green's rendition, it fails fully to undercut the lyrics' emphatic focus on a revenge that will be exacted by some force, God or conscience or, more likely, fate, which intercedes to even scores when lovers have been egregiously wronged. And while the speaker does not plan to seek retribution himself—though repeating his view that she's going to be punished for her actions does seem at least a bit sadistic—the burden shifts explicitly from the abandoned speaker in "Morning Sun" to the abandoning addressee of "Funny."

The album's next song, "You Ought to Be With Me," returns Green to the familiar ground of the hopeful supplicant, but the songs that precede it provide a context that makes his entreaties less palatable. Responding to the addressee's hesitance to enter into a relationship with him, a hesitance fueled in part, as we have already seen, by gossip concerning his unspecified transgressions, he attempts to reassure her, but his efforts have the unintended effect of potentially implicating him: "There's nothing to what they say / you ought to be with me, anyway." When he goes on to insist, "You ought to be the kind of girl / that can brighten this old world," the listener seeking connections between Green's songs recognizes in these lines a doubtlessly less poetic reference to the album's predominant metaphor, the morning sun. Recognizable, too, is the speaker's attempt to "change" his addressee, which the aggrieved lover of "Have You Been Making Out O.K." assures his ex he no longer wishes to do, to fit her against her will, in other words, into his romantic script. Considering the persona's efforts to determine his addressee's behavior in "You Ought to Be with Me" alongside the male dominance recalled in "Making Out O.K." and the bitter, vengeful perspectives in "Funny How Time Slips Away," it is difficult to side with a speaker who initially seemed to be the wronged victim of his addressee's inconstancy. His insistence that he doesn't "know the reason why" she might choose to be "with some other guy" appears either insincere or painfully lacking in self-reflexivity, and his entreaties, which appear dictatorial in the larger context of *Call Me*, suggest a circling back to behaviors and attitudes that doom the relationship mourned in "Making Out O.K.," the album's second song, and, possibly, help us to understand more precisely what the speaker of the title and opening track means when he says he had been "acting foolishly." And though "Stand Up" confidently suggests that self-reliance is the key to modifying one's self-destructive behaviors, taken together, the romantic songs on the album posit that its speakers are unable to transform themselves.

In *Take Me to the River*, the singer expresses faith that God will create a singular identity out of the disconnected selves who struggle for control of his being: "One day, He will do for Al Green what Al Green can't do for himself: heal that divided soul and make him whole" (8). Green's unanswered question about why he included "Jesus Is Waiting" on this album, suffused, as it is, with intertextual resonances, seems less daunting, I believe, when viewed in the context of *Call Me*'s repeated emphasis on personal and romantic disharmony. In light of Green's interest in forging a resolution of form, his thematic fascination with broken hearts, and his recognition that the resultant bitter and/or dictatorial tone conflicts with what Simon Frith might call the "essential 'personality'" that is "the basis of [his] popular appeal" (198), his investigation of his relationship to the divine—which his autobiography associates directly with nature—seems essential.

Hinson's *Fire in My Bones* articulates perspectives on religious performance that resonate with claims I am making both about Green's desires to achieve narrative coherence generally and about the relationship of "Jesus Is Waiting" to *Call Me*'s other tracks. Emphasizing the gospel singer's dedication to performing a series of songs as "a textured tapestry of music, motion, speech, and silence" that "com[es] . . . together to yield meaningful sequences" (4), Hinson argues that every testimony, every song, every stylized step and ecstatic shout . . . reflects and implicitly remarks upon related acts in other worship settings. Hence, a single song voiced at a gospel program might call to mind a testimony heard earlier that morning, a powerful sermon heard years ago over the radio, and the everyday performances of one's deceased mother who sang while she worked. All religious expression assumes this umbra of connotative reference, drawing the devotional universe together around an axis of personal experience. The step beyond singular event thus carries inquiry both *outward* to religious context and *inward* to motive and memory, thickening the descriptive texture while simultaneously grounding it in human experience. (5)

According to Hinson, gospel is a self-consciously intertextual sphere in which believers actively seek—and expect to find—thematic, spiritual, and imagistic traces of previously encountered texts or experiences in the praise songs and other forms of religious worship they witness or participate in at any given time. For singers and listeners, such acts of worship draw upon and are emblematic of a culture, a set of oft-repeated, shared and, hence, meaningful shouts, phrases, metaphors, and performances that bear witness to their living in a coherent, "whole" universe with likeminded people. Additionally, it is governed by a rigid set of behavioral standards that help to distinguish insiders and outsiders, as well as degrees of immersion in the church's cultural formulations.

Green's description of the mystery surrounding the composition of "Jesus Is Waiting" suggests that, at that point, he was clearly what Hinson calls a "gifted" singer—one who demonstrated "an easy command of tempo and tune, a deftness in improvisation, a nimbleness with harmony, a facility for learning by ear" (211)—whom God had seen fit to inspire to write the song. However, he had not joined the ranks of the anointed, made up of performers who can "minister to the *spirit*," as his moral bankruptcy and decadent existence offer indisputable proof that "'something was missing' in the lives of those with only the gift" (216). Those who have the gift "without the anointing can only minister to the *emotions*," because "they're too shallow, too grounded in self, too easily displaced by worldly concern" (218). Green could be perceived as one of a score of articulate secular singers who, according to Hinson, "sing just because they have a voice, or they're getting good money for it" (213), and whose songs generally "had the power to touch" the emotions but not the spirit of their listeners (68). Given his fundamentalist origins and his desire to heal divisions within himself and his artistic self-representations, Green will have to become both "gifted and anointed," a status that will allow him to create messages "filled with meditative substance" and capable of "carr[ying] . . . the mysterious power of Spirit, a power that saints say penetrates far beyond emotion" (218).

In "Jesus Is Waiting," Green's persona openly acknowledges his sins, flaws, and other human failings, positioning him as a "broken down," inconstant supplicant begging a merciful God for forgiveness rather than, as is the case on most of the album's other tracks, as a wronged lover struggling against bitter self-righteousness. To invoke some of the formulations of his quest for coalescence that dominate the final pages of his autobiography, *Take Me to the River*, he strives by means of this song to "knit . . . together the tatters of [his] life" (322), "to bind up all the different parts of Al Green back into something like wholeness" (324) so that "the singer and preacher, the entertainer and the evangelist, the man of the world and the man of the spirit come together to do a wondrous thing and call many to His name" (343).

Recalling—and strategically combining—the discourses of romantic angst and social uplift that precede it, Green's song begins by insisting that "Jesus is waiting" for both the broken down and those who have let themselves down, and is, like "Stand Up," concerned with self-improvement. But whereas, in his cliché-ridden foray into social commentary, Green's all-knowing speaker imparts advice about the wonders of self-reliance and helping hands to "everybody," in his gospel song, the humbled speaker acknowledges that, like the addressee, he needs both heavenly and human assistance. Indeed, divine encouragement of those who are unsure about life choices ("Standing right there behind you / Helping you to make up your mind") replaces both the vapid platitudes of "Stand Up" and lovesick, self-centered entreaties to former or part-time lovers advising them to change and dictating how they ought to be. Like "Morning Sun," "Jesus Is Waiting" (which is itself not above utilizing pat gospel and pop discursive formulations) clearly manifests a textual relation both to other songs on *Call Me* (note, for example, the lines, "I'll . . . do what I can / To stand up, and be a man," referencing both "Stand Up" and concerns registered in "Morning Sun" about what constitutes appropriate masculine behavior) and to popular songs of the time ("talking 'bout 'you've got a friend,'" "'Say a little prayer' just for me").

Synthesizing the themes, formulations, and even the words of his own and other songs, "Jesus Is Waiting" demonstrates the limitations of "Stand Up" as a reflection on how to improve the human condition and of his romantic songs as inquiries into heartbreak. If "love is the only salvation," as the speaker claims in "Jesus Is Waiting," the divine love he references here subsumes both sexual and platonic human love. In fact, the speaker is positioned, like the female addressees in the romantic songs, as the figure whose lack of commitment causes problems in the primary relationship that the track explores; Green sings, "I've been a fool, disregarding your love / But I wanna say this evening that I'm sorry, sorry, sorry, sorry." And while the song does include a human addressee, to whom the speaker pleads, "Help me, help me," the reciprocity of this relationship is significant only in the context of the characters' capacity to assist one another's efforts to prove themselves worthy of God's grace: "I want you to help me, and I'll help you / To save myself, and I'll save some for you."

Rather than being all-consuming, as it is in the angst-filled songs on *Call Me*, human love in "Jesus Is Waiting"—which may or may not be romantic in nature—is secondary to the speaker's love of God. Despite the speaker's flaws and neglect, Jesus has "been good to me," a constancy and devotion for which he thanks Him profusely. The song concludes with his recognition of the fact that "I might have a problem you can solve for me," and given this statement's placement at the conclusion of the last song of the album, that problem could be said to be Green's "divided soul" (and, perhaps, his album's apparently fragmented form). As the song fades out, Green can be heard to say, "I've come a long way," and that sense of progress can be seen as resulting from the apparent resolution introduced by "Jesus is Waiting" into the otherwise thematically circular album in which the cessation of the pain investigated in the songs is unimaginable. *Call Me* offers track after track whose emphasis is unfulfilled or, in the case of "Stand Up," improbably resolved longing. The gospel song contains Green's elegant embodiment of "surrendering feeling," but an instance where the surrender is appreciated and the surrendering soul is validated by the constancy and acceptance of the supreme Loved One.

If unfulfilled need is the primary theme of Green's romantic songs, without some alteration in his focus, that theme will necessarily clash in perpetuity with his desire for wholeness. In positioning the speaker as the figure who has neglected an inspiring, supportive, and divine love and is returning to it, he recasts the romantic narrative situations of "Funny" and "Making Out O.K.," signaling God's preeminence by marking Him as forgiving, patient, supportive, loving, and devoid of bitterness, states of being that the soul man's persona and addressees cannot successfully achieve in their romantic encounters. God—the unacknowledged presence "behind" Green's nature metaphors—is a synthetic force, resolving the tensions and satisfying the unfulfilled needs that Green's songs insist are an unavoidable consequence of human love when it is unmoored to the divine.

God, Man, Woman, and Nature:
The Synthetic Achievement of "Belle"

It could be said that Green leaves his quest for formal wholeness unresolved in *Call Me* because, while he uses situations in it from songs that engage the connections between humanity and nature, "Jesus Is Waiting" fails overtly to bring nature into the narrative. Certainly, the album manifests an Emersonian understanding of nature as a reflection of God and human states of feeling, but that connection is not made clear in Green's concluding lyrics, which otherwise invoke and comment tellingly on crucial situations and perspectives found in the album's preceding songs.

Now that we have a sense of his larger artistic project, we are better able to assess the full implications of locating his 1977 single "Belle" as the focus of Green's efforts to heal the sacred-secular divide. Unlike "Jesus Is Waiting," whose speaker's soul had only recently been reconciled with God, "Belle" records the perspectives of someone with a long-standing relationship with the divine ("The Lord and I have been friends for a mighty long time"). Firmly ensconced in God's graces, the speaker engages a beautiful woman who wants him either temporarily to stray spiritually or to abandon his faith altogether, a thought that "has never ever really crossed my mind." Promising to remain faithful to the Lord, and convinced that "the best thing we could do is have Him around," Green's persona—concerned that he and his addressee have totally divergent attitudes about religious faith—echoes parts of "You Ought to Be with Me" ("You don't have to waste my time / If you want to be a friend of mine") when he insists, "Let's not waste each other's time." And if his privileging of divine love over earthy passion in the line "It's you that I want, but it's Him I need" is as resonant as perceptive critics such as Robert Christgau, Brian Ward, and Craig Werner suggest, the song itself is best understood (in the context of Green's concern with artistic and thematic wholeness) in terms of its recognition of the divinity of and in nature. In fact, in privileging his love of God over his desire for his addressee, the spiritual novice in "Jesus Is Waiting" articulates essentially the same sentiment as the long immersed speaker in "Belle," which belies our sense that sustained spiritual engagement deepens one's knowledge and conceptualization of religious belief.

For my purposes, what is particularly striking about "Belle," however, is its synthesis of the major elements of Green's most acute autobiographical musings on his divided soul. The song seeks to resolve the possible tensions between romantic love and spirituality, proudly asserts its persona's status as a "little country boy," recognizes spiritual love as a source of happiness that romantic love can never be, and, most importantly, reaffirms, in what should strike listeners of *Call Me* and readers of *Take Me to the River* as familiar terms, nature's source and significance. In his autobiography, Green says that "music was the only way I knew of reconnecting to the nurturing love of God that I had once drawn from the breezes in the trees and the water in the brook and the birds chirping for their breakfast on a bright spring morning" (66). After situating the speaker as a "country boy," "Belle" makes that connection quite explicit. Having been brought "safe . . . through many drunken country bars," the speaker insists, "He's my bright morning star," "my everything," "such a brighter joy." By invoking the central metaphor of *Call Me* and connecting it explicitly not to an absent romantic object but to God's love, Green demonstrates how far he has indeed come in terms of his capacity to write about faith, in his efforts to inscribe resolutions of the sacred-secular divide, and as an artist seeking to create synthetic forms capable of containing all of his central themes.

In the first half of this track, where he speaks directly to Belle of his conflict, he employs the deeper registers of his voice in an almost robotic manner—a perversion, perhaps, of his "mannish" voice—which produces singing that is not nearly as engaging or pleasing as his performance of boyish vulnerability on his popular albums. That voice serves both a thematic and aesthetic purpose, offering aural evidence of Green's differentiation between romantic and divine love. The highlight of the song is a striking moment when, freed of the burden of romantic entanglement which he employs his deeper registers to relate, he expresses the religious joy his persona feels because of God's presence in the sun, the air, and his life. Using his steadiest, clearest falsetto, Green alternately holds, bends, unpacks, and repeats the divine referent "He"—heard during several improvisational moments throughout the song—manifesting the pleasures of life, faith, devotion, and deital love.

This brief but sustained moment yields what may be the most impressive singing Green offers on any of his seventies albums, perhaps because the aural and thematic contexts coalesce to permit him to articulate unambiguous joy. It's a performance that draws me in every time I hear it, makes me smile in appreciation of Green's gifts and in response to his pleasure, and touches me both emotionally and spiritually in ways that the work of few singers ever have. This striking "He" is the result of the "gradual and cumulative" process of "intensification of performance" that Glenn Hinson calls "elevation," a "strategic action and submissive receipt" wherein gospel singers both "are actively doing the elevating, consciously tightening their devotional focus and heightening the intensity of their presentation" and "are elevated, . . . as the Spirit joins the conversation and blesses the saints with inspiration, succor, and experiential uplift" (280–81).

Rhetorically speaking, "Belle's" and Green's "He"—"my morning star"—fills the song with loving presence, in direct contrast to "Your Love Is Like the Morning Sun," which is marked by the absence of the (human) object of affection and a telling incompatibility between nature and the speaker's state of being. Indeed, absence and incompatibility are reflected in his inability to make the song's lyrical references to the natural world and the addressee conform to the title's replication of our certainties about the meanings of nature. And while, certainly, the addressee in "Morning Sun" may, like Belle, be "all of these things," her (absent, inconstant) love can never compare with the morning sun, but—as "Belle" emphatically details—God's enduring love is manifested in that "bright . . . star's" regular, soul-warming, awe-inspiring appearance.

A consideration of white appropriation of black images . . . uncovers the extent to which mainstream American culture, no longer Anglo-American, has moved in the course of this century to becoming not only indebted to black aesthetic forms and traditions but itself profoundly African-American.
—**Susan Gubar**, *Racechanges: White Skin, Black Face in American Culture*

One of the most gifted voices of her generation, Phoebe Snow can do just about anything stylistically as well as technically. Her rich, throbbing alto, with its stratospheric outer limits, is a genuine phenomenon, and she backs up her technique with tough, gutsy emotionality. The question that's still un-answered is how best to channel such talent.—**Dave Marsh** and **John Swenson**, *The New Rolling Stone Record Guide*

[Phoebe Snow's] best work has always involved a blending of the two, rhythm and blues and pop, singing that's sweet and rough at the same time. It's certainly no coincidence that a healthy number of blacks always fre-quent her shows. "I feel like an honorary black and I'm flattered," she jokes. "But when they yell out, 'Get down, sis-tuh,' I tend to feel whiter than ever. 'Thank you,' I say. 'I believe I will get down now.'"—**Don Shewey**, "The Blues of Snow"

"Miss Snow, are you black?"

Second Childhood and the Cultural Politics of Musical
Style in the Post–Civil Rights Era

Between 1974 and 1976, the first years of what promised to be a stellar career, Phoebe Snow released her only gold single, "Poetry Man" (1974); "Gone at Last," a gospel-inflected duet with the legendary singer-songwriter, Paul Simon; two gold albums, *Phoebe Snow* and *Second Childhood*; and a third, *It Looks Like Snow*, that plainly con-firms critical perceptions of her as "a fabulous performer traversing styles and genres with ease and elegance" (Viglione). However, beginning with her next release, *Never Letting Go*, her albums came to be seen as

Phoebe Snow's second album examines the cultural implications of race in the post–civil rights era both in its cover art and in its juxtaposition of her singer-songwriterly tunes and remakes of songs associated with Billie Holiday, *Porgy and Bess*, and the Supremes.

"muddled" rather than accomplished attempts at a "synthesis of styles," commencing "a fall-off in both her commercial success and her artistic accomplishment" (Ruhlmann) from which she never recovered. Still, some critics, baffled by the failure of the best tracks from the latter releases to gain a significant audience, blamed Snow's diminished commercial success on Columbia Records, which, in their view, chose "not [to] have this material saturating radio across America" and "let her records find their audience without pushing them" because its marketing department could not "figure out whether she was a folksinger, a pop singer, a soul singer, or a jazz singer." For such critics, poor marketing by the only company to release more than one of her albums indicated that its employees had apparently forgotten "that Snow was a great singer" (Ruhlmann).

More than thirty years after she released her first album, the question of what type of singer Snow was and is no longer remains a hotly debated topic; indeed, because of her limited visibility, relatively small number of concert dates and new releases, and comparatively dismal record sales over the last two decades, it is unclear, at this point, how many people would recognize her as "a great singer" if, in fact, they recognized her at all. Certainly, compared to Aretha Franklin, arguably the important American singer of the last half century, and Al Green, a celebrated artist whose string of singles and albums during the 1970s was extremely popular and continues to be recognized as monumental, she is, at best, a minor figure. But given my concerns in this book with singers' uses of song covers to illuminate their public images and aspects of their social identities, Snow, whom critics came to regard as a mediocre songwriter but an inspired interpreter of R & B songs such as Sam Cooke's "Good Times," the Temptations' "Shakey Ground," Etta James's "At Last," and Barbara Acklin's "Love Makes a Woman," is as central as the aforementioned singers to my considerations. Fluent in a range of vocal styles, Snow — who claims to have grown up with little exposure to black music — has appeared since the downturn in her career fortunes, for example, both on a gospel album and on a tribute to blues great Muddy Waters. And in Philadelphia's expansive The Sound of Market Records, her releases are located in the R & B section, near the CDs of two Motown groups whose songs she has covered, the Supremes and the Temptations.

Of course, other white females who emerged during the 1960s and 1970s, including Valerie Carter, Bonnie Bramlett, Rickie Lee Jones, Laura Nyro, and Teena Marie, mined traditions of black expression to produce compelling records and, in Marie's case, to capture a sizable portion of the R & B audience. However, along with her production of numerous soul covers and the fact that observers often assumed she has African blood coursing through her veins, Snow's nuanced considerations of what it means to claim a connection (biological, experiential, or otherwise) to the culture out of which these musical styles emerged — considerations that never devolve into strictly defensive efforts to justify her artistic compulsions — make her an especially apt and intriguing subject.

During the 1960s and the 1970s — a period noteworthy in part because blacks (including Kenneth Gamble and Leon Huff at Philadelphia International, Al Bell at Stax, Curtis Mayfield at Curtom, and, of course, Berry Gordy at Motown) controlled, and profited professionally and economically from the production and, in many cases, distribution of forms of black expressive culture — whites were compelled to examine and rationalize their investment in black popular music. During this era, the compulsion to cross racial boundaries physically, spiritually, and psychologically was tempered, both for blacks and for white liberals and progressives, by an awareness of a baleful national history of profit-driven whites appropriating and overwhelmingly dominating the dissemination of Afro-American forms of expression. As a consequence, it was not important to many black industry insiders and soul aficionados that figures such as Jerry Wexler had made stellar contributions or, for that matter, that white singers such as Snow, Bramlett, Jones, Carter, and Nyro were deeply engaged in the aesthetics of R & B. What was important to such gatekeepers was the extent to which their engagement could be said to constitute exploitation of the kind that occurred during both the swing and rock 'n' roll eras, for instance, when white performers such as Benny Goodman and Pat Boone profited more than their black counterparts, whose styles and songs they appropriated. In an era when blacks theorized exhaustively about the necessity of seizing the means of production from whites of a product formerly referred to as race music, among other cultural entities, Snow's pursuit of black sounds placed her at the center of debates about the ethics, economics, and aesthetics of white participation.

These debates serve as the backdrop for my examinations of Snow's covers of black songs, particularly in her second album, *Second Childhood*. Various discussions of the place of whites in black music help us to consider, for example, Snow's debilitating struggles with notions of female beauty, her ambivalence about racial categorization, and some of the implications of the increased recognition of what, following Susan Gubar, we could call the "African Americanization" of popular music in the aftermath of the civil rights movement. Coming at the end of an era characterized by heightened race consciousness and racial tensions, concerted governmental efforts to address the effects upon blacks of centuries of enslavement and subsequent forms of debilitating oppression, and a willing acknowledgment of an indebtedness to "black aesthetic forms and traditions" (Gubar 45) by white acts such as Elvis Presley, the Beatles, and the Rolling Stones, *Second Childhood* is representative of a time when skillful, nonexploitative white participation in black traditions had come to be expected and, perhaps to a lesser degree, accepted. However, such efforts also became, I believe, analytically more challenging because of still entrenched notions of the relationship between race, power, and cultural performance.

Like Presley's practiced snarl and mesmerizing swivel, Paul McCartney's Little Richardesque "wooos," and Keith Richards's blues guitar riffs, Snow's inventive phrasing, note bending and twisting, savvy malformation of words, and rhythmic swing demonstrate that, in the age of integration and the democratization of the airwaves, whites could learn how to utilize black musical styles without having necessarily to establish intimate connections to its traditional spheres of cultural production. In her engagement in *Second Childhood* with familiar songs to which claims and labels of racial purity never could be easily applied—songs written by the Jewish composer George Gershwin for the black folk opera *Porgy and Bess*, performed by the Supremes (the authenticity of whose sound is frequently called into question) and reimagined by Billie Holiday (who transformed numerous Tin Pan Alley tunes into templates for the expression of blues sensibilities)—Snow compels us to consider some of the implications of the often discernible white presence in a good deal of twentieth-century black American music. If her mastery of black vocal aesthetics[1] is deemed insufficient, Snow's covers and discussions of her career implicitly suggest, she refused to justify her love in terms of a transgressive racial or gender politics that she was not, in fact, capable of performing.

"Something in Between":
Janis Joplin, Phoebe Snow, and the Appropriation of Blackness

The daughter of Jewish parents who were, in Don Shewey's phrase, "an arty duo"—her mother was for a time a member of the Martha Graham Company, and her father, "a stand-up comic in vaudeville," was "a real frustrated character actor" ("Blues of Snow" 76)—Snow was born in 1952, named Phoebe Laub, and raised in New York City and Teaneck, New Jersey. She emerged from the Greenwich Village club scene of the late 1960s and early 1970s with the name of a mythical train and a singing style which she describes as a result of an adult indoctrination overseen by her boyfriend, Charlie, who "turned her on to blues and old jazz" (Shewey 79). Her eponymous first album is the best evidence we have of an apprenticeship during which she learned to perform—and to combine—the musical sparseness of acoustic guitar–driven folk music, the love-so-right and love-gone-wrong repertoire and vocal styles of "old blues greats" (79), and her own intensely metaphoric, broodingly self-inquiring singer-songwriter compositions.

Indeed, *Phoebe Snow*, which kicks off with a rousing remake of Sam Cooke's "Good Times" showcasing the doo-wop group the Persuasions, to great effect, features engaging work by respected jazz musicians (bassist Ron Carter, saxophonist Zoots Simms, and pianist Teddy Wilson); two impressive, self-identified blues songs (Snow's own "Harpo's Blues" and the standard "San Francisco Bay Blues"); and a mysterious reference to death in "I Don't Want the Night to End" ("The dirty city mist seeped too deep inside / it took me on some kind of heady ride / it told me Charlie Parker died"), commemorating her deceased boyfriend, Charlie, to whom the album is dedicated, and the great jazz saxophonist, both of whom died of complications related to drug overdoses. But beyond its general lyrical inventiveness, its extremely popular, if (in Robert Christgau's view) "fatuous" hit single, "Poetry Man," and the clear, intoxicating musical accompaniment, this album's enduring power results from Snow's subtle, melismatic employment of her sweet, nasal, and seemingly self-satisfied voice to render blues modes, moods, and feeling. As Shewey emphasizes, *Phoebe Snow* features "a voice bigger than any song. Fluid, delicate, moody—instantly that voice had authority," manifested in "the breathy, girlish vibrato and the knowing, bluesy growl" she utilizes to such wonderful effect ("Blues of Snow" 74).

That style and those points of black cultural reference, along with Snow's bushy hairstyle, olive complexion, and non-Nordic features, have led even some of her fans to believe that she is a light-skinned black woman. Such misidentification persists, for example, both on a Web site where a black male record buyer's appreciation of soulful white female singers such as Lulu, Dusty Springfield, and Carole King refers to the belief "that Ms. Snow was really a black woman," and in a fan review of *Second Childhood* posted on amazon.com in July 2003 by a listener knowledgeable enough about her career to note an "incident on the 1977 Grammys, where Alice Cooper scared her to death," who says that "Phoebe Snow is one of the VERY few light-skinned black women performing out here at ALL!" (Kenyada). And Snow herself made a point of acknowledging, and registering her bemused or frustrated responses to, such identifications during live performances in the 1980s. During one such performance, at San Diego's Humphrey's By the Bay in the summer of 1989, Snow told her audience that she "used to get vaguely annoyed when people speculated about 'what' she was—'Is she black? Is she white? Is she something in between?'" but that she had learned to respond to such queries by claiming that she was "wicked, all the wicked you'll ever need."

In his review of *Second Childhood*, Robert Palmer discusses what another critic called her "cool, yet not blasé" singing, marked by "spontaneous melismatic invention" (Holden, Review of *Phoebe Snow*), as a distinguishing feature of "that voice that seduced us, that tender, sexy, little girl/ experienced woman voice" (Palmer). However "sexy" Palmer finds her voice, several of Snow's songs, and much of her own commentary about herself, emphasize her own sense of her limited sexual appeal and her lack of self-esteem. Describing herself as sometimes grossly overweight and "not a natural gorgeous person" who was, among other things, "a weird genius kid" ostracized by adolescent peers for being "fat and Jewish to boot" and sent clear signals by her parents that they "*suspect*[ed] you're never gonna be nothing," Snow admits that, early in her career, "I tried to flaunt whatever ugliness I could find [in myself] as a way of saying, 'I don't deserve this success'" (Shewey, "Blues of Snow" 76).

To my knowledge, neither Snow nor any music critic has attempted to connect her interest in black music to her sense of adolescent alienation from a white middle-class existence that made her feel as if she was an "odd girl out" who, as a consequence, "took to hanging around with other outcasts and getting drunk" (Shewey 76). In that regard, analyses of Snow differ markedly from those of another white female devotee of black music, Janis Joplin, who also experienced psychically debilitating ostracism during her youth. Gayle Wald speaks of Joplin, whose life reflected both a "fascination with and hatred of white bourgeois femininity," as "the prototypical outsider, a shy and chronically pimply faced girl from Port Arthur, Texas, whose college peers, in an act of breathtaking cruelty, once voted her 'Ugliest Man on Campus'" (159, 156). In Wald's view, Joplin's choice of black female blues singers as role models enabled her to address her own ambivalence about the white American middle-class community from which she emerged: "Joplin did not simply look to blues singers such as [Bessie] Smith for artistic inspiration; she also mediated her own feelings of outsidership from the 1950s-era 'feminine mystique' through her appropriation of a blues aesthetic that decades earlier had supported the production of a critical, oppositional, and public discourse of black female sexuality" (158). Joplin eventually sought empowerment through the "emotional fervor" of her own version of the blues aesthetic, which provided her with the means of mounting a critique of mid-twentieth-century norms that limited women's explorations of their emotional needs and sexual desires. Whatever one thinks of her singing (which Wald says "listeners today tend either to love or to despise" [156]), especially in contrast to "earlier white female vocalists—those 'nice girls' [such as Anita O'Day, Peggy Lee, and Lita Roza] who 'cleaned up' the blues—Joplin through her interpretations of a blues idiom . . . pioneered for white women a sexually assertive performance" (157) that, according to her biographer, Alice Echols, "seemed to embody the rebelliousness, spontaneity, honesty, and authenticity of her generation" (200).

Unlike Joplin, who appropriates blackness as part of her efforts to shape a "'let it all hang out' [style]—through voice, gesture, dress, hairstyle, and the like" (156), Snow appears not to have used attitudes evident in aspects of black expressive culture to mount a response to the white middle-class norms that led peers to ostracize her during her painful childhood. If Joplin "rejected rigid categories of identity" as evidenced by her "pursuing sex with men and women, proclaiming herself the 'first white-black person' . . . , drinking and carousing like one of the boys," and subsequently trying "to shield herself from the abuse that followed her rebelliousness by projecting a tough-girl ballsiness" (Echols xiii), Snow seems to have utilized black stylistic elements without attempting to project herself, either as a performer or as a person, as someone who embodies the attitudinal élan associated with some of its legendary practitioners. In other words, despite their similarly alienating upbringings and development of vocal styles that reflect their appreciation of Afro-American music, Joplin's "star story" is that of an artistic and social outsider whose rebelliousness emerges in part as a function of her appropriation of blackness, while Snow projects herself as a vocally "wicked" singer who, in her seemingly candid discussions of her personal life, appears much more like a painfully introspective, psychically tortured, self-flagellating singer-songwriter than a dissonant outcast imbued with a blues womanly "tough-girl ballsiness." Indeed, in her representations of her painful struggles with personal demons—including bouts of serious depression, the drug-related death of her boyfriend, the end of her marriage, the difficulty of balancing career goals and the demands of being a single mother of a severely brain-damaged child, the psychic scars that result from a lack of paternal nurturance, "her own inertia," and "a cycle of codependent relationships" that kept her "from nurturing her own self-worth" (Roos n.p.)—Snow might be said fully to embody the anxieties of white middle-class American females confronting the ambiguous freedoms of the post-sixties era. Those women generally sought self-fulfillment at a time when the norms of mainstream society and the entertainment culture continued to insist that women's worth was dependent upon their status as either sex objects or mothers.

Joplin's careful consideration of what it meant for her to appropriate blackness, which, as Echols claims, allowed "the quintessential 'nobody's girl'" (xii) to become a "white-black person" through the process of "transracial identification," is evident in her descriptions of the differences between the experiences of blacks who helped to shape the blues and her own difficult, but racially and materially privileged, upbringing. Joplin distinguished "between traditional blues and her blues" in the following way:

> "I don't know if this is grossly insensitive of me, and it may well be, but the black man's blues is based on the 'have-not'—I got the blues because I don't have this, I got the blues because I don't have my baby, I got the blues because I don't have the quarter for a bottle of wine, I got the blues because they won't let me in the bar. Well, you know . . . , I'm a middle-class white chick from a family that would love to send me to college and I didn't wanna. I had a job, I didn't dig it. I had a car, I didn't dig it." For a white woman like her, Joplin seemed to be saying, the blues weren't about material deprivation or, in the end, even about lost lovers but about existential loneliness and despair—"waking up in the middle of the night blues," as Sam Andrews puts it. (240)

Considered in the context of descriptions of the genre's philosophical underpinnings, the distinctions Joplin offers between "the black man's blues" and her own "existential" concerns underestimate the scope of the form's emphases. For example, Ralph Ellison describes the blues as "sung by such an artist as Bessie Smith" as an "autobiographical chronicle of personal catastrophe expressed lyrically" that reflects "an impulse to keep the painful details and episodes of a brutal experience in one's aching consciousness, to finger its jagged grain, and to transcend it, not by the consolation of philosophy but by squeezing from it a near-tragic, near-comic lyricism" (*Shadow and Act*, 78–79). While they originated as responses by imaginative blacks to poverty, romantic travail, and racial circumscription, the blues themselves engage triumphs and tragedies of human existence that are informed by, but not all explicitly tied to, racially specific experiences of economic lack, romantic woe, or the inequities inherent in America's imperfect practices of its democratic ideals. Of vital importance for my purposes here is the fact that Joplin sees herself as *appropriating* the blues, applying its sonic conventions and cultural wisdom—seen, in her age, despite Ellison's formulations and white rockers' vibrant engagement, as racially specific—to her own social, cultural, and material circumstances.

If the blues enabled Joplin to formulate the contours of her rebellion against rigid social norms, they also helped her to circumvent normative standards about the appearance of white female performers: "And then there was the question of Joplin's looks. As the record producer John Simon points out, '[Women] singers usually had to have that starlet look, and Joplin was pretty average-looking.' But in 1968 this worked for Janis, as did her boast that she'd always been an outsider, 'on the other side of society,' as she told *Vogue* magazine. The media fell in love with Joplin because she seemed to embody the rebelliousness, spontaneity, honesty, and authenticity of her generation" (Echols 199–200). The success of a "pretty average-looking" Joplin was contingent not on her having "that starlet look" or embodying what Naomi Wolf calls "the beauty myth" that shapes men's and women's sense of female worth by "assign[ing] value to women in a vertical hierarchy according to a culturally imposed physical standard" (12), but on the strength of her performance of wholesale transgression that, following Phoebe Snow, we could call wickedness. While Joplin's blues-inspired performances enabled her to become a superstar despite or because of her looks, more than a decade following her death, the career of Snow, a "once-in-a-generation" female vocalist blessed with what Shewey characterizes as a "knowing, bluesy growl" ("Blues of Snow" 76, 74), was curtailed, as the singer herself was well aware, by her physical appearance: "We both know that if she sang like Phoebe Snow but looked like [Blondie's] Deborah Harry, she'd be a superstar by now" (76).

Snow's apparent discomfort with the conventions of sexualized self-presentation, the stock and trade both of blueswomen such as Bessie Smith and Ma Rainey and of Joplin, whose "unapologetic sexuality proved irresistible" during her performances, which she "likened . . . to orgasm" and during which she "dressed like a psychedelicized hooker" (Echols xvi), is clearly on display during a 1989 concert in Germany that was recently released on DVD. Recognizing that her acoustic guitar opening to the title track of the album she was promoting, *Something Real*, might be perceived as a jazz prelude, she warns the crowd not to expect her to scat—the wordless jazz vocal technique employed by singers to approximate instrumental sounds and, on occasion, to fill space during concerts while the musicians were readying themselves to play the next song—because she "hated" scatting so much that she'd rather "run naked" than perform it. Although a male fan hoots suggestively at the idea, a response for which she thanks him perfunctorily but by which she seems unconvinced, the singer apparently wants simply to describe, by means of what she hopes will be a telling comparison, the most embarrassing scenario she can imagine in order to signal her disdain for this particular vocal technique.

Clearly, she did not reference nakedness to draw attention to her large frame, about which she had admitted feeling extremely insecure. And as she suggested, that insecurity was exacerbated by her participation in an entertainment industry in which commercial success is linked to physical attractiveness. While many of her white female contemporaries indeed possessed "that starlet look," which they utilized to define themselves and to sell their musical products—think, for example, of famous images like those of the smiling, model-thin, unself-consciously braless Carly Simon; Joni Mitchell's beauteous, shimmering emergence from a diaphanous pool; and the doe-eyed, alluring pout of Linda Ronstadt on the cover of *Rolling Stone*, with one of her negligee's spaghetti straps falling alluringly off of her thin, bare shoulder—Snow and/or her record companies chose often either not to place her image on the covers of her albums (*Never Letting Go, Natural Wonder*) or to lovingly caricature (*Phoebe Snow*) or obscure her face (*Second Childhood, Something Real*) in part, no doubt, because she was not thin and conventionally attractive.

Naomi Wolf says of the psychic pain that American women often feel as a result of finding themselves generally unwittingly engaged in a "beauty competition":

> It is painful for women to talk about beauty because under the myth, one woman's body is used to hurt another. Our faces and bodies become instruments for punishing other women, often used out of our control and against our will. At present, "beauty" is an economy in which women find the "value of their faces and bodies impinging, in spite of themselves, on that of other women's." This constant comparison, in which one woman's worth fluctuates through the presence of another . . . , forces women to be acutely critical of the "choices" other women make about how they look. (284)

Given these conditions and the emergence, in Wolf's view, of "the beauty myth" as a response to feminist critiques of social, cultural, and economic inequities that had begun to unsettle American society at the outset of Snow's career, the singer's choice to go "onstage in a ski parka, looking like the neighborhood baby-sitter" and appearance on a popular television concert series "look[ing] like a hot-dog salesman" (Shewey, "Blues of Snow" 76) could be interpreted, in the absence of contradictory evidence, as a sign of Joplinesque rebellion against the unrelenting objectification to which women generally and female entertainers in particular are subjected. But while we might want to view Snow's concert attire as a potent challenge to an oppressive paradigm, her comments in *Esquire* make it clear that her mode of dress was intended to cover an unglamorous physique, which, her culture insisted, rendered her unworthy of the success she was enjoying.

Snow's insecurities about her appearance—a "chubby" five-foot four-inch body that, after some eating binges, weighed "really close to two hundred pounds," a "funny," bespectacled, mole-filled, large-nosed and full-lipped face framed by wild, seemingly unruly hair—inspired doubts on her part about whether she deserved to be a star, doubts that led her to engage in acts of self-sabotage that she describes as symptoms of her "neurotic antisuccess thing." With what Shewey calls "the coolness of someone accustomed to digging into herself for her art and entertainment," Snow speculates that she "tried to flaunt whatever ugliness I could find as a way of saying, 'I don't deserve this success'" ("Blues of Snow" 76). Examined in the context of her own descriptions of her insecurities, her reference to anxieties about public nakedness seems to indicate that she neither expects nor feels she inspires the arousal of passionate fans' almost always distanced erotic desire.

Her 1989 comment manifests none of the awareness of sexual politics one would expect from an entertainer on tour to promote an album whose acknowledgments include a hilarious appreciation of "all the misogynists who did not become my boyfriends," and whose website and subsequent albums recognize her friendship with Gloria Steinem. As I have argued, Snow equates the indignities of disrobing with what she feels is a vacuous, ostentatious show of vocal technique used most famously by singers such as Louis Armstrong and Ella Fitzgerald to perform jazz sounds. Whatever else it is, scatting is a form of singing in which the primary distinction between the human voice and manufactured instruments played by even the most accomplished performers, the ability to render not just moods or even what is typically thought of as a musical vocabulary, but series of meaningful words, is rendered temporarily irrelevant. Consequently, Snow's discussion of shameful disrobing calls to mind for me not nubile female singers' increasingly conventional striptease, but modes of boundary transgression, during which disrobing or otherwise exposing that which is strategically hidden is avoided at all costs because such display would undoubtedly reveal the putatively inauthentic nature of the social identity that has been assumed.

I am thinking, in particular, of an *Atlanta Journal-Constitution* critique of Joss Stone's *Soul Sessions*, in which the reviewer's sense of the young white British singer's lack of racial and generational right to soul aesthetics is structured into the condemnation of what he considers an overhyped release. For the reviewer, Richard Eldredge, the album's cover art, "a tight shot of a female singer eclipsed by a large microphone and bathed in dark purple light" that harkens back to the minimalist look of soul albums of the 1960s and early 1970s, disguises the whiteness of "the latest musical manipulation by a corporate American record label" infinitely more concerned about the potential profitability of the gimmick—a "16-year-old from Devon, England" "vocally trying to establish residency in Detroit, Muscle Shoals and Memphis" by remaking "soul classics"—than about whether the singer actually had mastered soul vocal aesthetics.

Indeed, the issue of authenticity drives this review, especially in its negative comparisons of the young singer with not only the Queen of Soul, Aretha Franklin, whose composition, "All the King's Horses," Stone covers, but also with the "real R & B talent like Betty Wright, Little Beaver Hale and Timmy Thomas" who accompany her on *Soul Sessions*. To underscore his point that Stone is something less than a soulful talent, Eldredge juxtaposes the young singer and her origins to "real" performers (such as Wright and Thomas, best known for the songs "Clean Up Woman" and "Why Can't We Live Together" respectively, but who are not widely considered transcendent talents) and soulful American cities out of which R & B music emerged, and to the "classic" recordings upon which she draws (songs like "The Choking Kind" and "Some Kind of Wonderful" that are far less widely acclaimed than the work of Stone's black mentors; Franklin's 1972 album, *Young, Gifted, and Black*, on which the formally and lyrically experimental "All the King's Horses" appears). Whether readers and listeners agree with the Kennedy Center's organizers, who considered Stone worthy of serenading its 2003 inductee, James Brown, or with Eldredge's claim that her singing is marked by a "distractingly shaky pitch" and shows that "she doesn't yet have the depth or the life experience to convincingly sell" the songs she covers, is, for me at least, besides the point. Ultimately, such responses to Stone's appropriation of black songs and style and to her album cover reflect a persistent social uneasiness with what has become an undeniable fact: modes of performance, including black vocal styles which have permeated Western popular culture and successfully transgressed racial boundaries and national borders, can be persuasively adopted by people for whom they cannot be assumed to be culturally indigenous.[2]

Later in this chapter, I will explore the cover art of Snow's *Second Childhood*, which, like that of *Soul Sessions*, presents its singer as a figure of racial indecipherability. At this point, however, I want to return to Snow's 1989 concert discussion of modes of black vocal behavior she does not wish to perform. In her introduction to a performance that joins two songs with which she is associated, "Good Times" and "Gone at Last," into a single narrative unit, Snow implies that if her claim to blackness cannot be settled, once and for all, by looking at her, it may be resolved when others listen attentively. Resigned to the probability that her white, non-American audience will not "get the joke," she implores its members to "fake it," and then informs them of the question frequently directed at her by those Americans who assume "the right," as her "biggest fan[s]," to ask "the most intimate and personal question" she can imagine: "Miss Snow, are you black?" Unlike her response at the performance in San Francisco, where she insists that she is "all the wicked you'll ever need," she tells her German audience, "What I usually say is . . . , there's really only one answer to that question, and it goes something like this," at which point she begins a spirited rendition of "Good Times," a song composed and originally performed by Sam Cooke and which the DVD's distributors confuse with an earlier hit, "Let the Good Times Roll," written by Sam Theard and Fleecie Moore and sung by Shirley and Lee.

Given their titular and thematic similarities and the fact that, according to Daniel Wolff's biography, *You Send Me*, Cooke's composition intentionally "quotes from Shirley and Lee's 1956 hit" (287), assumptions that Cooke's record is a remake of the frequently covered "Let the Good Times Roll" are understandable. Still, the two songs are different in at least one significant respect: rather than achieving the unambiguous pleasure sought in "Let the Good Times Roll," Cooke's song is "bittersweet," "questioning," and contains what the biography calls a "touch of sadness" (Wolff 288) inspired by an awareness that the ecstasies promised by the earlier song may take "all night long" to arrive if, indeed, they can be achieved at all. Perhaps it is that melancholy "touch" that compels Snow to use Cooke's song both to begin her first album, *Phoebe Snow*, and as—in the words of one of her own later compositions, "Random Time"—the "punch line" to her concert "joke" that concerns her knowing participation in black vocal styles. Even if we recognize it as merely one of several party songs that Cooke composed and recorded (including "Having A Party" and "Twisting the Night Away") as part of a calculated effort to achieve mainstream success by moving away from gospel traditions he mined as lead singer of the Soul Stirrers—it goes so far as to offer the blasphemous suggestion that "good time," secular music, played energetically and expertly enough, could "soothe our souls"—the status of "Good Times" as "black" music is indisputable largely because the singer many consider the originator of soul imbues it with a "nice, lazy groove" (Wolff 288) and melismatic flourishes that he identifies as the genre's essence.

In her version of the song that appears on her first album, Snow counts out the beat ("one, two, three"), then, after a bluesy acoustic guitar solo that substitutes for the improvised "la-las" of the original, she adds the word "everybody" to the beginning of Cooke's lyrics. If the song's "good time" emphasis appears to conflict with the somber tone and pain-filled lyrics of much of the rest of *Phoebe Snow*, that is only because it is possible to ignore their doubts about whether secular pleasure can indeed approximate the soothing nature of spiritual comfort. Her concert performances of "Good Times," which on her first album helped to establish her credentials as a skilled practitioner of black vocal style, employ the first verse of the Paul Simon composition "Gone At Last" (which he sings on their duet), in place of the introductory verse of Cooke's song, which she also did not include in her studio track. The emphasis of the Simon-Snow duet is male redemption, as the "weary," "dejected" male traveler escapes the dark, wintry night by resting "at a truck stop" where he meets a wise, experienced woman able to recognize him as a "sweet little soul" and, consequently, to represent the possible end of his—and her own—"long streak of bad luck." The backing vocals by the gospel group, the Jessy Dixon Singers, the furious syncopated rhythms, the textured piano flourishes by Richard Tee, and the insistence that both figures "pray" that their angst will be relieved by an empathetic "somebody" who comes "out of nowhere" to "lift you higher / And your burdens will be shared" all suggest a relationship between secular and sacred realms, as well as between racial and mainstream musical forms, that is virtually the obverse of the Cooke song.

While the song's situation is clearly secular, its white singers—surrounded by and, in Snow's case, performing a gospel style—owe the possibilities of their salvation in part to its sacred sound; at the very least, it proves the most appropriate musical palette to express that movement, if not from sin to salvation, then from hopelessness to hopefulness. In the original, Simon sings in a slightly more animated voice than his generally engaging drone, but, as he himself has admitted, Snow's "great" singing "blew me off the record" because "I don't have a voice that's gospel" enough to enable him to manifest redemption vocally (Zollo n.p.). So in addition to performing the role of his sympathetic female "somebody," Snow serves as the perfect vehicle to represent the transformative joy accompanying the lifting of burdens that is a major subject of gospel music, upon whose themes and sounds Simon's composition draws heavily. In other words, taking her cues from the song's rhythms and background vocals—especially in the fadeout, where her accented "oooohs" demonstrate that she can, indeed, raise a joyous noise in a manner long practiced by singers in black churches throughout America—Snow evinces the capacity of a white artist not only to compose songs that utilize black idioms and gospel-influenced situations but also to embody that appreciation through her acts of cultural or stylistic transmogrification. In the original version of "Gone at Last," then, Snow serves as Simon's salvation both in the song's lyrics and in her performance of them that complements the redemptive black gospel contexts in ways Simon cannot.

In her concert use of the song, however, Snow assumes Simon's lines and (masculine) role, positioning herself as the "downcast," road-weary traveler in need of "sympathy" and recognition. That tale of romantic recognition resonates, to a significant extent, with her intentions to use her performance as a means through which her "soul," her mastery of styles of black singing, can be confirmed by her audience. Beyond allowing us to comprehend, in her conflation of Cooke's "Good Times" and Simon's "Gone at Last," their similar efforts to expand the possibilities of racial style, Snow compels her listeners to identify race as something other than a strictly biological category. In fact, she encourages them to see it—or, better perhaps, to *hear* it—as, among other things, a group of vocal behaviors from which talented singers of contemporary popular music choose in constituting their own styles. Rejecting scat singing as a part of her repertoire while embracing soul, gospel, funk, the blues, and other aspects of jazz, Snow identifies these forms of American music as crucial aspects of her own musical identity.

When they are applied to performances that rub up against certain supposedly well-established boundaries, measures of racial authenticity are utilized in an invariably subjective manner. When, for example, Richard Eldredge, the *Atlanta Journal-Constitution* reviewer, insists that Joss Stone "doesn't . . . have the depth or the life experience to convincingly sell" the songs she covers, he is referencing conventional beliefs that soul music directly reflects the lives of, and as a consequence should be performed by, mature blacks who have experienced and/or are able to place themselves imaginatively in the midst of the types of romantic situations about which they sing. Hence, we see white artists publicly embracing black culture as a defining aspect of their personal identities, including Janis Joplin, who proclaimed herself the "first white-black person" in order to authorize her use of blues songs and aspects of Bessie Smith's style; Johnny Otis, who, according to George Lipsitz, "participated so fully in the life of the African American community that he became 'black by persuasion'"; and the popular Euro-American balladeer Johnnie Ray, who was ostracized in such a painful manner because of his undiagnosed partial deafness that he turned for comfort and cultural wisdom to "those Negro spirituals which kept colored people struggling along in the days of yesterday and the Negro blues which gave them some release in the far-from-freedom days they still have to encounter" (*Dangerous Crossroads* 55).

In Lipsitz's view, such white artists recognized "the genius of African-American culture in nurturing and sustaining moral and cultural alternatives to dominant values," viewing it as "an important source of education and inspiration to alienated and aggrieved individuals [like themselves] cut off from other sources of oppositional practice" (54). He argues that the white musicians who participate most effectively in black expressive culture are outcasts of some sort in search of modes of oppositional critique and counterhegemonic practice. For the gifted cultural historian, the primary measure of the quality of whites' utilization of black musical style is not necessarily the music they produce, but the attitudes they articulate concerning their appropriative acts. Lipsitz is infinitely less interested in discussing whether Ray was a skilled participant in the black tradition, for example, than in the fact that, because "his disability gave him a sense of marginalization that made him think twice about the un-interrogated privileges he enjoyed as a white male," "unlike other white singers of his era, Ray could not in conscience appropriate Black music and fail to acknowledge his debts to it" (55–56).

Applying such criteria to the work of Phoebe Snow, who acknowledges her debts to black creative genius without necessarily embracing its "moral and cultural alternatives to dominant values," must we conclude that her intercultural excursions are as troubling ideologically as those of David Byrne (*Naked, Rei Momo*) and her one-time collaborator Paul Simon (*Graceland*), whose "enthusiasm and empathy," "creativity and curiosity . . . lead them to extremely important cultural creations" that are "carried out with[out] a self-conscious understanding of unequal power relations, of the privileges available to Anglo-American recording stars because of the economic power of the countries from which they come" (Lipsitz 61)? At the very least, Snow's primarily musical engagement with black culture presents us with something of an interpretive conundrum. Clearly, even if we recognize her sagacity in leaving the evaluation of the racial meanings of that engagement up to others, her status as "an honorary black" performer—conferred on her by black American audience members whose responses to Snow's production of familiar, familial sounds ("Get down, sis-tuh," and the like) made the singer "feel whiter than ever" (Shewey, "Blues of Snow" 80)—suggests that, in her case at least, whiteness and blackness are not mutually exclusive but, rather, coexist as a paradox that cannot easily be resolved. Her German audience is asked by an American Jew to confront the fact of a "white" person producing "black" sounds, while her Afro-American listeners' "flattering" approval of her sisterly performance serves to shock the singer back to a historical awareness of the wide gulf between herself and the people aspects of whose cultural aesthetics she has mastered.

In these cases, as well as with the examples of the colonizing white male stars whose attitudes Lipsitz critiques, the recognition and evaluation of difference remain significant features of the cultural exchange and the race changes in which the singers and their audiences engage. And even if Snow's performances—including her remakes of black songs on *Second Childhood* that I will examine in some detail—are deemed authentic by, among other groups, knowledgeable cultural insiders, as the two fascinating examples I discuss below suggest, such recognition may be abruptly withdrawn when it conflicts with what is perceived as the pressing ideological concerns of the race.

A Different World and the Exorcism of Whiteness

Before its first season, 1987–1988, the producers of the NBC situation comedy *A Different World*, a spin-off of the hugely popular *Cosby Show* that was set at Hillman College, a fictional southern, historically black school located somewhere below the Mason-Dixon Line, commissioned Phoebe Snow to sing the theme song. Along with Snow's languid melisma, the song's sparse instrumentation—acoustic guitar, percussion, and wailing harmonica—evokes the blues, a genre of American music that was created during times of violence-enforced segregation and concerned overwhelmingly with crafting resilient responses to romantic heartbreak and economic lack. The theme song's blues intonations conflict in fascinating ways with the lyrical emphasis on the comforts and consequences of parental nurturance for members of a post–civil rights generation:

> I know my parents love me
> Stand behind me come what may
> I know now that I'm ready
> 'Cause I finally heard them say
> "It's a different world, from where you come from."
>
> Here's our chance to make it
> If we focus on our goals
> If you dish it, we can take it
> Just remember you've been told
> "It's a different world, from where you come from."

By the time she recorded this theme, Snow's descent from the lofty heights of *Rolling Stone* covers, gold records, and "voice of her generation" salutations had been so precipitous that, in the midst of "nine years spent on what she called 'the unsigned-act circuit'" (DiMartino 238), she had literally become, in essence, a commercial singer for hire, heard infinitely more in jingles for companies like Stouffers and General Electric than as part of contemporary radio station rotations. The barely minute-long theme song, airing over half a decade after her self-described "three-chord rock 'n' roll record" (DiMartino 238) *Rock Away*, in which Snow abandons what Stephen Holden calls the role of "moody pop-jazz chanteuse" in favor of the pose of "a confident rock belter," afforded her more space to emote than the four-second proclamation "G.E. is Light." Snow's languid tempo, melismatic flights, and bluesy word-slurring locate the show in the South—and, less obviously perhaps, in histories of racial oppression—the region out of which the song's sounds originally emerged. Replicating a sparse musical setting associated with earlier forms of twentieth-century music, the song both evokes and distances itself from the dangerous racial tensions and limited opportunities for economic advancement out of which the blues emerge.

The struggles for which the Hillman College cohort generally and the show's central character, *Cosby* daughter Denise, in particular, need to be "ready" involve school work rather than economic deprivation and long gone, train-obsessed mates. Their "goals" are good grades and technical, cultural, and practical knowledge that will enable them to secure rewarding employment after college, and those doing the "dishing" are not racist whites or even, for that matter, no-good lovers, but professors well aware of the need to motivate many young students to live up to their intellectual potential. The evocative tones of the theme song place Hillman College—and, implicitly, the post–civil rights black middle class, whose numbers ballooned as a function of affirmative action legislation set up in part to redress the damages of the systemic oppression blacks experienced en masse just a generation earlier—in a telling historical context while suggesting that America has so significantly transformed its racial attitudes since the late 1950s that it indeed appears to have become "a different world."

The theme song served as another opportunity for Snow to show that she was a performer from whose mouth the conventions of an obsolescent Afro-American form still emerge smoothly and effectively. Nevertheless, in season two of the series, her version of the song was replaced by a bouncier, synthesizer-laden, more contemporary version sung by Aretha Franklin, whose voice had clearly become smokier and her phrasing more mundane than they had been on her Columbia albums of the early 1960s and classic Atlantic recordings from the mid-1960s to the early 1970s. In addition, the show's second season was notable because of the departure of two of its three central actresses: Marisa Tomei, who played Maggie Lauten, the only nonblack student featured in the show—who went on to a film career as a quirky, largely comedic character actress who won an Oscar for a hilarious performance in *My Cousin Vinny* (1992) — and *A Different World*'s initial raison d'être, the original *Cosby* kid Lisa Bonet, who "left the show . . . due to her real-life pregnancy" that was the result of her union with singer Lenny Kravitz.

Bonet's departure offered the producers the opportunity to transform a show whose first season was considered "so bad and so embarrassing that [its creator and executive producer] Bill Cosby threatened to have it taken off the air," despite the lofty ratings it garnered on Thursday evenings following the exploits of the larger Huxtable family (Gray 96). According to television scholar Herman Gray, the quality of the show improved dramatically in its second season because it was able to establish a more "distinct identity" and replace "antics and wisecracks" with plots whose "more serious academic credibility" helped to "bring some degree of dignity and integrity to its representation of black college life." In Gray's view, *A Different World* adopted a more self-determined and, hence, more complicated vision of blackness:

> From the opening visual montage, which rode over the catchy but powerful thematic hook sung by Aretha Franklin, the show explicitly commented on cultural difference and celebrated the social and cultural traditions of black college life. The opening montage, and the stories it frames, announced these differences (and similarities) without the primary requirement or expectation of identification on the part of white audiences. These representations invited identification, but not the kind of familiarity that necessarily assumes and privileges whiteness as the ideal subject position. They challenged analytic and interpretive positions that assume that for these televisions representations of blackness to work, they must be organized, structured, and deployed through whiteness. (95)

Even as the plots reflected an awareness of culture as a site of ongoing negotiation and sometimes energetic contestation, in Gray's view, the producers' "explicit turns towards blackness quickly established a clear identity for the show, one firmly rooted in African American social experiences and cultural sensibilities" (97).

That "firmly rooted" "identity" necessitated a less traditionally accommodating relationship to whiteness and to white cultural signifiers, whose most obvious representations, during the "bland" first year, were the ditsy white roommate, whose presence made the flighty Denise appear comparatively grounded, and the white singer of the theme song who, no matter how effectively she utilized black blues conventions, could never approach the symbolic appropriateness of the Queen of Soul. Whether or not we agree with Darnell Hunt's characterization of the show as evolving "into a lively, socially responsible" situation comedy that will "best be remembered for its cultural vibrancy, its commitment to showcasing black history, music, dance, fashion, and attitude," its replacement of Snow's blues with Franklin's synthesized contemporaneousness ironically limited the capacity of the theme to serve as an aural bridge between a post–civil rights sense of black middle-class plenitude and the materially lean, hard times that the blues traditionally references.

Owning Blackness, (Press) Releasing a "Single Note" of *Soul*

If Snow's erasure from the soundtrack of television's first extended examination of black college life is figured as a sign of progressive racial representation, such gestures failed to prevent others from featuring her voice as an authentic cultural sound. She appeared, for example, on Lou Rawls's wonderful 1993 album, *Portrait of the Blues,* sharing a microphone with the rich-voiced singer on a remake of the Clyde McPhatter song "A Lover's Question." Also, she contributed two lead vocals to *Good News in Hard Times* (1995), a gospel album by the Sisters of Glory, whose members include Thelma Houston and CeCe Peniston; released *I Can't Complain* (1998) on the House of Blues label, an album consisting largely of remakes of rock and R & B hits, including Joni Mitchell's "A Case of You," "Brand New Me" (which Kenny Gamble and Leon Huff composed and produced for the British singer Dusty Springfield in 1969), and "Piece of My Heart" (a minor hit for Aretha Franklin's sister, Erma, that became a signature recording for Janis Joplin); covered "Just to Be with You" for *A Tribute to Muddy Waters: King of the Blues* (1999); and, for Black History Month in 2003, contributed "resounding acapella vocals" to a "series of vignettes celebrating African-American heritage" that were conceived by Push Creative, the artistic arm of the Jesse Jackson–led civil rights organization, and televised on TNN (TNN press release).

For my purposes here, perhaps the most interpretively rich acknowledgment of her vocal style appears in New York University Press's promotional materials for the volume *Soul: Black Power, Politics, and Pleasure,* edited by Monique Guillory and Richard C. Green. The press release begins: "Soul is the stuff of our dreams, and our fantasies . . . , something that happens in altered states between consciousness and sleep. When Michael Jordan appears to defy gravity, when Phoebe Snow mesmerizes us with the tremor of a single note, we surrender our rational faculties to a feeling and a moment. Soul operates in that liminal domain of powerful nothingness where spirits, ghosts, and ancestors dwell." In their discussion of "the ubiquitous but elusive concept of Soul in a black cultural context," the volume's editors (and, I assume, the press release's primary authors) use as examples such central contributors to the art of black expressivity as James Brown, Alvin Ailey, and James Baldwin. Snow's inclusion in this pantheon is striking less because she is the only woman who is named explicitly—the introduction to the collection also discusses, for example, Aretha Franklin and Zora Neale Hurston—than because she is the only white person. Her presence serves as a telling response to questions that Guillory and Green insist continue to swirl around this ethereal formulation and "have proven to be legitimate grounds for battle": "who's got Soul and who doesn't, who stole Soul and who's faking it." According to this analysis, Snow is a legitimate sister of glory who brings the funk and swings the spirit in ways the aforementioned ghosts would approve and is, as a consequence, a "mesmerizing" example of the complexities of cultural—as opposed to merely racial—ancestry.

Soul features the editors' interview with Paul Gilroy, in which the black British scholar talks about whites' contributions to the music; his words manifest his sensitivity to possible Afro-American skepticism about his right to offer definitive judgments on the question of who an overwhelmingly black and American creation belongs to. In response to questions posed by Guillory—"So would you say that soul is something that is open to all—that anyone can possess soul, be soulful? Or is it racially marked?"—Gilroy replies with characteristic thoughtfulness:

> To make the music tell that story [that whites have not contributed significantly to soul music], you must do violence to the music. . . . The message that came to me from all of that [Sly and the Family Stone's, Miles Davis's, and Jimi Hendrix's traversing of stylistic boundaries] was that that quality of soulfulness was something that wasn't the specific property of blacks. . . . Now it certainly is the case that I recognized and still accept a kind of priority which is attached to the African American component in that

creativity. But I don't think that it's possible to argue that the music can be that exclusively, prescriptively. It just can't—it doesn't work. . . . The music showed me that race was limiting and offered concrete utopian resources in the struggle against racism. The presence and participation of white players was no obstacle to soul. In a sense, it may have even enhanced it by making "race" irrelevant and symbolizing the possibility of white agency against white supremacy. (257–58)

What interests me most about Gilroy's comment is not its acknowledgment of white contributions to soul—at least since Leroi Jones's insistence in *Black Music* that the successful appropriation of jazz by committed white musicians demonstrated "that the sub-cultural attitudes that produced the music as a profound expression of human feelings . . . could be *learned* and need not be passed on as a secret blood rite" (13), no serious investigator could argue that black musical performance is possible only for people who are tied by "blood" to Africa—but its delineation of the political implications of those contributions. Gilroy's stance differs, for example, from that of August Wilson, the author of an extraordinary series of plays (including *Ma Rainey's Black Bottom, The Piano Lesson,* and *Fences*) that draw extensively on the blues as subject and inspiration, who argues that black Americans enjoy exclusive epistemological access to and proprietary control over its cultural products. Indeed, while August Wilson insists that whites' involvement with Afro-American expressive culture limits black pursuit, on levels of production, consumption, and distribution, of the dream of American freedom and the theme of self-determination that the works themselves invariably investigate, Gilroy sees white contributions to soul as evidence of the viability of a "utopian" fantasy that, in their engagement with black musicians and black music itself, they will be inspired to display courageous signs of "white agency" that empower them to overthrow "white supremacy." If, for Wilson, white presence in the "altered states" and fecund fields of soul extends a history of commercial and artistic theft of the creative labor of enterprising black bodies into the putatively more egalitarian present, Gilroy sees that presence as a visible sign of the potential transcendence of race as a divisive social category and of the achievement of an interracial love of sorts, or at least experientially determined mutual respect.

Still, efforts abound to categorize the nature and implications of whites' participation in musical genres that were developed in what Wilson calls the "kiln" of Afro-American culture. In one such interrogation, Robert Hellenga's novel *Blues Lessons*, Reverend Taylor, a gifted country blues performer, debunks some of the myths surrounding the form for the anxious novice white bluesman Martin Dijksterhuis who is the novel's protagonist. Insisting, among other things, that Robert Johnson, around whom so much of the genre's mythology revolves, was at best a marginal and derivative talent, Taylor suggests that the wide dissemination of such myths forces performers "to tell people you sold your soul to the devil" because they "want to hear a story about a lonely old crossroad" where "the devil'll come and tune your guitar for you . . . , and after that you can play any song you want" (136–37). Rather than being the function of biology, racial oppression, or a supernatural pact with the devil, blues proficiency is, in Taylor's view, the result of the combination of common human experiences, musical talent, and diligent practice:

> "Of course," he went on, "you don't need any extra special feelings to play the blues. You already got all the special feelings you need. Any person alive in this world has all the feelings it needs to play the blues. What sets a blues musician apart from other people is not special feelings. It's the ability to play the music, to pick the guitar or blow the harp. You don't need any rarified feelings for that. What you need is talent, and a little bit of talent will take you a long ways. (133)

This fictional bluesman helps us understand that any truly useful discussion of white mastery of black musical forms must state clearly the terms of its assessment of the success or failure of white appropriation (and, for that matter, of black performance). To that end, Baraka praises the work of white jazz musicians such as the Original Dixieland Jazz Band and Bix Beiderbecke because it reflects the "attitudes that produced the music" and "signaled the existence of an American music, where before there was a Negro music" (13). Conversely, Wilson, who believes that artistic forms which contain "specific ideas and attitudes that are not shared on the common cultural ground . . . remain the property and possession of the people who develop them" (201), insists that they can be knowingly engaged only by members of the group that produced them.

Despite their divergent opinions about the verifiability of white achievement in this area, for these black intellectuals, the measure of successful appropriation is whether what they deem definitive black cultural "attitudes" can be discerned, either in the "broad cultural ground" or in the souls of white folk who are part of the commonality of American society. Whether this "attitude" is clearly manifested in the work of some "committed" whites, as Baraka and Gilroy hold, or not, as Wilson believes, given the nation's persistent devaluation of blackness and efforts of its capitalist custodians "to dilute and control [black expressivity] by setting themselves up as the assayers of its value and the custodians of its offspring" (203), white artists who seek to perform black styles do so because of what they hold to be their creative, cultural, and commercial advantages. On rare occasions, their efforts are judged to be attitudinally grounded enough to express—and haunt—"our dreams, and our fantasies" about black expressive particularity. But, as these examples suggest, evaluations of their effectiveness appear never to cease, allowing even as mesmerizing a singer as Snow to be removed from the fold either as part of an effort to foreground black multiplicity, in the case of *A Different World*, or, in *Soul*, when her mastery conflicts with an interrogation of the pitfalls of white appropriation.

The Color of the Soul of Jazz in
Black and White During "Overpoliticized Times"

Both Jon Panish's *The Color of Jazz* and Charley Gerard's *Jazz in Black and White* explore white proficiency vis-à-vis black expressive culture by investigating, among other things, various artistic endeavors that extend beyond jazz instrumental acumen: novels, poems, and essays in the case of Panish's book, and seminal R & B lyrics in Gerard's analysis. For example, Panish argues that, both for the analyst of black culture and the performer of its musical treasures, masterful engagement is possible only when "the white aspirant [recognizes that he or she] should study the people, the way of life, and the total experience of being black in America" (53). Examining works produced from the mid-1940s through the mid-1960s—a period when the notion of American cultural "color-blindness emerged . . . as the dominant racial discourse despite the power and popularity of the oppositional discourses that emanated from the Civil Rights Movement and urban bohemias like Greenwich Village" (xxii)—he finds representations of black jazz musicians by white writers such as Norman Mailer, Jack Kerouac, and Dorothy Baker lacking in comparison to those of the black writers Baraka, James Baldwin, and Ann Petry because they fail to recreate the ideological terms out of which black cultural forms emerge. "Because . . . Euro-Americans stood in a superior social and political position vis-à-vis African American culture," Panish argues, "they could appropriate or exploit those resources" (18), participating in a "form of romantic racialization that elevated their own sense of self and identity" over the "emphasis placed on race, community, and culture" (21–22, 143) in the writings of Afro-Americans and in the music produced by black musicians.

For Panish, such misappropriation is the result of whites generally being "unable or unwilling to recognize the subtle and profound ways in which that culture spun off different angles of vision on such cherished American ideals as individualism, freedom, and equality." As important, however, is the fact that whites often "were unable or unwilling even to put themselves in the position of subordinating themselves to black people and black culture. . . . Because of the inequality of racial categories in the United States (especially during this period), it was a different (and perhaps inescapably dominating) activity altogether for white men to forge a synthesis of white and black cultures than it would have been for black men and women to do so" (143). Unlike Panish, who focuses on the ways in which whites are empowered in and by their utilizations of black music, Charley Gerard emphasizes the fact that they "occupy an unenviable role in black music ideology. They are called thieves for making money from the music and exploiters for benefiting from African American talent" (6). In his survey of a variety of positions held by black musicians about the skills of white musicians and by white contributors about the degree of immersion in black culture necessary to produce authentic jazz, blues, and soul, Gerard includes those of jazz composer extraordinaire Duke Ellington, who "commended white musicians for growing close to the 'black soul'" (36); blues guitarist Michael Bloomfield, "a well off urban Jew [who] . . . never wanted . . . to be a white black guy" (105); and Dan Penn, a key contributor to Stax Records and composer of the lyrics of such seminal R & B songs as "Do-Right Woman, Do-Right Man" and "Dark End of the Street," who "notes that despite a strong influence of African American music, he is 'no blacker than the next white man'" (109). Indeed, Penn insists that he never thought much about the professional implications of his race "until he attended a music conference in 1969, the year after the Reverend Martin Luther King's death, [and]

. . . found out that African Americans in the music industry felt he had no business being where he was. Penn's eyes were opened by a meeting during which white rhythm-and-blues producer Jerry Wexler was hanged in effigy, and speakers demanded that African American artists work only with African American musicians and producers" (109–10). People who expressed desires for exclusively black zones of creative expression and economic profit did not necessarily presume that whites were incapable of creating or helping to produce black sounds—given Wexler's formative role in the careers of such prodigious talents as Ray Charles, Solomon Burke, and Aretha Franklin, such a view is patently nonsensical—but they did hold that black self-determination required that, to the extent it is possible, tight racial boundaries be drawn around the products emanated from the Afro-American soul.

In *Sweet Soul Music*, Peter Gurnalick also argues that King's assassination in Memphis signaled the beginning of the end of the interracial cooperation that had helped to propel that city's Stax Records into the status of soul music's perhaps most significant label. As the company's white cofounder, Jim Stewart, told the music historian Robert Gordon, this death "had a tremendous impact" on his employees, "put[ting] a wedge, or at least opened up that suspicious element, [within] the company. Although we tried to bond together and continue to work together, from that point on it changed considerably. There wasn't that happy feeling of creating together" (146). Similarly, Al Bell, a black part-owner of the company at the time who went on to purchase it outright in the early 1970s, suggests that the assassination, which took place just miles from the company's offices, "heightened internally the racial sensitivity amongst those of us at Stax. . . . We were there in the middle of the black community and here we were an integrated organization existing in a city where integration was an issue. Dr. King's death caused [some] African-American people in the community to react negatively toward the white people that worked for Stax Records" (Bowman 146).[3]

Both of the histories whose descriptions of a growing awareness the politics of racial difference I have referenced, *Sweet Soul Music* and *Soulsville, USA: The Story of Stax Records*, feature photographs of Janis Joplin, who performed in the Second Annual Stax-Volt Yuletide Thing on December 21, 1968. While Guralnick does not discuss Joplin, Rob Bowman explores her presence—both in Memphis and in the music business—in some detail. Bowman insists, for example, that Joplin's performance met "with tepid applause and a lot of silence" from a black audience that had thrilled to the sets of acts like the Staple Singers and Eddie Floyd and was waiting to hear Johnnie Taylor (167–69). According to Alice Echols, "King's assassination at the same Lorraine Motel [in which Joplin stayed in December 1968] . . . had ended all sorts of possibilities, including the cultural hybridity Janis Joplin and Jimi Hendrix represented" (231–32). Echols goes on to say that Joplin "wanted to sing soul, and her timing couldn't have been worse. King's assassination destroyed the dream of interracialism as Black Power and its critique of integration gained greater support and credibility within the black community—a shift that reverberated culturally as well as politically. . . . By the early seventies, many of the whites involved in southern soul music—most notably, Jerry Wexler, Rick Hall, and Phil Walden—left the field rather than be attacked for making money off black people" (237–38).

Despite their privileged status in American society generally, whites who participated in the production of black popular music during this period clearly faced daunting challenges. Among the consequences of agitation for black creative autonomy was the call for the exclusion from the field of experienced white professionals such as Wexler, who "felt angry, undervalued, scared, unsure of what to do or say" in "overpoliticized times" when "reasonable dialogue was an unreasonable expectation" (228). In such racially charged times, it is difficult to imagine that the appearance of Phoebe Snow on the Greenwich Village club scene, turned on to "blues and old jazz" and singing the songs of "old blues greats," could have been without complications. Though she has never to my knowledge indicated that she experienced racial hostility, it must have been stressful indeed for a self-described "vulnerable" young woman with "poor self-esteem, a poor self-image" (Lloyd n.p.)—who, "all of [her] life, when things got too difficult . . . , folded up the tent and went to bed" and who, "terrified of confrontation . . . , wouldn't get involved or fight back" (Roos n.p.)—to utilize black styles of music in the environment in which "white people doing black music carr[ied] a lot of guilt" (Echols 234) and in which one of soul's preeminent producers had been told that he had been marked for assassination.

In the period just before disco's explosion, some whites who performed soul did call attention to their race (e.g., Wild Cherry, in their recording "Play That Funky Music" and the Scottish group Average White Band, in their name), but numerous other white acts utilized soul and funk conventions in seemingly less self-conscious and defensive ways. Major hit songs of this type include Philly soul enthusiasts Hall & Oates' "She's Gone" (1974) and "Sara Smile" (1976), blues guitarist Elvin Bishop's "Fooled Around and Fell in Love" (1976), the Bee Gees' "Jive Talking" (1975), former Bluesology member Elton John's "Bennie and the Jets" (1974), folk pop duo Seals and Crofts' "Get Closer" (1976), and glam rocker David Bowie's "Fame" and "Young Americans" (1975). But while, for example, Bowie's mid-1970s grooves represent merely an important stage in a career marked by energetic experimentation, Snow perceived herself as trapped stylistically despite her superior vocal gifts and equally broad musical interests. As Shewey insists, "Phoebe's dazzling technique and extraordinary sophistication pegged her as a jazz singer from the outset . . . , but eventually she began to chafe under this narrow definition" (80). He sees her dissatisfaction as a function of the fact that "she realized that she was just going through the motions. 'I began to feel like a real supermimic. And the deeper I got into jazzy stuff, the more contrived it started to sound.' On her next four albums, Phoebe watched her musical direction grow more and more diffuse. When she called a halt to her recording career in 1979, it was because she had finally figured out exactly what it was she wanted to do: 'Rock.' She sighed—she remembers saying, 'I'm not a rock singer'" (80). This passage suggests that, despite an acute sense of her limitations—"I'm not a rock singer"—Snow believed that rock was a more appropriate milieu for and more authentic expression of her musical self than the forms of black music she had indeed mastered.

While she appears to recognize the paradox of claiming a natural affinity for a genre of music of which she is not a skilled performer, Snow seems unaware of the fact that her interests in rock derive from a "fantasy" of proficiency no less derivative or a transgression of firm social boundaries than her engagement with jazz. She says of her musical interests as a child:

> Before I met Charlie, rock's all I listened to. . . . Ask my mom. I spent every Saturday night at the Fillmore East. Give me Jeff Beck! Please, get Eric Clapton out here!
>
> . . . We all have fantasies of doing what Roger Daltrey does with the microphone, whipping ourselves into a frenzy. It's like wanting to be Superman when I was four. . . . That's the first superpower fantasy you have, and the

second is being a rock star. You can't deny that's a very viable fantasy. Everybody else was doing it, so I wanted to try. ("Blues of Snow," 80)

The fact that at least two of the performers she mentions, Clapton and Beck, strove for blues guitarist excellence indicates that Snow's formulations of her "supermimicry" of blacks and her "viable fantas[ies]" about replicating white male rock "frenzy" are not as easily differentiated racially as she implies. But by insisting that "everybody" wants to imitate Daltrey rather than, say, what Nelson George calls James Brown's "incredible, camel-walking, proto-moon-walking, athletically daring performance" (92), she assumes (perhaps correctly, given the article's appearance in *Esquire*) that white male rock cultural preferences are shared by all of its readers. Despite these views, Snow acknowledges that "something was still missing" in her 1981 rock album, *Rock Away*, and announces: "What I really wanna do, if the truth be known, is something I blatantly rejected on the last album. I guess I was nervous. On my new album, I'm gonna go back to funk" (80).

Snow does not spell out precisely the sources of her nervousness about pursuing her funk ambitions and, by extension, abandoning—at least temporarily—her rock fantasies. However, given her comments, we can safely assume that she is concerned that, like her earlier immersion in jazz and the blues, her performance of soul and funk would situate her in a musical environment in which, because of her race, she (and others) felt she did not belong. If aesthetic considerations had been the only factors she had to ponder, the choice between (white) rock and (black) funk, between the racially authentic and the expertly mimicked, between uninspired "frenzy" and "dazzling," "extraordinary" soulfulness, should have been easy. However, looked at in the context of debates in the early 1970s about race, art, and cultural authenticity—issues about which Columbia, the label that signed her after her golden successes on Leon Russell's independent Shelter label, was sufficiently concerned that it commissioned a 1972 study by Harvard's Business School in order to get expert advice about how best to make significant inroads in the R & B market—*Second Childhood*, Snow's first recording for this major company, assumes much greater historical and cultural import than being simply the singer's first attempt, after the success of *Phoebe Snow* and "Poetry Man," to consolidate her position as "voice of her generation."

For a record company that had failed in its efforts in the early 1970s to "penetrate the black market" (Sanjek 61), *Second Childhood* was a perhaps unanticipated opportunity to gain access to black record buyers. And for the insecure, gifted white female who was beginning to feel restricted artistically by the fact that listeners heard in her voice echoes of great black singers, her first major company release had the potential to allow her to acknowledge, and move definitively beyond, her debts to black musical traditions. Whatever *Second Childhood* represented for Snow, its success would be in part contingent on how masterfully she was able to sound and, indeed, appear to be black. In an industry so thoroughly dominated, in Salim Washington's estimation, by "cultural superstars" who enjoyed "their status not because of superior artistry, but primarily because of sufficient mastery of African American techniques and their 'whiteness'" (167), Snow's proficiency with both (white) folk pop and (black) bluesy soul styles could have given her the institutional authority if not to transcend race, to combine these styles in a definitive enough manner to have secured for herself the freedom subsequently to record any sort of music she desired.[4]

I have uncovered no direct evidence of how, if at all, Snow's music fit into Columbia's strategy to saturate black markets. But it seems unlikely that executives of the company that commissioned the Harvard Report would have failed to consider how best to maximize the economic gains and cultural capital they could accrue from the work of a white woman blessed with a "black" voice, given the increasingly hard "market segmentation" that David Sanjek, director of the BMI Archives, identifies in his analysis of this report (73). Such considerations appear to impact aspects of *Second Childhood*, including the singer's visual presentation on the album's cover and the choice to remake three songs that represent a range of popular black vocal styles during the preceding seven decades of the twentieth century. By obscuring—or covering over, if you will—Snow's whiteness both visually and through remakes of songs associated with *Porgy and Bess* ("There's A Boat That's Leaving Soon for New York"), Billie Holiday ("No Regrets"), and Motown ("Going Down for the Third Time," the B side of the Supremes' 1967 single "Reflections"), *Second Childhood* could be said to challenge both playlist segregation and received notions concerning the possibilities of being made over or reborn racially.

Don Shewey describes the image of Snow that graces the cover of her eponymous first album in the following way: "with a cloud of kinky hair topping a bespectacled face distinguished by full lips and seven promi-nent moles, you can't tell whether she's young or old, black or white" ("Blues of Snow" 76). The purported racial indeterminacy of the singer's visual rendering, of course, mirrors what Shewey considers the cultural hybridity of Snow's voice, suggesting either a natural or a staged syn-chronicity between her appearance and her capacity for both "black" and "folk" or "pop" expression.

While at most gesturing toward possible connections between her look and sound, Shewey insists that Snow's physical appearance matters com-mercially. Echoing the singer's own explorations in her first album's song, "Either or Both," of the perceived incommensurability between homely looks and feelings of social and romantic worthiness, he contrasts the "most famous picture" of the singer to the flesh-and-blood woman he is interviewing in 1982, concluding with the comparison to Blondie's lead singer that I referred to earlier: "Today, contact lenses have replaced the eyeglasses. And when she puts on a little makeup and changes into an em-broidered black pullover for dinner, she even shows a touch of real glam-our. But it's still a little awkward talking about her appearance. We both know that if she sang like Phoebe Snow but looked like Deborah Harry, she'd be a superstar by now" (76). If Snow could approach "real glamour" by discarding her glasses, covering over or removing facial imperfections, and dolling herself up with elegant clothing, because her looks could not be made to approximate the mainstream ideal of female beauty (unlike Blondie's lead singer who, in the three years before Shewey's article ap-peared, had sung the chart-topping singles "Heart of Glass," "Call Me," "The Tide Is High," and "Rapture"), her career was marked by obstacles that she apparently could not ultimately overcome.

If the subject of the cover art of *Phoebe Snow* is indeed racially indeter-minate, the elegant photograph that graces *Second Childhood* makes such identification even more profoundly difficult. The minimalist cover fea-tures the album's title at its top border, Snow's signature just underneath the title and to the left, and, in its exact center, a severely lit black-and-white photograph of the singer. Her body is positioned on the left frame of the photograph, and part of right side of her face—which is angled toward the camera—and the entirety of her neck in shadows, their blackness indistinguishable from the color of her dark garb and her afro, which appears significantly kinkier than in the earlier image. The dark areas of the photograph offer a stark visual contrast to the almost blinding whiteness of the rest of her serious, unsmiling face, her chest, and the glittering rose brooch affixed to her clothing. It is, I believe, this photograph, and not the image Shewey discusses, that, along with her voice's soulful textures, causes some fans to assume that Snow may be biologically connected to Africa.

Interpreting the cover art of *Second Childhood* requires that its viewers possess a general cultural knowledge and a willingness to surmise its artist's and sponsoring company's intentions. Compelling us to focus on the singer, it presents her strategically lit, miniaturized image in such a manner that we can barely make out her features. Indeed, while we can perceive essential characteristics in the photograph's subject—her earnest interrogation of her audience, the almost frightening seriousness suggested by her unsmiling, perhaps even unwelcoming, mouth—what the cover calls attention to, from my perspective, is (cultural) contrast.[5] The contrasts I have in mind are: between black and white; between nostalgia for a bygone era that the black-and-white image evokes and discomfort with the Technicolor Age in which it appears; between an unsatisfactory "childhood" and a "second" chance, a doubtlessly more pleasant constitution of the self that it promises to display, through older, perhaps even timeless, musical styles that are the aural equivalents of the cover's visual textures.

If, as Roland Barthes insists, "every photograph is contingent (and thereby outside of meaning)" and, as a consequence, "cannot signify (aim at a generality) except by assuming a mask . . . [that] makes a face into the product of a society and of its history" (34), what can we say of the mask made of Snow's face (by the viewer, the photographer, Columbia, and the singer herself) to ascertain its contingent meanings? Might we argue that it reflects post–civil rights racial crises that render her, a white singer touched by the expressive soul of ancestors not her own, a dangerous anomaly? That it foretells the demise of folk music as a mode of popular music, of the blues revival, and of the singer-songwriter as a viable category? That it imagines the daunting nature of its task to create a musical persona out of discarded fragments of these obsolescent genres? That, for a white female singer not blessed, say, with Linda Ronstadt's or Olivia Newton-John's sexy, girlish, wide-eyed face, pout, and figure, pop music can be an alienating, even traumatizing business? That cultural references other than exalted white female beauty would have to be attached to Snow if she is to have a career as significant as critics and her fans believe she is capable? Historicizing this cover, and Snow's career, allows us to recognize that all of these meanings can reasonably be attached its somber "mask."

In Barthes's view, the photograph "does not invent; it is authentication itself; the (rare) artifices it permits are not probative; they are, on the contrary, trick pictures. . . . Photography never lies: or rather, it can lie as to the meaning of the thing, being by nature *tendentious*, never as to its existence" (87). Considered in the context of early 1970s debates about the significance of race in the creation and performance of popular music genres, Snow's photograph is, indeed, a visual "lie," one that is, for me, what Barthes calls a "sting, speck, cut, little hole—and also a cast of the dice." Even if Columbia's employees, utilizing Snow as part of their efforts to increase the marketability of its product in black communities, did not compel Frank Laffitte to render the singer's image as racially indecipherable, the "tricks" used by the photographer contribute to the continued readings of her as a "light-complected black woman" whose vocal styles can then be deemed to be biologically compelled. If Snow has had to answer questions about her racial origins, those questions emerge not merely as a result of how and what she sings, but how her looks—and their meanings—have been manipulated.

Beyond "Layers of Metaphors and Obscure Imagery":
Soul and the Singer-Songwriter

If my discussion of Al Green confirms Stephen Holden's characterization of the singer-songwriter label as "selectively applied" in critics' descriptions of pop performers of the 1960s and 1970s, Snow is certainly a performer to whom it has been firmly (if, as we will see, somewhat problematically) attached. The generally acoustic-based work of participants in this genre, whose leading figures include Bob Dylan, Joni Mitchell, Neil Young, Paul Simon, and James Taylor, draws upon "the poetry of previous generations" and features "flattened" "pop melodies" that "accommodate the torrent of words and the limitations of the songwriters' untrained voices," "whose characteristic product was a confessional self-portrait comprised of a dozen or so thematically related pieces" (Holden 482). Its conventions "encouraged a greater intimacy in both songwriting and performance," especially in the "romantic-confessional realm" and the work of "romantic-visionaries who mythologized their personal experience" (483). And as the "Singer/Songwriter" entry in the *All Music Guide* suggests, it is a genre in which the singer—drawing "primarily from folk and country"—typically "performed alone with an acoustic guitar or a piano," delivering "lyrics [that] were personal, although they were often veiled by layers of metaphors and obscure imagery." Engaging predominantly white musical sources, the singer-songwriter produces "records [that] have a similar sound, which is usually spare, direct, and reflective . . . , [and] places the emphasis on the song itself" rather than, say—as in the case in black music generally—on the vocal prowess of the singer.

The most detailed discussion of *Second Childhood* I have encountered, Robert Palmer's *Rolling Stone* review (which appears six months after Snow—unsmiling, heavily made-up, in pink flapper's head garb, and photographed by Annie Leibovitz—graced the cover of the music industry's premiere publication), clearly identifies Snow as a singer-songwriter. According to Palmer, while her first album features "descriptions of adolescent insecurity and suburban nightmare," the second displays "a more mature, less neurotic Phoebe Snow" "wondering how these extraordinarily rapid transitions are going to affect her creativity," among other things. From his perspective, many of the songs on *Second Childhood* suffer as a consequence of "images [that] are too internalized and too fragmented to add up" and that are "subject to almost any interpretation," emotionally distanced personae who have not sufficiently processed the experiences they describe, and an indulgence in empty "wordplay" as a substitute for the singer's exploration of "her unique vocal potential." Rather than distanced, introspective, vocally muted folk sketches, what Palmer wants are clear descriptions of emotionally charged situations that push her to the sorts of engaged, soulful heights she displays in her duet with Paul Simon:

> She easily sings clear, bell-like tones an octave and a half above her normal range, but it took Paul Simon to get that facet of her talent on record, on the single they made together. There was nothing like that last, trium-

phant chorus of Simon's "Gone at Last" on *Phoebe Snow* and there's nothing like it on *Second Childhood*. Instead, strings, woodwinds and cunning but derivative jazz—by the Brecker Brothers' Dave Sanborn and Don Grolnick rather than Zoot Sims and Teddy Wilson—swirl around and over her voice, smoothing out its rough edges and too frequently vitiating its individuality.

Instead of the smooth, droll sameness of folk pop vocalizing, Palmer desires the "rough," emotional evocation of soul shouting of which Simon shows us Snow is capable.

As a devoted listener for three decades, I have enjoyed the singer-songwriter elements of *Second Childhood* much more than this review suggests I should, partly because I haven't generally felt compelled to "subject" her "obscure" lines to "any interpretation" whatsoever. Consequently, I have found it easy to appreciate Snow's voice—which, in Robert Palmer's words, "sings rings around voices with ten times the training and experience, and thrills us all the more because even at its most spectacular it sounds unforced and quite innocent of artifice"—without worrying about whether I was getting the full meanings of the combination of words she composed in her role as intellectual songwriter. But as a hopefully creative interpreter—my role here—I must admit that I agree with many of his points. Like Palmer, I feel that, compared to the lush musical accompaniment on *Phoebe Snow*, the instrumentation on her second album is generally sedate and appears muted, as if the music is being pushed through a filter rather than being allowed to distinguish itself within Phil Ramone's careful production. In addition, for better or for worse, her lyrics do offer what the *All Music Guide*'s entry on singer-songwriters calls "layers of metaphors and obscure imagery," in such lines as "the night queen fright Wig Street parade may fade / When we laugh at the statues of gods we have made" ("All Over") and "Help us Mary Jane / We are wandering out on this desert plain / We have no canteen / Can the thirsty stay sane after what they've seen" ("Two-Fisted Love"). And like Palmer, I'm not sure what the "internal," "fragmented" images of "Cash In" "add up" to, or that they add up at all. Finally, I, too, feel that Snow's voice remains harnessed for the most part, displaying what he calls a "dedication to vocal artistry" rather than to exploring its "potential." Certainly, her voice manifests throughout the album an admirable subtlety, its vibrato working overtime to highlight the sound, shape, and significance of key words and phrases, holding notes and displaying remarkable control over the art of artistic breathing, but offering little evidence of a soul on fire.

I agree with Palmer's assertion, then, that Snow fails generally to display the impressive volume, vocal power, and passion that distinguish her subsequent forays into styles of black music. But he is wrong, in my view, when he claims that such displays do not appear at all in *Second Childhood*. Indeed, they are certainly evident in the only song on the album he does not mention, "Going Down for the Third Time," in which the singer employs what, over the course of her later albums, become familiar stylistic flourishes to explore the soul potential of an album track that was written and originally produced for the Supremes by Motown's prolific team, Holland-Dozier-Holland. In addition, Snow's soul power appears—albeit briefly—on "Cash In," a song that Palmer says "sounds a little like Snow's friend Paul Simon and features the Jessy Dixon Singers, who have worked with him," before identifying (as I have indicated) Simon as the inspiration for the only recorded manifestation to that point of her capacity to reach the sort of ecstatic heights that he longs to hear from her more frequently. He fails to acknowledge, however, that Snow's singing of "Cash In," which is for the most part contemplative rather than inspirited, changes significantly at the song's end, when the Dixon Singers move to the sonic foreground, repeating the lines "Rolling out sevens / Leads away from Heaven / Jokers cash in / Gin." In effect, their emergence alters the musical environment sufficiently that Snow—as if freed temporarily from the constraints of the singer-songwriter form and her own artistic aspirations—allows her voice to rise to another register, swoop in behind and underneath the choir with seemingly rapturous "ooohs," and punctuate the line "Cash it in" with as much gospel fervor as the Dixon Singers, and certainly as much as she displays in her duet with Simon.

Second Childhood's self-penned, lyrically obscure, contemplative or "reflective," subtly delivered songs are, in my view, intellectually and aurally engaging. But other than moments like the fadeout of "Cash In," they position Snow in an overwhelmingly white genre (of the nearly one hundred singer-songwriters the *All Music Guide* lists as "key artists," only two—Joan Armatrading and Tracy Chapman—are black) rather than in the category of "black" singer she later comes close to claiming for herself. In the case of *Second Childhood*, then, such a claim certainly can be tested by investigating rare moments in songs she composed—like "Cash In," where her use of "her rich alto," in the estimation of Stephen Holden, "merits comparison with those of the great R & B shouters, like Big Mama Thornton and Ruth Brown" ("Rock Away"), or in "Two-Listed Love," which Palmer sees as "Snow at her best, a song that's verbally, emotionally and musically complex, and directly, unblushingly lusty." However, as I will show, it is infinitely more fruitful to test this claim in terms of her covers of black songs.

Music critics seem generally to agree with Shewey's contention, offered in a review of her last Columbia release, *Against the Grain*, that "when she interprets" others' songs, "Snow ignites, expands, takes outrageous chances, projects," but "when she contemplates [her own, often 'embarrassingly trite . . . , nerdy verses'], she withdraws, slows down, mumbles and gets dull." If it is indeed the case that, after her highly praised first release, her albums are undermined by her inability to resolve her quandary about whether to be a lyrically obscure, vocally staid—and aesthetically white—singer-songwriter or a more direct, vocally "outrageous" soul shouter (or, more precisely, how to be both and produce satisfying suites of music), the status of *Second Childhood* as "black" music (in addition to reaching number thirteen on the pop chart, Snow's second and final gold album also peaked at number ten on *Billboard*'s jazz chart and at number thirty-three on the R & B chart) can best be assessed by investigating, in some detail, Snow's three interpretations of songs associated with Afro-Americans.

As I have indicated, *Second Childhood* contains Snow's remakes of three songs: "No Regrets," a tune that became what Robert Palmer calls "the personal property of the late Billie Holiday" as a consequence of her nuanced performance of it in 1936; the relatively obscure "Going Down for the Third Time," which appears on *The Supremes Sing Holland-Dozier-Holland* and as the B-side of the Motown group's hit "Reflections" (both from 1967); and "There's A Boat That's Leaving Soon for New York," composed by George and Ira Gershwin, along with Du Bose Heyward, for *Porgy and Bess*, the "folk opera" that George Gershwin adapted in the 1930s from Heyward's 1927 novel, *Porgy*. As we will see, long before Snow interprets them in the context of her own compositions, these songs were all directly implicated in assessments of the ideological and aesthetic consequences of racial difference and, hence, can be accurately categorized as boundary songs.

The questions raised by these songs, their performers, and their writers—can a white composer create "black" folk sounds; to what extent can even the "greatest jazz singer" utilize the white middle-class male sensibilities of Tin Pan Alley composers to illuminate the concerns of blacks generally and black women in particular; and just how black is the music of the Supremes, Motown's crossover dream girls—reflect the desires of many people to position black popular music as an exclusively racial form of expression at the same time that its mass distribution enabled it to saturate and, indeed, reshape mainstream popular musical and sociocultural sensibilities.[6] The racial impurity of these boundary songs, sung by a singer who is frequently mistaken for (and comes close to describing herself as) black, then, is the focus of the following extended analyses.

On Gershwin, "Fake Authenticity," and
the Dangers of Leaving the Boat Too Soon

Porgy and Bess contains several songs—including "I Got Plenty of Nuttin,'" "It Ain't Necessarily So," and "the classic American lullaby" (Zinsser 96) "Summertime," which numerous singers, black and white, have recorded—that are widely perceived as essential American compositions. As Allen Forte argues in *Listening to Classic American Popular Songs*, such tunes, composed between the mid-1920s and the late 1940s, share "remarkable characteristics . . . that have kept them alive and popular over many years and that enable them to speak anew to each successive generation: the beautiful melodies and harmonies, the entrancing rhythms, the wondrous lyrics that are so often inseparably bonded to the musical notes in such extraordinary ways. These qualities, which evoke universal responses from sensitive listeners, inspired the use of the term 'classic' to convey the timelessness of the best of this music" (xii).

Forte insists that "sensitive listeners" respond to the supposedly universal characteristics of classic songs. Often, however, the parts and the whole of Gershwin's enduring "folk opera" are evaluated not solely in terms of their "melodies," "harmonies," or even "entrancing rhythms," but the perceived success or failure of its composer's efforts to translate, among other experiences, his immersion in Gullah culture during the summer of 1934 into dramatic scenes and musical texts that "portray the everyday life of an entire Negro community near Charlestown, South Carolina" (Zinsser 96).

Not surprisingly, the play's status as an authentic depiction of black life has been hotly contested. In his study of the history of the Broadway musical, Geoffrey Block concisely sketches the contours of the disputes concerning whether the play

> expressed the African-American experience. Criticisms of Gershwin's racial presumptions appeared as early as the 1935 Broadway premiere, but in con- trast to the gradual tolerance and eventual appreciation of his musical am- bitions and the work's length, the hubris of Gershwin's depictions has not diminished over time despite the proliferation of performances through- out the world. In fact, the growing "classic" stature of *Porgy and Bess* may actually have fueled racial controversies in recent years to a point where the problems brought about by what is perceived as cultural colonization and exploitation seems destined to remain central to the work in the minds of many for some time to come. (71–72)

Views of the racial authenticity of *Porgy and Bess*, its articulation of iden- tifiably black cultural and musical sensibilities, vary widely. Some hold that the play demonstrates "Gershwin's misunderstanding of the African- American character and experience" because the music "suggests sophis- ticated intricacies of attitude which could not possibly be native to the minds of the people who make up his story," and that it "perpetuates old stereotypes that right-thinking people have buried long ago" (Block 73). Others claim that it "possess[es] a 'fake authenticity' analogous to nineteenth-century slave narratives written by whites" and does not, as the "normally circumspect and polite Duke Ellington was reported to have said," "use the Negro musical idiom [and] . . . was not the music of Catfish Row or any other kind of Negroes" (Block 74). Still other critics believe that the play demonstrates its primary composer's ability "to freely adapt his own Russian-Jewish ethnicity into a personal interpretation of the African-American experience rather than slavishly imitate it" (Block 74), or that it offers evidence of similarities between black music and "good Jewish music" that allow Gershwin and his collaborators—who neces- sarily "compose out of who they are"—implicitly to demonstrate connec- tions between black folksongs and "Europeans' own folk songs and their own religious music" (Zinsser 99). These varied responses all hinge on a larger artistic and ideological question: can and should whites create "authentic" black music?

In Gershwin's play, "Boat" is a bouncy, promise-filled tune that crystallizes the efforts of the dope dealer and bootlegger, Sporting Life, to convince Bess—who earlier switched her romantic allegiance from the murderous alcoholic Crown to the sensitive cripple Porgy, who had been incarcerated in connection with the murder of Bess's jealous former mate—to become his lover. After supplying her with the news that she'll never see Porgy again and with a small quantity of the "happy dust" he sells to people seeking temporary escape from their difficult lives, Sporting Life offers her permanent respite from "them lonesome blues." If she accedes to his wishes, he promises that they will take a boat ride to America's most fabled metropolis, where they will live "that high life" in "the swellest mansion / Up on upper Fifth Avenue," go "strutting" through Harlem, the black cultural center, with her dolled up in "silks and satins / In the latest Paris style," and that he will work diligently to ensure that her blues will be a thing of the past.

Decca's recording of the original cast's version of "Boat" includes enough of the dramatic context—rendered in recitative or sung dialogue form that was disliked by critics and eliminated from many subsequent revivals—to offer the listener a clear sense of the song's import. Given Gershwin's status as a "classical" American songwriter, it is not surprising that many of his compositions are sung by a variety of singers in ways that display either no knowledge of or concern about their theatrical origins. So when jazz giant Louis Armstrong performs "Boat" for his and Ella Fitzgerald's recording of musical selections from the play, for example, Satchmo invests the song with smile-inducing vocals and his incomparable trumpet soloing, but his rendition reflects little concern with approximating the folk operatic origins of the lyrics and duplicating the malicious mischief that marks Avon Long's original performance. "Boat" is, in Armstrong's rendition, a compelling song from a play that has a hold on the American cultural imagination, one that he can both respect and bend to fit his own artistic vision.

Because questions persist about whether *Porgy and Bess* is indeed a "Negro opera," Snow's performance of "There's A Boat That's Leaving Soon for New York"—whose title she renders in Standard English, excising the original "dat's" and "leavin'"—positions her squarely in the middle of long-standing discussions about the efficacy of white participation in black music. Robert Palmer considers Snow's rendition of "Boat" "a gem," in part because she "gets inside it [the lyrics' meaning], touching that longing for the high life that's in almost everyone while illuminating the chord changes with gorgeous note choices and swinging like a veteran." In my view, however, it is more accurate to say that Snow does not merely "get inside" the song's lyrics, but transforms them in ways that render them appropriate for an urban, liberated, middle-class woman.

In place of the contextualizing recitative in the original recording, which is then followed by the song's chorus ("There's a boat dat's leavin' soon for New York / Come with me, that's where we belong, sister / You and me can live that high life in New York / Come with me, there we can't go wrong, sister"), Snow sings, above the song's casual, anticipatory first notes, her modern, feminized version of the first verse:

> We'll live in the swellest mansion
> Up on upper Fifth Avenue
> And through Harlem we'll go strutting, we'll go strutting
> And there'll be nothing too good for you.

In the play, Sporting Life insists to an extremely hesitant Bess that he'll use his ill-gotten gains to "buy you the swellest mansion," indicating his participation in a long-standing male tradition of currying the favor of typically less affluent women through gifts and other seductive displays of wealth. He then lists all the ways in which Bess will profit from his masculine largesse: "There'll be nothing too good for you," "You and me can live that high life," "I'll dress you in silks and satins," and "All the blues you'll be forgetting."

Positioning her persona as the figure who implores, "Come with me," and who strives to help her male addressee forget his blues, Snow does not totally flip the gender script—the male is still charged with the task of providing her with fashionable clothing—but she assumes a level of agency and economic self-sufficiency that would enable her to contribute, by means of something other than her mere assent, to her prospective lover's improved emotional and material condition. Certainly, throughout her "gorgeous" performance, in which she responds effectively to what we could characterize, to use Palmer's phrase, as "strings, woodwinds and cunning but derivative jazz," Snow skillfully utilizes recognizable musical codes and vocal conventions of big band singing. And if her appealing performance is, indeed, no more innovative than the "deriva-tive jazz" instrumentation that accompanies her, it demonstrates her ability to employ a classic musical discourse in ways that were deemed sufficiently authentic to place her rendition on the playlists of American radio stations that specialized in that musical style.

Seizing Personal Property:
Counterstatement in Billie Holiday's "No Regrets"

If her cover of "Boat" allows listeners to consider Snow's performance in the context of racial controversies surrounding *Porgy and Bess,* "the Mount Everest of American musical theater" (Zinsser 95), her remake of "No Regrets" invites comparisons with Billie Holiday. Holiday's version of the song established it as the "personal property," in Palmer's view, of the performer whom Robert O'Meally proclaims in his study *Lady Day: The Many Faces of Billie Holiday,* "the greatest jazz singer in history" (9). Holiday's stature, in O'Meally's estimation, is the result of her ability to "transmute . . . what she could use of her sorrows into the pure gold of her singing. She became an artist . . . because she worked hard to achieve her artistic voice and to master the timbres, turns of phrase, timings, and thousand other nuances that made her a singer whose records live on" (13). If her power as a singer results in part from her recognition that "every true jazz work may be likened to a poetic drama," that power manifests itself in her ability to "strip songs down to their bare essentials" in ways that "lured the listener into her tight emotional orbit" (33). Holi-day struggled "to magnificent effect" to interpret song lyrics in ways that would display the extent to which her "ideas fit together to create a won-derful musical unity: melody sustained mood, emotion sustained quality of voice" (36–37). One of her great strengths as a singer of sad songs like "Trav'lin' All Alone," O'Meally argues, is her capacity to make her voice sound "troubled in spite of the brightness in tempo. . . . It is a sad song rendered with poignancy appropriate to the lyrics; nonetheless the song's sorrowful sentiments are counterstated by a tempo and an overall treat-ment that says forget your troubles, *get up and travel with me. Let's dance*" (40–41).

O'Meally's formulation of Holiday's emphasis on the painful senti-ments expressed in song lyrics like those of "Trav'lin' All Alone," but obscured by bright, up-tempo musical arrangements, suggests an analytical approach that we can use to consider her performance of "No Regrets." Indeed, his notion of "counterstatement," of subversive vocal style, resonates with Angela Davis's view, offered in *Blues Legacies and Black Feminism*, that the "aesthetic dimension" of Holiday's songs generally manifests the singer's "simultaneous ability to confirm and subvert racist and sexist representations of women in love" (164). According to Davis,

> Billie Holiday's project—as that of a jazz musician who worked primarily with the idiom of white popular song—consisted largely in transforming already existing material into her own form of modern jazz. . . . She utilized the formative power of her jazz style to refigure the songs she performed and recorded, the great majority of which were produced on the Tin Pan Alley assembly line according to the contributed and formulaic sentimentality characteristic of the era. When she transformed these sentimental love songs into works that would become jazz standards, she relocated them in a specifically African-American cultural tradition and simultaneously challenged the boundaries of that tradition. (165)

Both Davis and O'Meally characterize Holiday as an artist who reshaped the meanings of lyrics and the relationship of words to music by subjecting them to, and filtering them through, a fierce intellect marked by profound awareness of the sexual and racial inequities of American society. In Davis's words, Holiday's transmutations of white male-authored songs "invited [her black audiences] to discover how white people acquired a consciousness of love and sexuality that was overdetermined by ideologies of male dominance and heterosexism" (171).

It may be difficult for all but a few of the most astute listeners to distinguish between what Davis considers Holiday's revealing critique of male dominance and her internalization of its ideology. What is generally accessible, however, is the fact that her art hinges in part on her capacity to use what Peter Dempsey calls her "bluesy whine" (*Wishing on the Moon* liner notes) to communicate levels of pain in highly dramatic, emotionally moving ways that are in subtle conflict with the social and, often, musical environs in which she operates. According to two of her former musicians, a full appreciation of the subtlety of Holiday's vocal technique depends on her audience's "listening to *what* she was saying and *how* she was saying." When "a singer like Ella [Fitzgerald] says, 'my man's left me' . . . , you think the guy went down the street for a loaf of bread or something. But when Lady says, 'My man's gone' or 'My man's left me,' man, you can see the guy going down the street. His bags are packed, and he ain't never coming back. I mean *never*" (O'Meally 52). If the perspectives of these musicians and of the aforementioned critics are accurate, Holiday's phrasing and impressive timing, the skill with which she works within her limited vocal range, her capacity to sing both squarely on and just behind the beat, enable her to portray the pain caused by male desertion even when, for example, the lyrics and musical arrangements of songs like "No Regrets" minimize the devastation of being replaced by "somebody new." And if Holiday "uncovers levels of feeling" (Palmer, review of *Second Childhood*) obscured by bright instrumentation and savvy phallocentric propaganda, her performance of "No Regrets" might be said to reflect a knowing skepticism of ideologies of transcendent romantic love that seduce women into believing that such love "will linger" despite, and may, in fact, be strengthened as a consequence of, their mates' wandering eyes and inconstant hearts.

Holiday's 1936 recording begins with the strumming of electric guitar chords which, after a brief silence, is followed by the singer's emphatic insistence that she has "no regrets"—a phrase whose three syllables are all accented equally—"although our love affair has gone astray." The musicians who accompany her—in particular, a bassoon player who projects a circus-like atmosphere, as well as a trumpeter and a clarinetist, both of whom comically end their respective solos by testing the physical limits of their instruments by playing what appear to be the highest notes they can—create a jovial mood that matches the song's lyrics and Holiday's singing before the instrumental break following her initial performance of the chorus and the first verse. But, after the pianist's minimalist tinkling cuts off the playful alternating instruments that dominate the break, Holiday's heretofore sweet girlish tone, offered at the highest octave she appears able comfortably to maintain, gives way to a deeper, more womanly register. It is as if, over the course of time—literally the minute and five seconds (nearly half the length of the song) of the break in which the band dominates the song; figuratively the time that feels like "forever" that her male lover remains "away" in another woman's arms— the bubbly, girlish persona has experienced the pain of her lover's desertion and, as a consequence, has come to recognize the problems of the romantic ideology she has embraced and is forced, both by social conventions and the scripted lyrics and musical notations, to repeat.

Holiday's use of her lower registers produces subtle changes in her enunciation of the words, lines, verses, and sentiments she articulated earlier. After matching her voice to the notes her musicians play during the smooth, swinging, girlish phase of her performance, she slows down her tempo so that she is noticeably off beat, singing, in a sense, a different song than either the musicians or her girlish former self, or singing the same song differently. As if emotionally depleted from her efforts to keep pace with her seemingly oblivious male musicians and the psychic demands of unrequited romantic love, Holiday comes to resist the bouncy tempo, carnivalesque flourishes, and gendered ideology that position her within a narrative in which her fate—sonically and culturally sealed, as it were—consists of waiting in perpetuity for her wayward lover's return.

"A Bopsinging Pollyanna":
Reimagining "No Regrets" in the Feminist Era

According to Palmer, Snow's version of "No Regrets" suffers in comparison to Holiday's because it is marked by "vocal grandstanding" that "negates the emotional weight of the Lady Day version by turning the song into an up-tempo virtuoso exercise. She's so pleased with her melisma on the first 'no' that she does it again before going on to 'regrets.' . . . Instead of uncovering levels of feeling [like Holiday], she skips blithely through the changes like a bopsinging Pollyanna." Insisting that Snow fails to infuse the song with "the emotional weight of the Lady Day version," Palmer asserts that, unlike Holiday, the younger singer does not discern complex "levels of meaning" in the lyrics and create, as a consequence, an overall synchronicity O'Meally speaks of as "musical unity." Palmer holds that Snow's is a flawed interpretation of "No Regrets" because the words are delivered with no sense of what O'Meally calls counterstatement or "double consciousness" (O'Meally 40), no felt difference between an initially naive persona's enduring faith in everlasting love and an older, more mature version's sense of romantic ideological entrapment. By fully embracing the lyrics' romance, Snow's singing simply mirrors and embodies, in Palmer's view, the persona's sunny response to what should be emotionally devastating news.

I believe, however, that Snow's performance reflects as knowing a take on the sociohistorical context in which it is produced—the mid-1970s, a period during which, in Joan Mandle's words, the hotly debated, but incontrovertible, cultural fact of "women's changing position in American society" is evidence of "how society alters over time" (147)—as Holiday's mid-1930s interpretation. As I have indicated, Palmer argues that Snow's first and second albums appear to be the work of "two different people," the first wrenched by "adolescent insecurity and suburban nightmares," the second noticeably "more mature, less neurotic." He prefers *Phoebe Snow* to *Second Childhood* because of the first album's freer, more "spare"—and better—jazz-blues instrumentation and the "remarkable immediacy, liquidity and control" of Snow's vocals. In addition, he feels that the singer's hard won satisfaction limits her capacity to achieve either a felt "immediacy" with or a knowing distance from the experiences her second suite of songs relates. Referencing O'Meally's formulations, we might say that, for Palmer, *Second Childhood* manifests, but does not come sufficiently to terms with, the sort of "double consciousness" that Holiday's art adeptly displays and resolves. Looked at in light of the gendered and racial contexts in which Snow's performance operates, however, her giddily naive performance of "No Regrets" is, in fact, extremely effective.

Rather than view Snow's "up-tempo virtuoso exercise" as an imperfect, "grandstanding" copy, it is more useful to consider her interpretation of Holiday's "property" as a parody, in Linda Hutcheon's use of that term. According to Hutcheon, parody "points to art . . . as inescapably bound to its aesthetic and even social past. . . . How do some representations get legitimized and authorized? And at the expense of which others? Parody can offer a way of investigating the history of that process" (101). While I have no interest in examining the process whereby Holiday was installed as "the greatest jazz singer" or the notion of subtle vocal "counterstatement" as a prized mode of cultural critique, Hutcheon insists that we recognize that such evaluations are historically contingent and, as a consequence, open to constant scrutiny. To "make a standard out of" Holiday's "No Regrets" is, to reference Barbara Herrnstein Smith, to establish it as "timeless by suppressing [its] . . . temporality" and, hence, to position it as a "canonical work [that] begins increasingly not merely to *survive within* but to *shape and create* the culture in which its value is produced and transmitted and, for that reason, to perpetuate the conditions of its own flourishing" (*Contingencies* 50). Holiday's profound impact on generations of performers is well documented, but her installment as *the* canonical jazz singer does not burden even the most reverential of her successors with the obligation of seeking to replicate her inimitable performances.

In her 1997 cover of "Ain't Nobody's Business If I Do," a quintessential Lady Day song for listeners for whom Holiday's personal tragedies are inseparable from her art because of its lyrics' combination of confident self-sufficiency and masochistic self-sacrifice, Dianne Reeves strips away both the big band arrangement and the romantic submissiveness which that arrangement supports and legitimizes. Accompanied only by Kevin Eubanks's acoustic guitar, the resulting languid blues interpretation deletes lines that confirm self-destructive tendencies in matters of the heart (including the notion that it's "nobody's business" if the persona is left "in a pickle" because she's given her man her "last nickel," and her promise that "I won't call no copper / If I'm beat up by my poppa"). While keeping virtually intact lines that refer to a general rejection of societal strictures, Reeves rewrites the song's formulations of love and trouble, replacing such sentiments with lyrics which demonstrate that its refashioned persona is unwilling to accept mistreatment of any sort from anyone, including her "man." Refusing the role of self-sacrificing, hopelessly devoted woman, Reeves proclaims, "If I dislike my lover / I'll trade him in for another." And rejecting outright the insistence in the earlier version that it is better to endure domestic abuse than abandonment ("I'd rather my man would hit me / Than him to jump up and quit me"), Reeves exclaims, "I'd rather my man quit me / Than for him to even rare up and even think about how he might even try to hit me."

Whatever else motivates these revisions, including, perhaps, an urge to speak in uncompromising terms associated with blues women such as Ma Rainey and Bessie Smith, they are also doubtlessly responses to the times in which Reeves lives, where enduring domestic abuse is seen as the very opposite of a sign of strength of character. If we can accept the fact that, in performing Holiday's famous song as something other than a reverential recapitulation, Reeves recasts and modernizes this canonical work without damaging her precursor's "personal property," we can perhaps reconsider the merits of Palmer's claim that Snow sings "No Regrets" "like a bopsinging Pollyanna" wholly unaware of the damage caused to women by ideologies of romantic love. Reeves's performance suggests that instead of approaching material associated with Holiday with reverence, singers may well need to adjust its sometimes troubling formulations of women's romantic lives to fit potentially more egalitarian gendered contexts. Adjustment of this kind may take many forms, including parody, which, in the case of Snow's version, may be as subtle an approach as Holiday's "counterstatement" proved to be in her time.

To recognize Snow's interpretation of "No Regrets" as a critique of Holiday's rendition, we must, like Hutcheon, understand that, "through a double process of installing and ironizing, parody signals how present representations come from past ones and what ideological consequences derive from both continuity and difference" (93). Viewing Snow's cover as "critical" of Holiday's, as a counter-counterstatement, if you will, is not the same as suggesting that it fails to recognize the earlier version's strengths. Indeed, we could argue that, after its vibrato-tinged, even hesitant introduction—efforts on the part of the singer, perhaps, to shake herself free of contemporary formulations of the unacceptability of giddy female self-sacrifice in order to perform sentiments of a bygone era persuasively—Snow's version replicates, albeit within the framework of her own vocal strengths and limitations, the girlish attitude of Lady Day's interpretation of the first half of the lyrics. In my estimation, Snow invokes aspects of that performance in ways that underscore her own and Lady Day's significantly different historical circumstances. Holiday's performance is appropriate for a time before women's liberation and other civil rights struggles to reform an American society whose laws and institutional practices overwhelmingly benefited men who were white and affluent. In such an age, there was limited reward for direct ideological confrontation, so that Holiday's claim, "I hate straight singing" (*Stormy Weather* 136), can be read not only in the context of an aesthetics of counterstatement, but as a sign of her recognition of the potential costs to her career of "straight" musical talk about gendered and racial inequities.

However, to expect Snow to replicate Holiday's version is to ask her to respond neither to her own aesthetic urgings nor to the ideological struggles that were being waged all around her to benefit women, struggles that helped to engender, among other things, "changes in women's personality and economic and family position" (Mandle 147). Indeed, in addition to Helen Reddy's anthem, "I Am Woman," a number of songs of the period, particularly by black women such as Millie Jackson and Ann Pebbles, directly articulated dissatisfaction with the ideologies of romantic love that supported baleful gendered inequities. As Brian Ward argues, female soul singers "began to offer increasingly bitter, often darkly humorous, critiques of black male inadequacies, coupled with proud assertions of female rights to better treatment at home, at work, and in bed. Laura Lee, for example, boldly stated her claims for equal rights to sexual satisfaction in 'Women's Love Rights' and, like the philandering black man, had no compunction about getting them outside the marital bed in 'Wedlock Is a Padlock'" (383). In such an environment, "counterstatement" might be, at best, counterproductive and, at worst, a relic of a time when women's critiques of male hegemony were energetically repressed. If, like Angela Davis, we view women's expressivity in both political and aesthetic terms, we can recognize, in ways that Palmer perhaps does not, the historically contingent nature of Holiday's performance. That is not to say that Lady Day's "No Regrets" loses its effectiveness—listening repeatedly to it in order to construct this analysis, I now understand the enthusiasm of her devotees much better than I ever have—but also that the song can be said to signify differently in a noticeably different era. And to reference, again, the halting introduction, which Palmer sees as motivated by the younger singer's desire to flaunt her vocal chops rather than by sound artistic reasoning, Snow's version can be said to reverse the movement from innocence to experience that distinguishes Holiday's "No Regrets." While, in Holiday's version, the persona comes to—and is moved to perform—an awareness of her former naïveté, Snow's initial hesitance could be seen as her way of registering conflict; instead of constituting "virtuoso" play, her twice-repeated, melismatic "no" may be said to signal ideological resistance beyond which she must move if she is to approach Holiday's daunting "property."

To consider Snow's version a parody of Holiday's, then, is to recognize how, in Hutcheon's words, "present representations come from past ones and what ideological consequences derive from both continuity and difference." A virtual pastiche of jazz style—the music's modulation from slow to mid-tempo; the singer's vocal grandstanding, her self-satisfied display of her multioctave range, her turning of the twice-repeated "no" into an amazing singing exercise; her Ella-like swing; her running together of the words "babydon'tyourememberyoutoldmetohave," followed by an impressive display of melisma and vocal control when she follows this mouthful with a boisterous "no regrets"; her final utterance of the phrase, "somebody new," that sounds almost celebratory because of the vocal play that accompanies its articulation—Snow's physically exhausting performance of the girlish giddiness of "No Regrets" offers her virtually no time to breathe, and very little time to reflect on the meaning of the lyrics. Given the proliferation and wide availability of vociferous feminist counterstatements to such romantic sentiments by the mid-1970s, it makes perfect sense that this classic song—whose continued value, beyond its estimable melodic sway and its lyrics' sonic play, its fascinating rhythms and internal rhymes, depends in large part in its association with the distinguished pasts of jazz, classic American music, and, of course, Holiday—would yield the sorts of responses Palmer criticizes in Snow's interpretation. Unlike "There's A Boat That's Leaving Soon for New York" or "Ain't Nobody's Business If I Do," "No Regrets" leaves little space for lyrical updating that reflects the values of a noticeably changed time marked by, among other things, greater cultural and economic equity for women. Consequently, in the context of its time, Snow's "straight singing" of the lyrics, is, in fact, parodic in the most complex meanings of that term.

"Mush-Mallow" Masculinity:
The Supremes' "Going Down for the Third Time"

In his essay, "Motown Crossover Hits, 1963–1966, and the Creative Process," Jon Fitzgerald challenges pejorative descriptions of the music that emerged from calculated efforts to situate that fabled company's stable of black artists as, in the words of its motto, "the voice of young America." His musicological refutation of "regular attack[s]" from critics who consider Motown's overall product "white bread soul," "corny," "appalling . . . , ill conceived mush-mallow" (2) establishes stylistic affinities between gospel music and the popular singles produced by the legendary team, Holland-Dozier-Holland, and recorded by such acts as the Four Tops, Mary Wells, and Marvin Gaye. In the process, he explores their utilization of traditional black musical elements such as "syncopation, . . . call-response, melismatic melodies, varied and expressive vocal tone, vocal dexterity, melodic variation and improvisation, repetition, percussive playing technique, hand-clapping and footpatting, use of piano and tambourine" (4). Fitzgerald concludes that records like the Four Tops' "Baby I Need Your Lovin'," Martha and the Vandellas' "Nowhere to Run," and the Supremes' "You Can't Hurry Love" are examples of "a new style of mainstream popular song—thoroughly based in gospel and conceiving of song structure in an innovative way, where the hidden architecture supporting the melodic/lyric hook is now primarily rhythmic" (8). Motown's use of gospel features and its "concentration . . . on details of the 'groove,'" both infinitely more evident in the company's singles, according to Fitzgerald, than in its recordings of popular show tunes, remakes of Beatles and Sam Cooke songs, and its own writers' less stellar efforts, brought an "infusion of new musical elements into the pop song" (8). Because of this glaring difference, Fitzgerald believes, along with Tony Cummings, author of the aforementioned "mush-mallow" remarks, that "most of Motown's top acts maintained . . . 'a double identity: on single the performers of virile pop-cum-soul music, on album the performers of middle of the road mush'" (1).

Establishing Motown's racial authenticity by emphasizing its products' musical structure, the skills of the influential studio musicians, the Funk Brothers, or, for that matter, the black traditions evident in the lead vocals that grace "Heat Wave," "Standing in the Shadows of Love," and "How Sweet It Is," however, cannot convince its detractors that Berry Gordy's most popular recording act, the Supremes, produced soulful black cultural sounds rather than "mush-mallow." Between 1964 and 1968, the group released a string of alluring hits, including "Where Did Our Love Go," "Stop! In the Name of Love," "Back in My Arms Again," and "You Can't Hurry Love," that emphasized smooth pop elements that were the perfect complement to lead singer Diana Ross's girlish voice. Ross had kittenish stage presence, mainstream appeal because of what Dave Marsh calls a "confectionary," "glitzy effervescence" (375) and a singing style that Hirshey describes as "adenoidal keening" (163). While agreeing generally with Marsh and Hirshey, Brian Ward's assessment is much more generous, as he refers to the Supremes as "the perfect black crossover act" and to Ross's vocals as "much lighter and breathier than Martha [Reeves]'s on chart-topping songs such as "Where Did Our Love Go?" and "Baby Love" (263).

The Supremes were, indeed, "the perfect vehicle for Motown's ride into the mainstream, to Las Vegas, to the Copacabana, to the network variety shows" (154), because its members' staged innocence and charm school enunciation evinced little connection to the grit, power, and aggression of the emotionally wrenching deep soul style that helped to make arresting performers of such label mates as the Temptations' David Ruffin, the

Four Tops' Levi Stubbs, the underrated Brenda Holloway, or, for that matter, fellow Detroit resident Aretha Franklin. If the popular songs created for them by Holland-Dozier-Holland contain prefunk beats, jazz touches, and elements of gospel urgency, the rhythmic effects that accompany Ross's "confectionary" vocals on *The Supremes Sing Holland-Dozier-Holland*, the album on which "Going Down for the Third Time" appears, were created by, among other instruments, suspended cymbals, bells, and tambourines. Instead of the Funk Brothers' deep rhythmic bottoms and propulsive uses of thumping bass lines and alternately light and firm drum licks, the downbeats on well-known hits from this album and *More Hits by the Supremes* ("Love Is Here and Now You're Gone," "You Keep Me Hangin' On," "Nothing But Heartaches," "Stop! In the Name of Love," and "Back in My Arms Again") are brassy percussive pings. While these rhythmic effects clearly evolved from the same musical family, they give Ross's group a "softer, less soulful sound" (*The Motown Album* 140) than Martha and the Vandellas, whom Supreme Mary Wilson calls "more soulful than us . . . , more R & B," "tough," and "masculine" (Hirshey 179).

It would appear that black vocal masculinity, an attribute reserved not merely for men, is marked both by deep soul musical grooves and by the willingness of male and female singers to deliver dramatic, gut-wrenching, highly emotional performances. For Wilson, then, propulsive musical tracks and assertive, lower octave lead vocals made songs such as "Heat Wave" and "Dancing in the Streets" more "virile" or stylistically "masculine" than the Supremes' hits, which were characterized by the combination of Ross's girlish purr and feathery percussive effects. Looked at in light of Cummings's description of the "double identity" of Motown acts who produce "virile" singles and "mush" filler, the Supremes' hits seem not to fit what is otherwise a persuasive and well-conceived formulation. While these records do indeed manifest a "concentration . . . on details of the 'groove'" that classifies them as part of a black music tradition, their manifest lack—indeed, their overt rejection—of "virile" elements suggests that that gendered quality is not a necessary feature of rhythm. If deep, "virile" grooves compel listeners to get down, the sweet rhythmic sensations utilized on the Supremes' hits, so light that they appear almost to float above the rest of the songs' elements, demand bodily motion, too, but of a more cerebral, less sweat-inducing, less funky variety. The music on these hits is grounded in black traditions, but to describe it convincingly in such a way requires that we recognize forms of cultural authenticity that extend beyond the masculine registers of Cummings's remarks.

Considered in the context of Fitzgerald's and Cummings's identification of the soulfulness of Motown's hits, what is remarkable about "Going Down for the Third Time" is how thoroughly it deviates from the soulful hit, mushy-filler pattern the critics suggest we should expect if we compare it to popular songs on the album on which it appears, *The Supremes Sing Holland-Dozier-Holland*. For example, the Supremes' number one hit, "Love Is Here and Now You're Gone," features an insistent but light beat provided by tambourines and other brass percussive effects that complement Ross's use of the highest registers of her voice—by which the singer admitted to Hirshey she was embarrassed two decades later (163)—to describe her insincere former male lover, who "just walked away" after he "persuaded me to love you," and the emotional consequences of his inconstancy. Having been left "all alone" to remember his appeals for her affection and to wrestle with the pain of his abandonment, the speaker asks him only to recognize the impact of his betrayal—"Look at me, see what loving you has done to me / Look at my face, see how crying has left its trace"—not to keep promises he had made to share his life with her.

By contrast, the persona of "Going Down," having twice endured the devastating conclusions of romantic relationships, admits to her current, apparently wayward lover that she's "drowning in the fear that my arms you're leaving," and implores him to "save me" from having to experience that misery "for the third time." Ross's singing here is much more assertive and authoritative, her voice much deeper than in "Love Is Here" and features her emphatic delivery of crucial words (alternately, "I'm," "down" and "third") as she insists that he "bring back that love we knew," that he "start showing" "a little tenderness," and that she will "forgive your lies and alibis" if he agrees in exchange to cease the behavior that is causing her so much pain. The musical accompaniment is also much more "virile," featuring an insistent beat that relies on assertive drum strokes rather than brassy pings which, while present throughout the song, fail to become the dominant rhythmic element that they are on a large number of the Supremes' hits.

"Going Down for the Third Time" is vocally, rhythmically, and thematically as "masculine" as the Supremes sound on any recording I've heard. If calling the album on which this song appears *The Supremes Sing*

Holland-Dozier-Holland is meant to highlight the creative talents of this team of songwriters-producers whose work, along with that of Smokey Robinson, dominated Motown's incredibly productive first phase, those talents are manifested less, in my view, in the popular representations of passive female romantic suffering that Ross had already proven she was adept at performing than in "Going Down for the Third Time," which demands from her gritty vocals and attitudinal aggressiveness that conflict with the kittenish debutant image which she had cultivated and begun to market so skillfully. And while her vocal limitations and persistently bourgeois diction ensure that she will never be compared favorably to label mates Levi Stubbs or Martha Reeves (whose groups' respective hits, "It's the Same Old Song" and "Heat Wave," the Supremes cover in unremarkable ways in the second half—the "filler" portion—of this album along with "Going Down"), Ross demonstrates herself to be a versatile enough singer to offer a "virile pop-cum-soul" performance.

Again, I'm not suggesting that the Supremes' hits lack cultural authenticity, but that they are stylistically different, distinguished not by "masculine" flourishes, but by strategically "feminine" sonic elements that typically are not recognized by Motown's critics as soulful. If the hits on *The Supremes Sing Holland-Dozier-Holland* are redeemed from critical derision when we attend to their subtle gospel elements, so, too, is the more deeply soulful "Going Down for the Third Time," which provides Ross with the opportunity to experiment with a "masculine" vocal style.

"Who the Hell Do I Think I Am?":
"Going Down" and Covering Nondefinitive Songs

"No Regrets" and "There's A Boat That's Leaving Soon for New York" are cultural treasures as precious, in their own way, as "Piece of My Heart," a song which Phoebe Snow includes on *I Can't Complain*, her 1998 album of blues, R & B, and rock 'n' roll covers. Snow says of covering material linked with figures like Janis Joplin:

> Maybe a good alternate title for the record is "Who the Hell Do I Think I Am?" . . . I mean, "Piece of My Heart"? C'mon. Am I out of my mind? I think you have very mixed feelings when you cover a song because you know the definitive version has basically been done. But just being able to

> do some of those really landmark songs from my childhood and formative years—to try and put my own spin on them—is such a thrill. It's probably like every garage band that's said: "We're going to do a Jimi Hendrix tune just because we have to. It's a love thing." (Roos n.p.)

Her discussion of the "thrill" of engaging other artists' work helps to explain why "Snow ignites, expands, takes outrageous changes, [and] projects" in her soul covers. But however excited she might have been about recording "Going Down for the Third Time," that feeling had nothing to do with covering a "landmark" song whose "definitive version has basically been done." While the Supremes had been extremely popular during her "childhood and formative years," and while Snow might have enjoyed the song when she encountered it either on *The Supremes Sing Holland-Dozier-Holland* or on the flip side of "Reflections," covering this largely unknown "filler" could hardly have proven a daunting task if her primary worry in such situations is competing with interpretations that are deemed definitive by large numbers of listeners. In fact, "Going Down for the Third Time" was so little known that although reviewers for the *All Music Guide* and *Rolling Stone* associate the famed production and songwriting team's composition with Motown, neither attempt to connect it to any of its specific artists.

Perhaps Palmer fails to mention the song in a review that deals with all of *Second Childhood*'s other tracks because of his unwillingness, as a well-regarded music critic who is aware of the origins of "There's A Boat That's Leaving Soon for New York" and of the definitive version of "No Regrets," to appear less than authoritative in his knowledge about the most contemporary of the songs Snow covers. My own fruitless initial searches of record guides, Internet sites, and compact disc stores led me to believe that, no matter how well stocked his and *Rolling Stone*'s record libraries were, Palmer may not have been able to discover which act had indeed recorded "Going Down for the Third Time," which he knew was a Motown tune because its writers were Holland-Dozier-Holland.[7] But whatever motivated it, his silence allows him to evade the challenge this track offers to his argument that Snow's performances on *Second Childhood* "stopped short of her unique vocal potential." As I have suggested, Palmer links that "potential" to her being able to produce gospel-inspired, "clear, bell-like tones an octave and a half above her normal range." It seems to me, however, that Snow explores another aspect of her "potential" in her cover of Supremes' "virile" filler: the deeper registers and soulful intonations of her voice. With the possible exception of "Good Times," the track on her first two albums that best foretells her subsequent engagement with forms of black music that emerged after World War II—R & B, soul, and funk—is her remake of the Supremes' song, where she pursues more energetically than Diana Ross's "lighter and breathier" voice allowed her to the stylistically masculine features of the song. These features, at odds with the group's hit format, provide Snow with the opportunity to transgress categorical boundaries—in this case, between "masculine" and "feminine"—which, in the areas of both race and gender, her album confronts in engaging ways.[8]

In her introduction to *Sexing the Groove: Popular Music and Gender*, Sheila Whiteley argues that figures such as Mick Jagger and Madonna and phenomena such as cross-dressing, in whose boundary-transgressing performances theatricality and radical self-invention are essential components, demonstrate the highly malleable nature of social identities. Referencing Elaine Showalter's contention that "socially-constructed gender roles may be reshuffled, and that no one with the divine spark need be relegated forever to single sex," Whiteley identifies popular music as an arena in which artists can challenge the normative standards that have led us to behave as if masculinity and femininity were both essentially polarized and fixed social categories. She goes on to insist that gender's complex implications can best be discerned by means of "fresh analytical explorations of the ways in which musical discourses work in tandem with lyrics, performance styles, gendered identities and consumer positions" (xvi). With such criteria in mind, I've examined the Supremes' "Going Down for the Third Time" as an attempt to navigate a black masculine realm in figuratively spiked heels; as a black girl group working in a musical genre whose male and female performers alike relied on "masculine" self-presentation, its femininity had to be (over)produced, enhanced by— and performed through—mousy vocals, charm school enunciation, and sweetened instrumental accompaniment, which, while still categorically black, matched preconceived notions of the natural sounds of the fairer sex.

The success of Snow's earth-shoed cover hinges not on her capacity to perform black masculinity as well as Ross, the ultrafeminine bourgeois crossover dream, but (to cite "Changed," which appears on her 2003 album, *Natural Wonder*) "to sing the blues like an old blind guy." Unlike

Janis Joplin, then, whose idolization of Bessie Smith is specific and same-sexed, Snow locates a black male type, whose age and visual handicap underscore its status as authentic sufferer intimately acquainted with the blues, as having established the standards in American popular musical vocal performance.[9]

Snow's cover pursues the song's rhythm and blues possibilities, beginning with a funky interchange between organ and acoustic piano (both played by Richard Tee, whose riffs also enhance her duet with Paul Simon). Eliminating the largely pop arrangement of the Supremes' original, Snow and her musicians dig deeply for musical grooves that match the persona's fear of drowning "in a sea of emptiness" without her lover. Singing at least an octave lower than normal, she explores, and in a recognizably bluesy fashion, the meaning and sonic potential of words and the range of her voice. Whereas Ross identifies the import of the sounds and meanings of selected words either by punctuating their syllables emphatically, followed by a brief silence, or by holding notes on a sustained pitch, Snow runs up and down the scale, approximating, in her pronunciation of the word "down," for example, the fall and rise of an emotionally desperate and, perhaps, sexually frustrated lover who, because she is "all alone on a raging sea"—with "sea" the subject of the torture-filled crescendo that demonstrates the grit in the singer's voice—is willing to forgive any transgression. As the piano and organ play, augmented, from time to time, by blues guitar riffs, Snow breaks up the beginning and end sounds of the word "third" with a breathy squall, attacks "down" with a vibrato that turns the word into a three- and sometimes four-syllable utterance, and, in part because it matches the internal vowel sounds of the word that follows ("fast") more effectively, transforms the word "sinking" into a grammatically incorrect present participle, "sanking," with the grace and vocal charm of a singer for whom Standard English phrasing is not the measure of discursive excellence, as it appears to be in the Supremes' version, particularly when it stands in the way of her getting across her emotional point.

Snow's funky version of "Going Down for the Third Time" emphasizes its soulful "potential"—to use the term Palmer's employs to suggest the vocal qualities he feels are missing from *Second Childhood*—while at the same time pursuing the "masculine" directions of the Supremes' version. To say that Snow's spin on the song, her soulful wailing, demonstrates that a particular white woman can sing blackness more effectively than a particular black woman is, according to the Supremes' harsh critics, to say very little indeed. What Snow shows is not that she is a better performer than Ross, but that she recognizes transgressive possibilities that distinguish the Supremes' version; with the able assistance of her musicians and producer, she is able to use her skillful voice and mastery of established black vocal conventions in order to maximize those possibilities.

"My Last Try": Race, "The Phoebe Idea,"
and Failed Synthesis

Phoebe Snow was not able to turn her soul offerings into hit records, as did Hall & Oates, or claim the moniker of soul singer either wholeheartedly, like Teena Marie, or as merely part of her musical identity, as David Bowie was able to do during moments in both the 1970s and the 1980s. As important, she was not able to continue to create popular or critically acclaimed black and blues–based music oriented toward a white rock audience, as the Rolling Stones and many other acts had been able to do. As a consequence, she has become a quintessential journey(wo)man singer, a voice for hire, and is no longer widely considered a major talent whose gifts far surpassed those of the great majority of singers who emerged in the wake of the racially turbulent 1960s, Motown, and the singer-songwriter movement. Certainly, she was not as physically attractive as Linda Ronstadt and Olivia Newton-John, lacked the musical pedigree and generic identification of Natalie Cole and Bonnie Raitt, and couldn't shake her "groove thang" as well as Donna Summer or disco's innumerable one-hit female wonders. And her lack of traditional sex appeal, coupled with her insecurities and her inability to tour extensively because of her rumored psychological travails and her daughter's serious birth defects, may explain her marginal status far better than any combination of record company blunders.

Instead of reaching for psychological explanations, however, I want to suggest that her limited popular success may be attributed to a simple, indisputable fact: she just wasn't as skilled at creating radio-friendly ditties as other singers who emerged during the same period. And after *It Looks Like Snow*, the quality of her work diminished precipitously; between 1977, when her third album appeared, and 1989, when her comeback effort, *Something Real,* was released, she did not produce consistently engaging records. Indeed, when *Something Real* was released—her first album in nearly a decade—its title track's proclamation, "This time when I reach out / It might be my last try," seemed as much a comment on Snow's own career frustrations as on the persona's romantic misgivings. But while the album demonstrated that she was capable of producing first rate material (her voice never sounded better than on the title track, and many of its songs, including "Touch Your Soul," "Soothin'," and "Stay Away," are quite engaging), it had become clear that, absent an improbable Bonnie Raitt- or Santana-like rediscovery, her days as a pop star had long since passed.

Unlike Mariah Carey, Snow had neither traditional photogenic sex appeal to enhance her musical profile nor a verifiable black ancestry to authenticate her in the minds of skeptics. And unlike Janis Joplin, Snow seems, in Gayle Wald's words, not to have "mediated her own feelings of outsidership" from conventional norms of white womanhood "through her appropriation of a blues aesthetic" or to be engaged in what George Lipsitz calls "discursive transcoding," "the process by which white artists 'disguise' their own subjectivities in order to 'articulate desires and subject positions' that they cannot express in their own voices" (158). By the mid-1970s, women artists were being encouraged by feminist activists and intellectuals to express their desires and subject positions in their own voices, and while obstacles to such expression continued to exist and performers such as Olivia Newton-John and, to a lesser extent, Minnie Riperton were being rewarded for voices that embodied girlish innocence, the sounds of white women roaring in rock and pop songs, at demonstrations in support of the Equal Rights Amendment and reproductive rights, were so commonplace that no one could rationally argue that Linda Ronstadt needed to imbibe the black oppositional energy of Betty Everett's "You're No Good" before she could mount a critique of male-centered romantic ideology through, among other things, her cover of the song. We cannot quantify the extent to which its source was black women's long-standing "production of a critical, oppositional, and public discourse" that resented misogyny and resisted phallocentricism, but a constitutive element of white womanhood during and after the emergence of the contemporary women's movement was its resistance to male hegemony. Consequently, however much she admired her work, Snow had no need to look to Aretha Franklin (whose monumental "Do-Right Woman" she has covered and whose remake of Sam Cooke's "Good Times"—which, like "Do-Right Woman," appears on *I Never Loved A Man*—may have inspired Snow's) as an ideological role model in the ways that Janis Joplin looked to Bessie Smith. Instead, despite and because of the politically charged nature of her times, she could credit black singers for perfecting a style that had become quintessentially American, and experiment with its conventions in an effort to find the stylistic range of her own voice.

Finding one's voice seems to require that a novice undergo a period of mimicry during which one learns to express oneself through already established texts and styles—an activity with which Snow expressed her discomfort as it relates to jazz and blues—until, in the case of the most accomplished artists, one develops the capacity to synthesize aspects of these styles that enables one to express one's own artistic self. Shewey recognizes his subject's fundamentally synthetic impulses as a young artist, insisting that Snow's "best work has always involved a blending of the two, rhythm and blues and pop, singing that is sweet and rough at the same time. It is certainly no coincidence that a healthy number of blacks always frequent her shows. 'I feel like an honorary black, and I'm flattered,' she jokes. 'But when they yell out, "Get down, sis-tuh," I tend to feel whiter than ever. 'Thank you,' I say. 'I believe I will get down now'" ("Blues of Snow" 80). But if honorary sisterhood is powerful, it remains for Snow, at most, a partial musical identity, a means of categorizing some but certainly not all of her vast musical interests.

Lacking a signature, all-encompassing style, Snow seemed always in pursuit of a mode of artistic self-presentation that distinguishes her and reflects her complex musical inheritance. The following passage from Shewey's article for *Esquire* helps to clarify the nature of this pursuit:

> Phoebe loves to talk about other singers. She listens to everything, for fun and profit. "I'm looking for a sound," she confesses, shoving aside her watermelon rind. "You know in *The Glenn Miller Story* where James Stewart goes to New Orleans and listens to Satchmo, then hears a regular dance band, then goes to a strip club, and he tries to score all that music for his band? Then he crumples up the paper and goes, 'That's not it! That's not *the sound!*' It's so Hollywood, but every time I see the movie I wait for that identity crisis. "I do have a sound in my head," she says, "but I've never gotten it." She brightens up like a model in a tv commercial. "It's the Phoebe Idea." (80)

"Miss Snow, are you black?"

In Shewey's view, Snow's work over the course of her career—in folk, jazz, blues, R & B, rock, pop, and funk—demonstrates "that the Phoebe Idea keeps changing," and that may very well be the case. Whatever their various merits as artists, performers like Paul Simon, Rod Stewart, and the Rolling Stones have succeeded in large part because of their capacity, relatively early on, to "blend" "rhythm and blues and pop," or, more generally, various types of "black" and "white" music, in ways that allowed them to create identifiable styles and "voices" which shape their work throughout their careers. For example, Simon's efforts from "Me and Julio Down By the School Yard" and "Loves Me Like a Rock" to "Gone at Last" and *Graceland* suggest that his solo career can be seen, in large part, as an attempt at what Lipsitz calls "trans-cultural musical collaboration" (57). Listeners can hear stylistic affinities between "Loves Me Like a Rock" and "You Can Call Me Al" that allow them to identify the songs as recognizable products of Paul Simon, but Snow's constant journeying from one musical port to another does not enable similarly easy associations. Unlike Simon's sound, Snow's tends to be shaped by the various musical shores she encounters, and reflects, among other things, her inability to develop or sustain a firm sense of a marketable musical "identity."

The Rolling Stones, Rod Stewart, and Paul Simon "Idea" defined their acts from an early point in their formation (in Simon's case, following his split from Art Garfunkel), and was not something that they were scurrying around to discern midway through their careers. Snow's adventurousness may be a function of the fact that the musical styles she mastered became obsolete (folk, blues), unappealing to her (jazz), or were so racially overdetermined (R & B, funk) that she felt compelled to redefine herself in order to participate, while it has been demonstrated, over and over again, that audiences would not or could not embrace her as a rock singer. As *Second Childhood* and others of her recordings demonstrate, she is indeed a gifted "soul" singer, but unlike someone like Teena Marie, whose first albums bore the imprints of their producers, the popular funkster Rick James and the late Minnie Riperton's husband-producer, Richard Rudolph, and of Motown, Snow never appeared comfortable—and, commercially speaking, was never as successful—applying that label to herself. And in the racial fields in which she has toiled, there appeared to be no room for an artistic exploration of white identity.

"going home"

In 2003, Al Green, Phoebe Snow, and Aretha Franklin produced albums that reflect their continuing concerns with issues
that inform my discussions of their careers and earlier work. Green's and
Snow's efforts were heralded as especially significant: *I Can't Stop*, his first
soul recording since 1995's *Your Heart's in Good Hands*, marks Green's re-
union with Willie Mitchell, his mentor and producer of his major albums
and classic singles;[1] and *Natural Wonder*, Snow's second album in fifteen
years, constitutes her return to the self-exploratory emphases of her early
releases, but instead of quiet revelations colored with blue notes and jazz
and folk idioms, we encounter louder, less vocally nuanced performances

accompanied by "a lot of rock guitars" and other rock sounds. (Ollison in the *Baltimore Sun*). And while Franklin's *So Damn Happy* lacks an attention-grabbing sales hook, because her promotional efforts stress the autobiographical nature of the title song, it clearly continues her efforts to separate herself from the image of blues sufferer.

Green has translated his status as the Last of the Great Soul Men, mentioned in virtually every article and review concerning his "remarkable comeback" album (Schinder n.p.), into a position of prominence in contemporary American culture befitting a musical legend. His music is featured on television, including the theme song for Showtime's drama series *Soul Food*, and on soundtracks of such movies as *Dead Presidents*, *Crooklyn*, *Notting Hill*, *Ladies Man*, and *On The Line*.[2] Additionally, "Love Is a Beautiful Thing," a track from *Your Heart's in Good Hands*, has assumed a level of cultural visibility nearly equivalent to the most beloved of his classic singles, appearing both at the conclusion of the film *Two Weeks Notice* and as the beauteous sounds of Almay's 2004 commercial campaign. Featuring a positive theme, bouncy music, and Green's ecstatic delivery, all of which nicely complement the upbeat situations in which it is employed, "Love Is a Beautiful Thing"—of which he is not credited as a cowriter—ends with an act of calculated reiteration even more extensive than in "Your Love Is Like the Morning Sun," as he sings the titles of six songs he has recorded, all but one of which he had at least a hand in composing: "Let's stay together, let's stay together / 'cause I'm still in love with you / call me, for the good times, / tired of being alone, here I am."

Despite the fact that the last four songs Green mentions are, in fact, concerned with romantic heartbreak, the newer song and its title effectively recast the received meaning of these conjoined songs and symbolize his cultural role—the singer of beautiful love songs—even though, in truth, his output is far more wide-ranging. Unable, to a large extent, to control how his hits are thought of and used or, for that matter, his own urge to perform that music, Green uses reiterative gestures to present listeners what they have come to see him as—the sum of all his popular recordings—in the course of creating new music that he hopes can have a similar commercial and emotional impact. In essence, such gestures allow him to acknowledge predominant elements of his "star story" while striving still for what he discusses in his autobiography as "wholeness," for the integration of personal and professional selves and identities, as he endeavors to add a significant new chapter to the constantly evolving book of his life.

Clearly, however, even Green's more inventive forays into the secular world can be seen as something other than part of a complex quest for wholeness by onlookers with longer or fuller memories than fans for whom his *Greatest Hits* distills the essence of his career. Such onlookers include his contemporary Teddy Pendergrass, who, like Green, is an ordained minister whose early solo albums include tracks such as "Somebody Told Me," whose persona is a religious leader called by God at age ten to minister to a fallen world. The tall, handsome, charismatic lead singer of Harold Melvin and the Blue Notes when Green was at the height of his popularity, Pendergrass seemed uniquely positioned, when he embarked on a solo career in the mid-1970s with the power of Philadelphia International Records behind him, to succeed Green as *the* great male soul singer. That artistic trajectory was halted, in my view, not by the 1982 car accident that left him a quadriplegic, but by his descent into love man caricature that preceded it, the turn-off-the-lights, close-the-door, do-me-do-me Teddy Bear persona that was, however lucrative, restrictive artistically for a gifted singer who too often substituted the vocal equivalent of chest thumping for nuanced delivery.[3] When asked in 2002 if his physical infirmities had compelled him to "lead a more sacred life," he answers by referencing Green's sacred-secular dilemma: "I don't mean this negatively but I'm not Al Green trying to split hairs. I don't want to be called Reverend Pendergrass today and Teddy tomorrow. That's not my course. I'm not comparing myself to Al, so please don't write that I am. He's an incredible artist. It's just that when someone needs to do A and then B, it looks as if he's unsure. I know what I want to do and who I am" (Amorosi 40). Pendergrass's qualifications notwithstanding, clearly he perceives Green's tortured efforts as evidence of the inability of "an incredible artist" to determine "who I am."

Interestingly, *I Can't Stop*, written largely by Green and Mitchell, is the work of a performer who appears not to be struggling with tensions between religious and secular urgings, one whose romantic musings, in fact, reflect little or no knowledge of an animating spiritual force. Apparently unable, as the title song suggests, to "stop loving," "holding," and "hanging on" to his secular career, he embraces its demands fully, foregrounding the pleasures and pain of romantic love and suppressing any mention of its potential religious dimensions and demands. In "Rainin' in My Heart," for example, he offers familiar associations between love and nature as his lonely persona, as despondent as his predecessor in "Your Love Is Like the Morning Sun," finds himself "looking at the sun" and unable to coordinate its positive received meanings with his internal state. But his latter, fully secular persona, devoid of biblical knowledge, declares—in obvious contradistinction to Green's religious convictions— "I don't know how life begins / I sure don't know where life might end." Self-consciously employing the conventions of the genre and the discourse of his earlier romantic songs,[4] Green, whose gospel catalogue is nearly as sizable as his secular corpus, demonstrates his comfort with the fact that he is performing love songs rather than manifesting the entirety of his being. "Rainin' in My Heart" conveys sentiments that do not gibe fully with those of the Reverend Al Green, who constructs a heartbroken persona he embodies temporarily to perform an earthly role.

But if what his autobiography describes as "the glory of the natural world" is evident at moments in this recording, its representation lacks both the animating tension provided by the religious subtexts and, aesthetically more important, what Green himself identifies as the "soft, tender vulnerab[ility]" of his classic songs in which he uses his "voice to cry out with a need [that] can't be filled." Al Whitman insists "that Al has lost something in the vocal department," as his "normal register just isn't what it used to be" (Whitman n.p.). Having heard Green numerous times over the course of the last five years, including a performance during an outdoor concert on Philadelphia's Penn's Landing in the summer of 2003 where he sang "Take Me to the River" within yards of one of America's famed rivers—the Delaware—and seemed not to notice it, and read his discussions of having to be compelled by Mitchell to abandon his deeper, more mannish vocal potential in favor of softer, higher, more boyish tones, I'm less certain than Whitman that the differences are a function of deterioration than of a choice not to sound like his earlier self.

Critics insist that *I Can't Stop* is "a good, nearly great, album" that is "a clear attempt to recapture the old magic" (Whitman n.p.). Certainly, as a chapter of the book of his musical life and of his life in music, it is fascinating.

⊙ ⊙ ⊙

Phoebe Snow's *Natural Wonder* reflects desires that crystallized in the late 1970s when, as Don Shewey relates in his *Esquire* article, "she had finally figured out exactly what it was she wanted to do: 'Rock.'" In her estimation, "the rock 'n' roll thing" of *Rock Away* (1981) "worked and it didn't work—something was still missing." However, she felt similarly about her R & B efforts, which, while inspired by her admiration for artists such as George Clinton, James Brown, the Ohio Players, and Sly Stone, were no more an actualization than her rock album of the unattainable "blending" of pop, blues, jazz, rock, folk, and R & B styles that she imagines and characterizes as "the Phoebe Idea" (80). That "Idea" involves, among other things, performing her own compositions, as she does extensively on her most commercially successful albums, *Phoebe Snow*, *Second Childhood*, and *It Looks Like Snow*, with "let-it-all-go belting" (Ollison n.p.) that critics came to prefer and that Shewey insists she employs only in her interpretations of others' material.

Condemnation of her songwriting became intense following her first album, as critics insisted that her lyrics, which they deemed nerdy and "often so banal they can stop the momentum of a killer side (or concert) dead in its tracks" (Shewey, review of *Against the Grain* n.p.), needed to be "considerably more direct" to be truly effective (Holden, review of *Rock Away*). Given her decision, following *Second Childhood*, to reduce the number of her own compositions on her albums, she seemed to have come to similar conclusions about her songwriting limitations and interpretive strengths. As the work of a performer in search of "the Phoebe Idea," an amalgam of styles that would yield authentic self-expression rather than stylistic mimicry, Snow's *Natural Wonder* reflects her efforts to resolve artistic dilemmas that have plagued her career: how to escape the impression that she is a "banal" lyricist and reestablish herself as a thoughtful singer-songwriter; how to unify the acclaimed jazz-oriented style of the beginning of her career and the talent for "belting" with a "rich alto [that] really merits comparison with those of the great R & B shouters, like Big Mama Thornton and Ruth Brown" (Holden, review of *Rock Away*); how to recognize her debts to black popular music without being mistaken for black or imitating black artists.

In its review of *Natural Wonder*, *Billboard* deems her efforts a resounding success: "Phoebe Snow's first original album in 14 years finds the veteran songstress in finest fettle—both as a singer and songwriter. Sometimes understated, other times intensely atmospheric, the production spotlights her autobiographical and personal lyrics while never losing sight of one of the most powerful voices in pop." An opposing perspective is offered in an amazon.com fan review of the album, which reads:

> Phoebe Snow has a frustrating and erratic recording career, made more so by the enormity of her great talent and her lack of direction. Unfortunately, more often than not, she uses her powerful voice to oversing, pummeling the song instead of caressing it. . . . She desperately needs a producer to reign in her excess, and show her versatility as demonstrated on her first two classic albums, "Phoebe Snow" and "Second Childhood," and on her underrated late '80s Elektra album "Something Real." The songs on "Natural Wonder," mostly co-written by Snow, are in a rock/blues mid-tempo groove, and play mostly to her flaws. The final track, "Going Home" bears the most charm, and the first half of her cover of "Baby, I Need Your Loving" is controlled and soulful, and immediately grabs your attention because it is the best melody on the album.

Black artists' formative role in rock has been so widely discussed that it is unnecessary for me to argue here that Snow's efforts do not necessarily constitute an evasion of black cultural styles. And rightly or wrongly, rock has long been considered a veritable sonic melting pot, one that accommodates both traditional forms and challenging innovations in ways that none of the canonical subgenres of American music (including country, folk, and R & B) appear equipped to do.

However, guitar-driven rock has been viewed since the 1960s as the province of white artists, no matter how clearly their output bears the cultural imprint of the blues and R & B. When black musicians such as Jimi Hendrix, Joan Armatrading, Living Colour, and Lenny Kravitz utilize rock vocal and instrumental styles, their music is deemed "white" and, hence, inappropriate for placement among the R & B holdings and play lists of record stores and radio stations, respectively. So while hard-core black music enthusiasts have on occasion been able to embrace the infusion of rock elements into their music (Ernie Isley's Hendrix-influenced guitar riffs, Michael Jackson's "Beat It," Run DMC's "Walk the Way," Janet Jackson's "Black Cat," En Vogue's "Free Your Mind," and Dionne Farris's "I Know" come readily to mind), they are unwilling to accept these elements as essential features of the soul musical repertoire.

Snow describes the tracks on *Natural Wonder* as "rock, I guess," both because of the presence of "rock guitars" and other musical elements and because, rather than strive for melismatic rapture as in her performance of "His Eye Is on the Sparrow" or the blues intonations in her remakes of Etta James's "At Last" and Muddy Waters's "Just to Be with You," the singer utilizes the clipped snarl of the rock vocalists she admired as a child. Her stated desire to "sing the blues like an old blind guy" notwithstanding, it is only in the soulful cover of the Four Tops' (and, three years later, Johnny Rivers') hit and her charming "Going Home," which recalls her mid-tempo R & B grooves such as "Soothin'" and "Love Makes a Woman," that Snow sings in ways that listeners would identify with the blues. These soulful concluding moments of her album can be viewed as her most contemporary explorations of what is natural and what is not, what is her stylistic home and what styles constitute for her, at best, temporary respite.

I spoke in my chapter on Snow of her contempt for current radio format practices that insist "that everything has to be categorized." In a comment she offers to a newspaper columnist, she suggests both that *Natural Wonder*, the album that she characterizes defensively as rock ("rock, I guess"), is an actualization of her "Idea" of musical synthesis and that it is merely an expression of one facet of her identity: "This album is really who I am, one part of who I am" (Ollison n.p.). If her latest work is "rock," according to musical categorizations that date much further back than she is willing to admit, to state "This album is really who I am" is to categorize herself as a "white" singer, which she is clearly loathe to do because her goal is an amalgam of black and white styles. However, to call it simply "one part of who I am" is to acknowledge that, despite its rock vocals and instrumentation and the generally accessible lyrics she is largely responsible for composing, this album, too, fails as a manifestation of "the Phoebe Idea." Like Green, whose performances on the "Al Green Interlude" and "Put It on Paper" demonstrate his continuing concern with how to connect the sacred and the secular, Snow appears to remain fascinated with and troubled by the implications of her participation in various popular musical genres. But while Green seems comfortable enough with his own unresolved compulsions to produce a wholly secular album which goes so far as to claim ignorance of fundamental biblical truths, Snow's dedication to her (synthetic) "Idea" is seemingly derailed by her album's penultimate track, a remake of a classic R & B song first recorded by the Four Tops, one of Motown's core group of artists.

If Snow's album of covers, *I Can't Complain*—which contains, in her infectious remake of Blind Willie Johnson's "Lord, I Just Can't Keep from Cryin,'" her efforts "to sing the blues" of, if not exactly like, "an old blind guy"—confirms her talents as "an interpretive singer" blessed with a "voice . . . so distinctive that she had no trouble making such material her own" (Ruhlmann n.p.), *Natural Wonder* constitutes her effort to demonstrate she can "ignite" *her own material*. After her first album, her compositions were deemed "banal," "corny confessionalism" (Shewey, review of *Against the Grain*) so uninspiring that one critic went so far as to advise her either to "study songwriting or devote more energy to interpretation." The critics who deplored her earlier lyrical efforts may not feel as inclined as the *Billboard* reviewer to see her compositions on *Natural Wonder* as a significant step forward, but clearly she is attempting, with the help of five collaborators, to establish herself as a singer-songwriter (and coproducer) who can indeed "belt" her own songs. Certainly, no one can suggest that "Ever Surprised," "Above the Band," and "Key to the Street" are songs on which—as Shewey claims about her performance of her earlier compositions—"she withdraws, slows down, mumbles and gets dull."

In this context, her performance of "Baby, I Need Your Lovin'" is significant in part because of the appreciable differences between her "interpretation" of its well-known lyrics and her own songs. After eight aggressive rock vocal performances of her own compositions (she had no hand in writing a ninth track, "Lightning Crashes"), Snow's sumptuous reading of a classic song that, like "Going Down for the Third Time," was written by Holland-Dozier-Holland, is anything but anomalous. And unlike her other soul covers, she approaches it as something other than an opportunity to "sing . . . like" a black singer. Perhaps the existence of Johnny Rivers's pop version, more commercially successful than the original, removes the compulsion she displays in other covers to replicate or improve upon soul styles. Snow slows the mid-tempo tune down, turning what was originally a song of black male dissemblance ("when you see me smiling / You'll know things have gotten worse / Any smile you might see / Has all been rehearsed") into a poignant ballad that affords her the space both to emote soulfully and to kick ass like the rock vocalists she loved as a child. It is a performance capable of inspiring rock's and soul's often-divergent fans alternately to yell "rock on" and "get down, sistuh," and may be the closest she has come to actualizing "the Phoebe Idea."

This encounter with classic soul gives way to the final song, "Going Home," an undeniably funky mid-tempo tune, which Snow cowrote. Despite the soulful features of her "Baby, I Need Your Lovin'," the final track seems jarringly out of place on this "rock" set. One possible reading of its presence and placement on a "rock" album is that Snow—listed, for the first time, as a coproducer of her music—is attempting to satisfy fans enamored of her earlier "black" performances for whom the album's other songs, and moments of the Four Tops cover, may be unappealing. I read its dissonant presence, however, as part of an ongoing exploration on her part of "home" sounds.

Natural Wonder constitutes another attempt by a nomadic singer to achieve "The Phoebe Idea," to find a (musical) home, stylistically speaking, in which she is able to sing "naturally" and express who she is, rather than feel as though she is mimicking established modes of expression. But what, indeed, is Snow's musical home? Does the rock genre she wants to master and which dominates this album provide her the possibility of resolving her (musical) ambivalence? Or is home the soul groove with which she concludes the album and in which she sounds—to my ears at least—significantly more comfortable? What is the point of concluding a rock (or white) album with a soul (or black) song? Is home an accommodating place to whose cultural forms she returns "for a holiday" from "Idea[l]" rock pursuits, or is it where she "belongs" and where she'll stay?

Given the position of "Going Home" on Snow's album, are we to believe that she is now any more equipped to abandon soul than she was in 1982 when Shewey interviewed her for *Esquire*? Perhaps "Going Home" signals her recognition, arrived at after she fulfills her rock fantasies, of the fact that soul is home. Perhaps, having come as close as she can imagine to "The Phoebe Idea" in "Baby, I Need Your Lovin'," she positions the final track of *Natural Wonder* as the beginning of a less conflicted return to R & B, soul, and funk. Whatever conclusion seems most plausible, if albums are structures that can communicate coherent ideas—in this case, Snow as "rock" singer—our responsibility is to attempt to discover the meanings of its apparently intentional introduction of incoherence, its self-consciously dissonant concluding sounds.

⊙ ⊙ ⊙

In March 2004, *Ebony* published an article entitled "Aretha Franklin: The Queen Still Reigns" that "offers a glimpse into the royal life" of the Queen of Soul, a life which the magazine chronicled through "the ups and downs, the pitfalls and triumphs, the joy and sadness" "from the time she sang backup with her renowned father [and] . . . the release of her first record in 1956," from hits like 'I Never Loved A Man' . . . on through 'A Rose is Still a Rose' in the '90s." An update trumpeting a new release, this piece details her hobnobbing with politicians and musicians at a holiday celebration in Detroit, "pursu[ing] jewelry in Tiffany & Co.," and having "tea at the ritzy Fairmont Hotel in Chicago" (62, 64). Using the title of *So Damn Happy* as its theme, it claims that the album's artistic success can be attributed to the fact that her "fans delight in the joy and exuberance that she expresses on the recording and especially on the title song" (62).

The focus on Franklin's opulent lifestyle and cultural power gives way to discussions of career plans and her personal life. Insisting that she's "so *damn happy* about the new album" and that she "'absolutely' still loves to perform," she lists as her future professional goals "a recording of classical arias," "another gospel album," and "more acting projects" if her agent is able to find "something nice and meaty, something [she] can sink [her] teeth into" (64).[5] Near the end of the article, "a reflective" Franklin speaks of being "disenchanted at this point" because of the recent end of a romance. Sounding less like the "so damn happy" persona she has adopted and slightly more like the deeply sad woman that critics, friends, and family members have described her as being, she speaks of her surprise that she has remained "this naïve and gullible at this point in my life," able still to be so blinded by love that "it's sometimes kind of hard to see everything that you need to see." But having come to this insight, "a few days later, she tells cheering fans at a concert that she has made three significant resolutions for 2004: 'I'm going to lose weight, get more organized, and I'm going to leave these bull-s—— men alone!'" (64)

It seems highly unlikely that, in the long run, *So Damn Happy* will be deemed a significant contribution to her oeuvre. But rather than comment further on her album or the obvious cracks in her construction of herself as a contented woman no longer in need of a bridge over troubled waters, I want to conclude with a discussion of the final moments of her performance at a 2003 Black Entertainment Television event honoring her career. Taking the stage after a bevy of contemporary singers pay tribute to her by performing many of her well-known hits, Franklin informs the audience that she's about to take them back to the beginning of her career. She then launches into her initial R & B hit, "Today I Sing the Blues," which she first sang on the demo record that impressed John Hammond so much that he signed her to a contract on Columbia Records. Her performance was a boisterous display of her regal pipes rather than the type of subtle, contemplative reading that distinguishes the original. Her boisterousness was purposeful; before a crowd of adoring fans and admiring colleagues, many of whom certainly had never heard the song before, Franklin reaches an unearned state of vocal frenzy that seems to leave her body overwhelmed by the weight of the blues. Rather than fall to the floor, like James Brown at similar moments in his concert performances, Franklin throws off her wig in a dramatic gesture the audience appreciated at least as much as her singing.

The fact that most of the audience members did not know the song was not important, nor was their ignorance of the fact that, in going back to her "roots," Franklin was self-consciously referencing her mentor Clara Ward who, "caught up in the fervor of the song 'Peace In The Valley,'" which she performed at the funeral for one of Aretha's aunts, "grabbed the hat off her head and hurled it to the ground," a display of "spirit" and "stirring emotion" that "stayed with her [Franklin] for a long time" (Bego 17). However they read Franklin's gesture, and however much I reveled in both her acknowledgment of a largely unremembered great song from her distant past and her tribute to Ward, watching her made me worry. I recalled the diet pills that killed Dinah Washington, MisterLucky's comment about Franklin's "exhausting series of relationships," and her own resolution "to leave these bull-s— men alone," and I worried about the excessive physical and psychological weight Franklin appeared to be carrying.

In a lengthy September 29, 2003, *Jet* article, Franklin insisted that she was "damn happy" not only with her boyfriend (whom she had stopped seeing when she was being interviewed by *Ebony* three months later), but "with the progress she's making with her weight" (Waldron n.p.). I think I understand why Franklin claims happiness in her personal life as intense as that which she communicates in "So Damn Happy," even as she acknowledges that the song's inspiration is not the then current (and soon-to-be former) beau who is making her "so damn happy" (Waldron n.p.): she has endured three and a half decades of being described as suffering with the blues. Similarly, I think I understand Snow's need to display her rock chops as well as her inability to abandon the soulful strut of black expressivity. And I believe I comprehend Green's desire, at a point when he accepts that he cannot resolve long-standing tensions between religious and secular imperatives, to ignore his religious convictions temporarily in order to assume once again the mantle of Soul Man.

I don't claim to understand them as human beings, and I am not foolish enough to see the most apparently self-revelatory of their songs as representing and communicating the unadulterated truth about their lives. Singers are performers who take off and put on lying and grinning masks, assume sighing and sinning personae, more frequently than their fans change their socks. I suspect, for example, that Snow—who insists in interviews that she has only recently learned to stand up for herself and who has been accused of mumbling her own lyrics—refers to her own life and career in the track on *Natural Wonder*, where she adopts a persona who insists that crafty resilience and informed outspokenness enable you to "survive past your 15 minutes" and be heard "above the band," but I know better than to make too much of that suspicion. In this book, I've tried to communicate some of what three singers—working in genres of American popular music in which the capacity to offer gut-wrenching performances of a range of emotions is essential, and endeavoring to make already-known songs conform to their evolving notions of their own musical identities—appear to be attempting to say in their uses of sounds, words, tradition, genre, religion, and notions of identity, love, and loss.

notes

1 The resemblance that the young Washington resisted was less vocal than physical and temperamental—both she and Smith were considered "unattractive, rough-hewn, and moody." Washington sought to evade comparisons to this long-dead, mythic cultural figure, about whom colorful stories continued to circulate within black and blues communities even though her recordings no longer dominated their airwaves and phonographs. In Cole's case, her still vibrant precursor Franklin, on the other hand, was firmly entrenched as the "Queen of Soul," so that the resemblances for which both she and her producers strove were seen not simply as a form of flattery but as the theft of the resources of a contemporary.

Whatever negative response Washington had to being deemed as physically and temperamentally "unattractive" as the dark-skinned, big-boned blues Empress, particularly at a point in American history notable for the wide circulation of images of the light complexions and Nordic features of seemingly refined entertainers such as Lena Horne and Dorothy Dandridge, who were thought to epitomize black beauty and elegance, she did not have to contend with a living-and-breathing Smith or a bitter rivalry with a "rough-hewn" idol.

2   Using Grammy recognition as a measure, Franklin was not able over the course of the next decade to reestablish herself as the undisputed Queen of black female singers; members of the National Academy of Recording Arts and Sciences recognized (in addition to Cole again in 1976) Thelma Houston, Donna Summer, Dionne Warwick, Stephanie Mills, Franklin, Jennifer Holliday, and Chaka Khan (in both 1983 and 1984). Franklin was honored by Grammy voters in 1985 for the rollicking "Freeway of Love" and again in 1987 for the wretched album *Aretha* and for "I Knew You Were Waiting (for Me)," her duet with George Michael. Cole is the offspring of a legendary entertainer, whose vocal elegance clearly influenced such singers as Ray Charles, Sam Cooke, and Marvin Gaye (indeed Gaye, who aspired to be a crooner on a par with Cole, in an attempt to satisfy that longing recorded *A Tribute to the Great Nat King Cole* for Motown in 1965 following his idol's death). Nat "King" Cole was the first black person to host a national variety show, and he released versions of "Mona Lisa," "Unforgettable," "Straighten Up and Fly Right," and "White Christmas" that left an indelible mark. Partly, no doubt, because of her parentage, Natalie Cole was treated by audiences and critics as if she had been born to wear the female soul singer's crown. Not as gifted vocally as Franklin or, it could be argued, the performers with whom she shared recognition at the onset of Franklin's quasi-official and commercial demise, Cole was nonetheless viewed by many as the next great black female singer. During an immensely successful three-year period, she recorded three albums that achieved platinum sales; became, according to an engaging study of the Grammy awards, "the first black ever voted Best New Artist"; "officially end[ed] Aretha Franklin's eight-year monopoly of the category" of Best Female R & B Vocal Performance (231–32); and was widely regarded as a charismatic live performer with great prospects for a lengthy and successful career. As she discusses at length in her autobiography, she developed a serious drug habit that limited her subsequent success.

3   Bloom's formulations of influence speak also to the burdens facing the post-Enlightenment author writing with a full awareness of "the diminishment of poetry" after "the giant age before the flood, before the anxiety of influence became central to poetic consciousness" (*Anxiety* 11), and before it became the responsibility of the "strong" to stave off "the death of poetry" (10). Bridgewater's contemporary jazz singer, like Bloom's modern poet, is an artist seeking to situate herself vis-à-vis an imperiled tradition, and is similarly burdened with the seeming impermanence and cultural marginalization of her form of expression. As we have seen, Bridgewater appears acutely aware of her own belatedness, her

entrance as a player on the jazz stage after Fitzgerald's, Holiday's, Vaughan's, and McCrae's deaths, and after the passing of the material, social, and aesthetic conditions that enabled their modes of vocal art. As a consequence, she sees her fight to preserve the "diminish[ed]" and dying art of traditional jazz singing as admirable, even noble, but doomed to fail. Like the poet "rebelling more strongly against the consciousness of death's necessity than all other men and women do" (Bloom, *Anxiety* 10), it could be argued, Bridgewater performs jazz in order to immortalize herself, but her tribute to Fitzgerald is, as much as anything else, a condemnatory response to an age where the art form of which she sees her idol as the prime exemplar has been neglected, devalued, left to die like the artistic parent she claims to have believed would always be both vibrantly alive and widely celebrated. The younger singer constructs her predecessor as possessed of a seemingly indestructible body, despite her lengthy illnesses and obvious frailty during the last decade of her life, because she wants her readers and listeners to see Fitzgerald as a symbol of a seemingly indestructible music for whose marginalization, "diminishment," and imminent death they are responsible as members of an age that exalts less emotionally resonant styles while refusing to support artists whose work keeps alive, and builds upon, the monumental traditions that Fitzgerald helped to establish. Striving to preserve Ella and the jazz traditions she exemplifies, Bridgewater is, in essence, fighting for her own survival at a time when, particularly in the United States, that endeavor is more likely to be accompanied by "woes," "hardship," and "problems" than by critical and popular acclaim, appropriate financial recompense, or artistic immortality.

4 As the reviewer correctly notes, when Franklin is called upon to recall psychologically and/or emotionally charged incidents from her life, her recollections become markedly more "filtered," leading her to claim "she can't remember specific details of why a particular relationship ended or she breezes over the breakup of her parents." At other moments, including her consideration of her inability to parlay her popularity as a singer into significant film roles à la Barbra Streisand and Diana Ross, Franklin refuses to acknowledge a capacity on her part for envy or for "petty or jealous" feelings, representing herself as "a saint, gently accepting God's will."

5 The black male singers who ruled in Dinah Washington's era along with her and in the period following her demise, including Bobby Blue Bland, Ray Charles, B. B. King, Sam Cooke, Jackie Wilson, Otis Redding, James Brown, Solomon Burke, and Wilson Pickett, engaged in sometimes contentious battles to resolve the question which of them was the most accomplished artist. However, despite the fact that they all recorded songs of deep heartbreak, their public personae—which ranged from deeply devoted husbands (Cooke, "love man" Redding), to serious men of God working in secular fields (Cooke, Burke), to "midnight hour" lovers of multiple women (Charles and Pickett)—indicate that they weren't forced to embody a singular notion of black and blues masculinity. However soulfully these men-and-a-half, these geniuses, originators, kings, and godfathers of black

and blues music performed, and whatever tragedies indeed befell some of them, their success certainly did not revolve around their capacity to project images of inescapable angst off the stage.

6   Franklin also asserts that she remembers few of the details of the "big confrontation in Muscle Shoals between Ted White and one of the musicians" (109) that interrupted perhaps the most important recording session in which she was ever involved. Brought to the Deep South, the birthplace of the blues, soul, and gospel sounds that Wexler hoped he could help her to produce in a more commercially appealing fashion than she had at Columbia, she was forced to stop recording because of the chaos that ensued when, according to Guralnick, an unnamed white trumpet player, who had earlier "made a smart remark to the artist which the artist's husband vociferously objected to," "either got smart with Aretha again or 'pinched her butt'" (*Sweet Soul Music* 341–42). We may believe this account or, for that matter, Wexler's slightly different version, which locates a sometimes nemesis, the Alabama-based producer Rick Hall, as the source of the tension. Wexler chides Hall for heightening racial tensions in the studio by failing to follow the producer's instructions to hire a black or at least racially integrated horn section and for, after a "'dozens' duel" between White and an equally inebriated horn player, entering into what Hall himself characterizes as "a full-blown fistfight" (210–11) with Franklin's volatile husband that sent the couple back to the relative safety of the North with only "I Never Loved A Man (The Way That I Loved You)," which would become her breakout hit from her first Atlantic album, having been recorded. Still, what does strain credulity is Franklin's assertion in *From These Roots*—in response, no doubt, to Ritz's questions about her recollections of the particulars of this much-discussed event—that because "it's been so long and so many things have happened since those days, I really don't recall" (109). She does recall, however, aspects of this experience that place her in a more favorable light, including feeling agitated enough the following morning to leave her hotel room and head to the airport without her husband.

7   Franklin's account of her early Atlantic career also fails to credit Otis Redding as the writer and original performer of "Respect." Franklin also claims that "Until You Come Back to Me" was a "song Stevie Wonder wrote for [her]" (Bego 159) despite the fact he recorded it years before her version appeared.

8   Franklin's initial appearance on the R & B chart occurred in 1960 with "Today I Sing the Blues," which rose to number ten; Knight's first chart entry with the Pips was the chart-topping "Every Beat of My Heart" in 1961. According to Joel Whitburn's R & B singles and albums compilations, Franklin is the second most popular singles artist from 1942 to 1995 and the second most popular album maker from 1965 to 1998, while Knight is eighth on both lists, primarily because of her work as the lead singer of Gladys Knight and the Pips. But music critics generally insist that Franklin is more talented, if not always as focused; for example, Guralnick endorses Russell Gersten's assessment of Knight as a "smart and wise and well-developed and sometimes great" singer, and of Franklin as an inconsistent performer who, when she is inspired, communicates with a "won-

derful clarity" of which more "earthbound" artists like Knight are not capable (346).

9   One interesting facet of the history of "Cold, Cold Heart" is the involvement of Jerry Wexler who, a year earlier, in his role as what he calls a "tune tout," suggested to "Jack Rael, who managed Patti Page," that she record "Tennessee Waltz," her "career song" (*Rhythm and Blues* 66), which went on to sell nearly five million copies. The southern connections of the New York-based Wexler would become quite extensive in the 1960s, partly because of Atlantic's distribution deal with Memphis's Stax Records, but are important for a discussion of Aretha Franklin because he chose Muscle Shoals, Alabama, as the location of her first recording session with him, feeling that, because she "was a natural for the Southern style of record" (208), being in the South would help to release her deep soul artistry that her first record company was unable consistently to tap. Even though he recognized that "Cold, Cold Heart" was "far from the jazz, blues, and rhythm and blues [he] loved best," he brought Williams's song to the attention of Columbia new executive, Mitch Miller, who orchestrated a successful pop recording that "added momentum to mainstreaming country music" (67). While acknowledging that Miller himself supports this version of events, Escott also details the infinitely more appealing "mythology that, against all odds and against the deeply ingrained resistance of the pop music oligarchy, Wesley Rose [the son of Fred Rose, whose partnership with Williams's idol, Roy Acuff, Acuff-Rose Publications, was partially responsible for Hank's accumulation of significant wealth because it sold his sheet music and handled his publishing rights] went to New York and persuaded Mitch Miller to record 'Cold, Cold Heart' with Tony Bennett" (142).

10   In a paradigmatic formulation of black artistic lineage, expressed, interestingly for our purposes here, in the form of contentious racial negotiation, Ralph Ellison explains his own efforts to move beyond the limitations of what he considers to be the didactic, rage-filled narratives of his artistic "relative," Richard Wright, in favor of the more compelling perspectives of "a greater artist" like Ernest Hemingway. Ellison suggests that, unlike the author of *Native Son*, Hemingway "was imbued with a spirit beyond the tragic with which I could feel at home, for it was very close to the feeling of the blues, which are, perhaps, as close as Americans can come to expressing the spirit of tragedy" (*Shadow and Act*, 186). Because he believes Hemingway's reflections on "the tragic" more closely approximate the "spirit" of the blues than the work of Wright, whom he accuses of not knowing "anything about the blues" (186), Ellison positions these important American authors as opposing voices in what he calls "an argument over the nature of reality" (165). Indeed, in his explorations of his sense of his artistic influences and the necessarily contentious battles in which contemporaries engage over "the nature of reality," Ellison offers a claim that "all novels of a given historical moment . . . are, to an extent, criticisms each of the other" (165) that seems to me applicable, at least in some respects, to the phenomenon of song covers, which are fundamentally in conflict with one another about how best to interpret the combination of lyrics and music. While the arguments suggested by compet-

ing versions of songs are not always particularly profound—Motown's choice to release Marvin Gaye's version of "I Heard It Through the Grapevine" a year after Gladys Knight and the Pips' major hit left the charts comes immediately to mind; certainly, we might consider their different tempos, use of background vocals, and the formulations of gender that inspires Gaye to exclaim, "I know a man ain't supposed to cry," in place of Knight's plea to her wayward addressee "Take a look at these tears in my eyes," but the interpretive yield of such considerations would be slight compared to the sorts of philosophical and moral differences that Ellison identifies. When they involve important issues like the politics of making "countrified" art acceptable to "citified" audiences, such arguments can illuminate the degree to which remakes serve both as recognition of the power and "criticisms" of the limitations of earlier performances.

11   Note, for example, such sentiments as "Atlantic provided TLC—tender loving care" (Franklin and Ritz 108) and offered "so much more room [than Columbia for her] to be creative"; "the enthusiasm and camaraderie in the studio were terrific, like nothing I had experienced at Columbia"; "this new Aretha music was raw and real and so much more myself"; and "putting me back on piano" (a "key difference between my Columbia and Atlantic sessions") "helped Aretha-ize the new music" (108–9). Earlier, however, she suggests to Bego that while marketing blunders and creative differences did indeed negatively impact her during her time at Columbia, for which she admits she produced "a lot of good stuff," "the move from Columbia to Atlantic was about commercial success" (77).

"something like wholeness"

1   Black performers' remaking of popular songs by white rock artists is, indeed, a little examined phenomenon of the 1960s and 1970s, and is perhaps best exemplified by the Isley Brothers, a then journeyman group whose only significant hits during the 1960s were 1962's "Twist and Shout" (recorded two years later by the Beatles at the beginning of their reign), the 1966 Motown-Tamla hit, "This Old Heart of Mine," and the self-produced smash of 1969, "It's Your Thing." Seeking material that might best showcase their version of "black rock," an emphatically guitar-driven fusion of rock embellishment of R & B rhythms and vocal styling, between 1971 and 1974 the Isleys covered, with wildly divergent degrees of success, songs by such white artists as Bob Dylan ("Lay Lady Lay"), Carole King ("It's Too Late"), Stephen Stills ("Love the One You're With"), James Taylor ("Don't Let Me Be Lonely Tonight"), Seals and Crofts ("Summer Breeze"), and Todd Rundgren ("Hello It's Me"). Interestingly, after the platinum success of 3 + 3, which featured remakes of four white artists' songs, including their superb versions of Taylor's and Seals and Crofts' tunes, and whose title formally recognizes the group's reconstitution as a combination of the three original brother-vocalists and three musicians who were younger members of the family, the Isleys became a frontline R & B recording and concert act that, with one notable

exception—1974's "Hello It's Me"—eschewed this practice in favor of producing albums that featured their own compositions for at least the next decade. In 2003, the group's lead singer, Ronald Isley, who during the last decade has found his third—or fourth—musical life as Mr. Bigg, the R. Kelly foil and creation, made an album of covers of Burt Bacharach compositions, produced by Bacharach himself, entitled *Isley Sings Bacharach*, which I find unlistenable.

2   One way Green calls attention to the importance of songwriting is by nam-ing his autobiography after one of his compositions that he does not feel he was able to sing as effectively as he might have. While he insists that his version of "Take Me to the River"—which was never released as a single—is one of the high-lights of his seventh album, *Al Green Explores Your Mind*, he reminds us: "Another Hi artist, Syl Johnson, would get a hit off [it] in '75. . . . I always preferred Syl's version to my own" (307). The song describes a young man who is clearly in the throes of an all-consuming lust he mistakes for love and who is unable to face the fact that the woman responsible for his sexual initiation on his sixteenth birth-day subsequently treats him "so bad" because she is neither similarly naive nor smitten. Pleading for, at the very least, another totally immersing sexual liasion with the object of his desire—"dip me in the water"—the song's youthful persona seems convinced that what he views as pleasurable intimacy's baptism-like plea-sures will "cleanse my soul." If Simon Frith is correct that, generally, listeners assume an essential connection between singer and the song's persona whose narrative he or she vocally embellishes, the lyrics' emphasis on the youth of the persona serves to create an unmistakable distance between the twenty-eight-year-old singer and "Take Me to the River's" sixteen-year-old supplicant, whose story emerges as a toe-tapping parable of the foibles of youthful romantic naïveté. In this song, Green is uncharacteristically removed from the pains that accompany human passion, linked, in his capacity of distanced observer, with members of his audience who typically can imagine that the mininarratives he usually offers as communicating the singer's own heartaches. While this is an interesting rhetorical strategy, that distance seems to limit Green's engagement in the words, and, as a result, for me at least, he seems to rush through most of the lyrics like he does on his novice remakes rather than linger suggestively on the sonic possibilities and emotional resonances of phrases and syllables as he does in his best work.

Still, even if we agree with Robert Christgau's contention that "Take Me to the River" is Green's "acknowledged masterpiece" (466)—like Green himself, I prefer Johnson's slightly funkier version—we might also consider the strategic significance of naming his life story after a song whose ironic marrying of pain-ful romantic circumstance and soul-cleansing religious imagery represents per-haps the most poignant lyrical manifestation in all of his popular albums of the struggle between "sin and salvation," which he hopes against hope that his audi-ence will begin to believe animates even his familiar romantic songs. Manifesting a narrative distance unachieved by his song's lusty young persona, a mature (but, in keeping with biblical formulations concerning the omnipresence of tempta-tion, still susceptible) Green seeks to convince listener-readers of the problems of failing, like the sixteen-year-old subject, to move beyond their fantasies in order to assess the nuances of their realities—and of him—with a clear-eyed, perhaps even self-protective, objectivity. To continue to view him solely in terms of romantic fantasy is to remain fixed in the sort of cognitive dissonance that the song for which the narrative of the singer's life is named clearly exposes as cognitively flawed, spiritually and emotionally damaging, and downright stupid. Green seeks to let the reader in on the secret of his success, to give him or her fuller understanding of the dangers of wishing to continue to be dipped in obviously murky waters.

3 Perhaps Green's continual underplaying of the sexual aspect both of his relationships with Juanita and Laura and of his encounters with his countless female conquests might best be read as possible confirmation of rumors whispered in black communities at the height of his popularity that Green may be gay. (To cite one example: a colleague informed me that people in his community interpreted the lines "Forgive me baby if I do wrong / I haven't been a true man for so long," in his single "Look What You Done for Me," as his resolution to give up the "wrongs" of his transgressive lifestyle and become "a true man.") Certainly there are numerous perplexing moments in *Take Me to the River* related to issues of gender, sexuality, and identity, including his suggestion that during his relationship with Juanita, he found "comfort and security, . . . safety from the storms of life" in "the fancy boudoir we called home—with its colored lights and satin sheets and beguiling baubles—. . . a dollhouse where we hid from the real world and its terrible responsibilities" (146). In that relationship, he learned to discern "the sexual preference of each regular customer" by watching his prostitute girlfriend work with "the dark and depraved side of the human animal," memories of which "left a scar on my soul, one I'd rather keep to myself" (137). At the very least, he seems to be aligning himself suggestively with those who resist traditional societal notions of gendered behavior, as when he claims that "clothing was another of the common bonds we shared and we were constantly borrowing one accessory or another from each other—a scarf or a belt or a piece of jewelry—to finish off one of our more flamboyant costumes" (131) just before describing visiting "one of Juanita's favorite haunts" (132), "a basement club" whose "floor show featured some of the biggest and ugliest women I'd ever seen doing some kind of a bump and grind dirtier than I could ever have imagined" (133). These performers, whom his girlfriend "called . . . Claude and Monroe or some such unmistakable masculine names," turned out to be "a pair of transvestites," and the occasion marked "the first time I'd ever seen men dressed up in women's clothes and the sight both fascinated and repelled me" (133).

"Miss Snow, are you black?"

1 Proof of Snow's skillful appropriation of black vocal style might be seen if we contrast her charming remake of Barbara Acklin's minor 1960s hit, "Love Makes

a Woman," with Linda Ronstadt's perhaps most soulful release from her period of huge popularity, her evocative version of "Blue Bayou." However successfully Ronstadt approximates sadness or impressively she holds the title phrase's final syllable, these accomplishments differ if not qualitatively, then in terms of their cultural resonances, from Snow's majestic fadeout, where, over the space of less than half a minute, she changes octaves, volume, and tonality in a seemingly effortless manner. Snow's mastery of forms of black singing is evident in her joyous, gospel-inspired "woooos" and "oohs," her use of the phrase "Yes it's love" as a vocal aside that sums up the song's central message, and her mimicking of the accompanying saxophone, rendering the ecstatic mood wordlessly by virtually eliminating the language elements of this phrase and approaching it as a series of sounds that are both almost indecipherable and sonic manifestations of a liberating emotional clarity.

2   Stone herself has acknowledged the possibility that her "voice doesn't fit [her] body," but goes on to suggest, somewhat naively, perhaps, "Music has no color. How can it have a color, because you can't see it? How can you say that I sound black or white, or purple or pink or whatever?" (Moody 36).

3   Duck Dunn, a bass player in the instrumental group, Booker T. and the MGS, and one of the company's most important contributors, describes an incident during which policemen "jump out [of their cars] and pull out their guns" because they believed members of a group of black Stax employees that included Dunn's long-time colleague Isaac Hayes, "were doing something to hurt us [Dunn and his wife] because we were white" (355). So when we read that Hayes, whose year-long creative block following King's murder is frequently mentioned in histories of soul music, "was filled with so much bitterness and anguish, till [Hayes] couldn't deal with it" (355), we understand that those feelings might be attributed, in part, to a belief that he had to reformulate his notions of the place of race in black music creation and distribution. Hayes emerged from this creatively fallow period to record several important albums, including *Hot Buttered Soul* and *To Be Continued*, whose spoken raps, jazzy instrumental riffs, and radical break from the convention of the three-minute song inspired artists such as Marvin Gaye, Stevie Wonder, and Millie Jackson to utilize the soul album as a medium for sophisticated, thematically unified artistic expression. Perhaps because of the personal and professional trauma he experienced as a result of King's assassination or in recognition on his part of his artistic and social importance, Hayes began to clothe himself with iconic racial accoutrements—chain shirts that signified black enslavement; the moniker "Black Moses" (which he used, also, as the title of a wonderful mid-seventies double album that was packaged with a large foldout cardboard image of Hayes dressed in striped, hooded garb Hollywood has taught us to associate with biblical times, his arms extended like Christ on the cross)—despite the fact that his songs rarely, if ever, engaged the subject of black oppression in America.

4   In his essay on the Harvard Report, David Sanjek, director of the BMI Archives, summarizes the conclusions of Nelson George's seminal study, *The Death*

of Rhythm and Blues, concerning both the report and the costs of black mainstream success in a manner that has obvious relevance for my own discussions of Snow. As Sanjek insists, "George argues that assimilation by African-Americans into the commercial mainstream demands too many sacrifices, and that the Harvard Report is a notable example of how that perilous exchange takes place. More often than not, he believes, black individuals lose an unrecoverable portion of their identity in the process. 'Pursuing an anglicized self-image,' George writes, 'these "transformed" black people, with their belief that anything can be sacrificed to generate more capital, are one of the most disturbing triumphs of assimilation'" (61–62).

5   Roland Barthes speaks of the "'details' which constitute the very raw material of ethnological knowledge" in *Camera Lucida*, his provocative study of the "duality" or "co-presence of two [seemingly contradictory] elements" of compelling photographs (23, 22, 28). One "dual" or contradictory image that Barthes explores is by the Dutch photographer Koen Wessing, and features nuns traversing the rubble of an obviously bombed urban landscape along with armed, helmeted soldiers. He goes on to discuss his belief that two contrasting elements are apparent, and in some tension with each other, in all compelling photographs. He characterizes the first element, the *studium*, as "average" because it is perceived "as a consequence of my knowledge, my culture; this field can be more or less stylized, more or less successful . . . , but it always refers to a classical body of information" which results "almost from a certain [cultural] training" that leads him to interact with the photograph with "a kind of general, enthusiastic commitment . . . , but without special acuity" (26). According to Barthes, this "average," cultural element is invariably disturbed in photographs that fascinate him by "a second element . . . which rises from the scene, shoots out of it like an arrow, and pierces me." He labels this element *punctum*, a Latin word that means "sting, speck, cut, little hole—and also a cast of the dice. A photograph's *punctum* is that accident which pricks me (but also bruises me, is poignant to me)" (26–27).

For Barthes, a photograph's *studium* allows the viewer to "encounter the photographer's intentions . . . , which animate his practices . . . , to read the Photographer's myths . . . [which] obviously aim (this is what myth is for) at reconciling the Photograph with society . . . by endowing it with functions, which are, for the Photographer, so many alibis. These functions are: to inform, to represent, to surprise, to cause to signify, to provoke desire. And I, the *Spectator*, I recognize them with more or less pleasure: I invest them with my *studium* (which is never my delight or my pain)" (28).

6   One example of this saturation is the fact that two-fifths of the top one hundred artists on Joel Whitburn's *Billboard* list of pop singles acts between 1955 and 1999 are black; the work of a number of the white acts—including top fifty entries such as Elvis Presley, the Beatles, the Rolling Stones, Madonna, Pat Boone, Rod Stewart, Hall & Oates, and George Michael—was heavily influenced by black music (886).

7   It is also possible that, given Motown's practice of having multiple acts

record the same song (the most famous instance of which is "I Heard It Through The Grapevine," which both Gladys Knight and the Pips and Marvin Gaye produced impressive—and stylistically quite different—hit recordings of in the late 1960s), this lack of attribution on Palmer's part could indicate that other acts with whom Holland-Dozier-Holland worked also recorded the song. However, I have not been able to find a version of this song by another Motown act.

8   In a 2003 interview with a *Baltimore Sun* reporter who speaks of Snow as "fearlessly musical, her work sweeping through the blues, gospel, jazz, pop, folk—sometimes within one song," Snow makes the point that "one of the things that got the music industry confused and under the weather right now is that everything has to be categorized. It's killing everything. It always has" (Ollison n.p.). Manifesting a characteristic resistance to limiting generic characterization, she insists that *Natural Wonder*, which "has a lot of rock guitars," "is really who I am, one part of who I am,"and expresses her doubts about whether her work will find its way onto "rigidly formatted" "radio play lists," whose quality pales in comparison to the supposedly more eclectic radio formats of the 1970s.

9   The pervasiveness of this trope is confirmed, for example, by the Smithsonian collection of classic blues singers, *The Blues*, which includes, along with Ray Charles, four male singers whose stage names emphasize their sightlessness: "Blind" Misters Lemon Jefferson, Willie Johnson, Willie McTell, and Boy Fuller.

coda

1   One reviewer, Andy Whitman, who claims that Green "is [his] favorite male vocalist, and has been for many, many years," erases *Your Heart's in Good Hands* from his corpus, asserting that the new album is "his first 'secular' album in 27 years" (Whitman n.p.).

2   Indeed, in the romantic comedy *On the Line*, Green is a major presence and plot device: the meeting of the lead characters revolves around their shared affection for his music; one of the obstacles to their union—her caddish boyfriend—is removed when he is exposed as unromantic because he chooses work over joining his girlfriend at the Al Green concert he'd promised to attend; and in addition to his performance of "Love and Happiness" in the concert scenes, his joyous rendition of "Let's Stay Together" during the closing credits represents the highpoint of a drearily scripted, poorly acted film.

3   Two exceptions among many fine songs: "Love TKO" and "You're My Latest, You're My Greatest Inspiration." My point about Pendergrass resonates with the formulations of Martha Bayles, whose controversial study of American popular music, *Hole in Our Soul*, argues, among other things, that a "headlong hedonism" was "the preferred response" to "the official post-1960s mood" of "despair at the dashing of utopian hopes" (269), and that its clearest, and most artistically devastating, manifestation in black music was the emergence of "unadulterated love man music" (272). This music, she argues, replaced the "self-indulgence and pre-

tension" of the pursuit of "Art" by innovative artists such as Isaac Hayes, Marvin Gaye, Donny Hathaway, and Stevie Wonder, who sought to expand the possibilities of the soul album with the "self-indulgent and pretentious" emphasis on "Sex." In Bayles's view, the "piercing emotional intensity of soul was left behind as soul men became 'love men'" for whom "love [was not] really the point," as evinced in songs—including Pendergrass's wildly popular Teddy Bear tunes—that communicate "the sound of a man so enamored of his own powers of seduction that his partner is reduced to a faint chorus of orgasmic chirps" (270–71). I think Bayles paints with too broad a brush here, ignoring scores of male acts that continued the soul tradition of "piercing emotional intensity," but it is undeniable that the male and female "sound[s]" she identifies did come to constitute a very large part of the soul canvas after the early 1970s. For example, the soul trope of the simulated orgasm appears on New Birth's otherwise remarkable ballad "It's Been a Long Time" and the vocally challenged Major Harris's "Love Won't Let Me Wait." Generally speaking, many of the most popular love man tracks now seem dated and a little silly (as do such love woman equivalents as Sylvia's "Pillow Talk" and Donna Summer's "Love to Love You Baby"), though I must admit that I appreciate "the lengthy, drawn-out monologue, half-spoken and half-sung against a dense, throbbing, quasi-orchestral background" (269) much more than Bayles. But if some of the songs are now barely listenable, if even "Let's Get It On" has devolved into parody, as evinced by Jack Black's performance in the film *High Fidelity*, many songs of this genre—including Marvin Gaye's "You Sure Love to Ball," whose moans and flawed equation of love and sex position it in the center of the tread Bayles identifies as helping to cause the demise of black music—remain quite compelling to me.

4   Green repeats the line "Stop the rain, stop the rain" that he uses at the close of "What a Wonderful Thing Love Is," a marvelous track from *I'm Still In Love With You*.

5   I can't imagine there are many "meaty" roles available to a dangerously overweight black woman in her sixties who, unlike singers such as Natalie Cole, Gladys Knight, and Patti LaBelle, has failed to build even a spotty acting resume (excluding "the two successful Blues Brothers movies" ["Aretha Franklin" 64]), nor is it clear how someone who "hasn't been on an airplane since 1983" would be in any better position to pursue such roles than she was in the mid-1980s, when she abandoned the musical on the life of Mahalia Jackson.

bibliography

books and articles

Amorosi, A. D. "Q & A: Teddy Pendergrass." *Philadelphia City Paper*, October 10–17, 2002, 40.

"Aretha Franklin: The Queen Still Reigns." *Ebony*, March 2004, 60–64.

Bakhtin, Mikhail. *The Dialogic Imagination*. Edited by Michael Holquist, translated by Caryl Emerson and Michael Holquist. Austin: University of Texas Press, 1981.

Barthes, Rolande. *Camera Lucida: Reflections on Photography*. Translated by Richard Howard. New York: Hill and Wang, 1981.

Bayles, Martha. *Hole in Our Soul: The Loss of Beauty and Meaning in American Popular Music.* Chicago: University of Chicago Press, 1994.

Bego, Mark. *Aretha Franklin: The Queen of Soul.* 1981; New York: Da Capo Press, 2001.

Block, Geoffrey, *Enchanted Evenings: The Broadway Musical from Showboat to Sondheim.* New York: Oxford University Press, 1997.

Bloom, Harold. *The Anxiety of Influence.* New York: Oxford University Press, 1973.

———. *A Map of Misreading.* New York: Oxford University Press, 1975.

Bowman, Rob. *Soulsville, U.S.A.: The Story of Stax Records.* New York: Schirmer, 1997.

Brackett, David. *Interpreting Popular Music.* Berkeley: University of California Press, 1995.

Breithaupt, Don, and Jeff Breithaupt. *Precious and Few: Pop Music of the Early '70s.* New York: St. Martin's, 1996.

Christgau, Robert. *Growing Up All Wrong: Great Rock and Pop Artists from Vaudeville to Techno.* Cambridge, Mass.: Harvard University Press, 1998.

———. *Robert Christgau's Guide to the 1980s.* New York: Pantheon, 1990.

———. *Rock Albums of the '70s: A Critical Guide.* New York: Da Capo Press, 1981.

Cole, Natalie, with Digby Diehl. *Angel on My Shoulder.* New York: Warner, 2000.

Collins, Jim. *Uncommon Cultures: Popular Culture and Post-Modernism.* New York: Routledge, 1989.

Dahl, Linda. *Stormy Weather: The Music and Lives of a Century of Jazz Women.* New York: Pantheon, 1984.

Davis, Angela. *Blues Legacies and Black Feminism.* New York: Vintage, 1999.

DeCurtis, Anthony, and James Henke, with Holly George-Warren, eds. *The Rolling Stone Illustrated History of Rock & Roll.* New York: Random House, 1992.

DiMartino, Dave. "Phoebe Snow." In *Singer-Songwriter: Pop Music's Performer-Composers, from A to Zevon*, 238. New York: Billboard Books, 1994.

Du Bois, W. E. B. *The Souls of Black Folk.* 1903; reprint, New York: Signet, 1969.

DuBus, Andre, III. *Bluesman.* New York: Vintage, 1993.

Echols, Alice. *Scars of Sweet Paradise: The Life and Times of Janis Joplin.* New York: Henry Holt, 1999.

Edmonds, Ben. *What's Going On? Marvin Gaye and the Last Days of the Motown Sound.* Edinburgh: Mojo Books, 2001.

Eldredge, Richard. Review of Joss Stone, "Soul Sessions." *Atlanta Journal-Constitution*, October 21, 2003, E7.

Eliot, T. S. *Selected Essays.* New York: Harcourt, 1950.

Ellison, Ralph. *Invisible Man.* New York: Random House, 1952.

———. *Shadow and Act.* New York: Vintage, 1964.

Emerson, Ralph Waldo. *The Selected Writings of Ralph Waldo Emerson.* Edited by William Gilman. New York: Signet, 1965.

Escott, Colin. *Hank Williams: The Biography.* New York: Little Brown, 1995.

Fitzgerald, Jon. "Motown Crossover Hits, 1963–1966, and the Creative Process." *Popular Music* 14.1 (1995): 1–11.

Forte, Allen. *Listening to Classic American Popular Songs*. New Haven: Yale University Press, 2001.

Franklin, Aretha, and David Ritz, *Aretha: From These Roots*. New York: Villard, 1999.

Frith, Simon. *Performing Rites: On the Value of Popular Music*. Cambridge, Mass.: Harvard University Press, 1996.

George, Nelson. *The Death of Rhythm and Blues*. New York: Dutton Obselisk, 1988.

George-Warren, Holly, and Patricia Romanowski, eds., Jon Pareles, consulting ed. *The Rolling Stone Encyclopedia of Rock & Roll*. New York: Fireside Press, 2001.

Gerard, Charley. *Jazz in Black and White: Race. Culture, and Identity in the Jazz Community*. Westport, Conn.: Praeger, 1998.

Graff, Gary, Josh Freedom du Lac, and Jim McFarlin, eds. *MusicHound R & B: The Essential Album Guide*. Detroit: Visible Ink Press, 1998.

Gray, Herman. *Watching Race: Television and the Struggle for "Blackness."* Minneapolis: University of Minnesota Press, 1995.

Green, Al, with Davin Seay. *Take Me to the River*. New York: HarperEntertainment, 2000.

Gregory, Hugh, *The Real Rhythm and Blues*. London: Blandford, 1998.

Gubar, Susan. *Racechanges: White Skin, Black Face in American Culture*. New York: Oxford University Press.

Guillory, Monique, and Richard C. Green, eds. *Soul: Black Power, Politcs, and Pleasure*. New York: New York University Press, 1998.

Guralnick, Peter. *Sweet Soul Music: Rhythm and Blues and the Southern Dream of Freedom*. New York: Harper and Row, 1986.

Haskins, Jim. *Queen of the Blues: A Biography of Dinah Washington*. New York: William Morrow, 1987.

Heilbut, Tony. *The Gospel Sound*. New York: Simon and Schuster, 1971.

Hellenga, Robert. *Blues Lessons*. New York: Scribner, 2002.

Henke, James, ed. *Rock Facts: Rock and Roll Hall of Fame and Museum*. New York: Universe Publishing, 1996.

Hinson, Glenn. *Fire in My Bones: Transcendence and the Holy Spirit in African American Gospel*. Philadelphia: University of Pennsylvania Press, 2000.

Hirshey, Gerri. *Nowhere to Run: The Story of Soul Music*. New York: New York Times Books, 1984.

Horstman, Dorothy. *Sing Your Heart Out, Country Boy*. Nashville: Country Music Foundation, 1986.

Hoye, Jacob, ed. *VH1's 100 Greatest Albums*. New York: Pocket Books, 2003.

Hurston, Zora Neale. *Their Eyes Were Watching God*. 1937; reprint, New York: Perennial, 1990.

Hutcheon, Linda. *The Politics of Postmodernism*. New York: Routledge, 1989.

Ignatiev, Noel, and John Garvey, eds. *Race Traitor*. New York: Routledge, 1996.

Jackson, David. "Al Green Changes Hearts and Minds." *Village Voice* 20 (January 1979): 53–54.

Jones, Leroi. *Black Music.* New York: Da Capo Press, 1968.

Jones, Quincy. *Q: The Autobiography of Quincy Jones.* New York: Harlem Moon/ Broadway Books, 2001.

Knight, Gladys. *Between Each Line of Pain and Glory.* New York: Hyperion, 1997.

Lawler, Jennifer. *Songs of Life: The Meanings of Country Music.* St. Paul, Minn.: Pogo Press, 1996.

Lipsitz, George. *Dangerous Crossroads: Popular Music, Postmodernism, and the Poetics of Place.* London: Verso, 1994.

Longhurst, Brian. *Popular Music and Society.* Cambridge: Polity Press, 1995.

MacKinnon, Catharine. *Toward a Feminist Theory of the State.* Cambridge, Mass.: Harvard University Press, 1989.

Mandle, Joan D. *Women and Social Change in America.* Princeton: Princeton University Press, 1979.

"Mariah Carey." *Ebony*, April 1994, 55–60.

Marsh, Dave. *The Heart of Rock & Soul: The 1001 Greatest Singles Ever Made.* New York: Plume, 1989.

Marsh, Dave, and John Swenson, eds. *The New Rolling Stone Record Guide.* New York: Random House, 1983.

Middleton, Richard, ed. *Reading Pop: Approaches to Textual Analysis in Pop Music.* New York: Oxford University Press, 2000.

Moody, Nekesa Mumbi, "So Rare: Rocker Fefe Dobson among New Breed of Singers Ignoring Musical Boundaries." *Philadelphia Daily News*, December 18, 2003, 35–36, 42.

Morgan, Thais. "The Space of Intertextuality." *Intertextuality and Contemporary American Fiction*, edited by Patrick O'Donnell and Robert Con Davis. Baltimore: Johns Hopkins University Press, 1989.

Neal, Mark Anthony. *What the Music Said: Black Popular Music and Black Public Culture.* New York: Routledge, 1999.

Ollison, Rashod D. "Snow Storms through Music's Many Genres." *Baltimore Sun*, July 10, 2003.

Olney, James, ed. *Autobiography: Essays Theoretical and Critical.* Baltimore: Johns Hopkins University Press, 1980.

O'Meally, Robert. *Lady Day: The Many Faces of Billie Holiday.* New York: Arcade, 1991.

O'Neill, Thomas. *The Grammys: The Ultimate, Unofficial Guide to Music's Highest Honor.* New York: Pedigree Books, 1993.

Panish, Jon. *The Color of Jazz: Race and Representation in Postwar American Culture.* Jackson: University of Mississippi Press, 1997.

Pollard, Alton B., III. "The Last Soul Singer in America." *The Theology of American Popular Music*, edited by Jon Michael Spencer. A special issue of *Black Sacred Music: A Journal of Theomusicology* 3.2 (1989): 85–97.

Pruter, Robert, ed. *The Blackwell Guide to Soul Recordings*. Oxford, U.K.: Basil Blackwell, 1993.

Ritz, David. *Divided Soul: The Life of Marvin Gaye*. New York: McGraw Hill, 1985.

Rolling Stone: The Complete Covers, 1967–1997. New York: Harry Abrams, 1998.

Rolling Stone 500 Greatest Albums of All Time Special Collectors Issue. Issue 937, December 11, 2003.

Rucker, Leland, ed. *Music Hound Blues: The Essential Albums Guide*. Detroit: Visible Ink Press, 1998.

Sanjek, David. "Tell Me Something I Didn't Already Know: The Harvard Report and Soul Music Revisited." *Rhythm and Business: The Political Economy of Black Music*. New York: Akashic Books, 2002.

Scholes, Robert. *Protocols of Reading*. New Haven: Yale University Press, 1989.

Shapiro, Peter. *Soul: 100 Essential CDs*. London: Rough Guides, 2000.

Shepherd, John. "Music, Culture, and Interdisciplinarity." *Popular Music* 13.2 (1994), 127–41.

Shepherd, John, and Peter Wicke. *Music and Cultural Theory*. Cambridge: Polity Press, 1997.

Shepherd, John. *Music as Social Text*. Cambridge: Basil Blackwell, 1991.

Shewey, Don. "The Blues of Snow." *Esquire*, May 1982, 74–81.

Smith, Barbara Herrnstein. *Contingencies of Value: Alternative Perspectives for Critical Theory*. Cambridge, Mass.: Harvard University Press, 1988.

———. *Poetic Closure: A Study of How Poems End*. Chicago: University of Chicago Press, 1968.

Smith, Suzanne E. *Dancing in the Street: Motown and the Cultural Politics of Detroit*. Cambridge, Mass.: Harvard University Press, 1999.

Stepto, Robert. *From Behind the Veil*. Urbana: University of Illinois Press, 1979.

Vincent, Rickey. *Funk*. New York: St. Martin's Griffin, 1996.

Wald, Gayle. "One of the Boys? Whiteness, Gender, and Popular Music Studies." In *Whiteness: A Critical Reader*, edited by Mike Hill. New York University Press, 1997.

Waldron, Clarence. "Aretha Franklin: Returns with Soulful CD, 'So Damn Happy'—Interview." *Jet*, September 29, 2003.

Ward, Brian. *Just My Soul Responding: Rhythm and Blues, Black Consciousness, and Race Relations*. Berkeley: University of California Press, 1998.

Werner, Craig. *A Change Is Gonna Come: Music, Race, and the Soul of America*. New York: Plume, 1999.

Wexler, Jerry. *The Rhythm and the Blues*. New York: St. Martin's, 1994.

Whitburn, Joel. *Billboard's Top 10 Charts, 1958–1995*. Menomeonee Fall, Wisc.: Record Research, 1995.

———. *Top Pop Singles, 1955–1999*. Menomeonee Fall, Wisc.: Record Research, 2000.

———. *Top R & B Singles, 1942–1995*. Menomeonee Fall, Wisc.: Record Research, 1996.

Whiteley, Sheila, ed. *Sexing the Groove: Popular Music and Gender*. New York: Routledge, 1997.

Wilson, August. "I Want a Black Director." In *May All Your Fences Have Gates*, edited by Alan Nadel. Iowa City: University of Iowa Press, 1994.

Wolf, Naomi. *The Beauty Myth*. New York: Morrow, 1991.

Wolff, Daniel, with S. R. Crain, Clifton White, and G. David Tenenbaum. *You Send Me: The Life & Times of Sam Cooke*. 200–204. New York: Quill, 1995.

Zinsser, William. *Easy to Remember: The Great American Songwriters and Their Songs*. Jaffrey, N.H.: David Gordine Publishers, 2001.

internet articles

Ankeny, Jason. "Phoebe Snow." Biography, discography, and other information. http://www.allmusic.com.

Farley, Christopher John. "Lady Soul: Singing It Like It Is." *Time*, June 28, 1968. http://www.time.com.

Holden, Stephen. Review of *Phoebe Snow*. January 2, 1975. http://www.rolling stone.com.

———. Review of Phoebe Snow, *Rock Away*. http://www.rollingstone.com.

Hunt, Darnell. "A Different World." On Museum of Broadcafst Communications Web site. http://www.museum.tv/archives.

Kenyada. "Interracial . . . Record Buying." On Mr. Kenyada's Neighborhood Web site. http://kenyada.com.

Lloyd, Jack. "Phoebe Snow Is an Avid Fan As Well As a Class Act." On the fan Web site of Virginia De Bolt. Article reproduced from the *Philadelphia Inquirer*. www.vdebolt.com.

MrLucky. Review of Aretha Franklin, with David Ritz, *Aretha: From These Roots*. http://www.mrlucky.com.

The New TNN Highlights "Purpose," "Action," and "Triumph" during Black History Month. February 2003. http://pushcreative.tv/media/tnnpress.pdf.

New York University. "NYU Press Features Books for Black History Month." July 13, 2003. www.nyu.edu/publicaffairs/newsreleases/b_NYU_P1.shtml.

Palmer, Robert. "Making It in the U.S.A." Reprinted from *Penthouse* magazine, March 1979. http://www.ronstadt-linda.com.

———. Review of Phoebe Snow, *Second Childhood*. April 8, 1976. http://www.rollingstone.com.

Pitts, Leonard, Jr. "Bush Plan 'Let's Get Married'/Ways and Means Hearing." April 4, 2002. http://listarchives.his.com/smartmarriages.

Roos, John. "Phoebe Snow Emerges from a Long, Wintry Spell." On the fan Web site of Virginia De Bolt. reprinted from the *Los Angeles Times*. September 1, 1998. http://www.vdebolt.com.

Ruhlmann, William. Review of Phoebe Snow, *Against the Grain*. http://www.allmusic.com.

Schinder, Scott. "It's Too Late for Al Green to Stop Now." Spring 2004. http://songwritershalloffame.org.

Shewey, Don. Review of Phoebe Snow, *Against the Grain*. www.rollingstone.com.

"Singer-Songwriter." http://www.allmusic.com.

Tucker, Ken. Review of Phoebe Snow, *Never Letting Go*. December 1, 1977. http://www.rollingstone.com.

Viglione, Joe. Review of Phoebe Snow, *It Looks Like Snow*. http://www.allmusic.com.

Whitman, Al. Review of Al Green, *I Can't Stop*. Issue 7, no date. http://www.pastemagazine.com.

Zollo, Paul. "The Solo Years—The Songwriter/The Songs." On the IT University, Centre for Digital Media and Higher Education (Göteberg, Sweden) Web site. 1992. Page no longer available.

compact discs and albums

A Tribute to Curtis Mayfield. Warners 9-45500-2, 1994.

A Tribute to Muddy Waters. Hybrid Records HY 20016, 1999.

A Twist of Motown. Verve 44007-60312, 2003.

Beatles. *Sergeant Pepper's Lonely Hearts Club Band*. EMI 7777-46422-2, 1967.

Belle, Regina. *Reachin' Back*. Columbia 7464-66813-2, 1995.

———. *Stay with Me* 1990. Columbia 7464-44367-2, 1989.

Bennett, Tony. *16 Most Requested Songs*. Columbia 74644-0152, 1986.

Bridgewater, Dee Dee. *Dear Ella*. Verve 314-537-896-2, 1997.

Burke, Solomon. *The Best of Solomon Burke*. Rhino Atlantic and Atco Masters 8122-72972-2, 1998.

Cole, Natalie. *The Natalie Cole Collection*. Capitol 7777-46619-2, 1987.

Conception: An Interpretation of Stevie Wonder's Songs. Motown 44006-73142, 2003.

Cooke, Sam. *Portrait of a Legend, 1951–1964*. ABKCO Records 18771-92642, 2003.

Franklin, Aretha. *Amazing Grace*. Atlantic 7567-81324-2, 1972.

———. *I Never Loved a Man the Way I Love You*. Rhino Atlantic and Atco Masters 02122-71934-2, 1995.

———. *Jump to It*. Arista 7822-19602-1, 1982.

———. *The Queen in Waiting*. Legacy/Columbia 9699-85696-2, 2002.

———. *So Damn Happy*. Arista 82876-50174-2, 2003.

———. *Unforgettable: A Tribute to Dinah Washington*. Legacy/Columbia 7464-66201-2, 1995.

———. *Who's Zooming Who?* Arista 7822-18286-1, 1985.

———. *Young, Gifted, and Black*. Atlantic SD 7213, 1972.

Freelon, Nnenna. *Tales of Wonder: Celebrating Stevie Wonder*. Concord Records CCD-2107-2.

Gaye, Marvin. *Marvin Gaye: The Master 1961–1984*. Motown 31453-0492-2, 1995.

————. *A Tribute to the Great Nat King Cole*. Motown 1965. 374635162, 1965

————. *What's Going On*. Motown 5010-92815-1, 1971.

Green, Al. *Al Green Gets Next to You*. 1971 Hi Records. The Right Stuff 0777-7-66709-2-8, Reissue 1993.

————. *Call Me*. 1973 Hi Records. The Right Stuff 7243-8-28538-2-4, Reissue 1994.

————. *Greatest Hits*. Hi Records T2-30800, 1975.

————. *Green Is Blues*. 1972 Hi Records. The Right Stuff 0777-7-66710-2-4, Reissue 1993.

————. *I Can't Stop*. Blue Note 243-5-93556-2, 2003.

————. *I'm Still in Love with You*. 1972 Hi Records. The Right Stuff 7243-8-27627-2-0, Reissue 1993.

————. *Let's Stay Together*. 1973 Hi Records. The Right Stuff 7243-8-27121-2-1, Reissue 1993.

————. *Live . . . Tokyo*. The Right Stuff 7243-8-31975-2-1, Reissue 1995.

————. *Livin' for You*. 1973 Hi Records. The Right Stuff 7243-8-29791-2-8, Reissue 1994.

————. *Take Me to the River*. Hi Records. The Right Stuff 72435-28679-2-9, Reissue 2000.

————. *Your Heart's in Good Hands*. MCA 08811-13502, 1995.

Holiday, Billie. *Wishing on the Moon*. ASV Ltd. 43625-52772, 1999.

Howard, Miki. *Miki Sings Billie: A Tribute to Billie Holiday*. Giant Records 7599-24521-2, 1993.

Isley, Ronald. *Isley Meets Bacharach*. DreamWorks Records 0044-50500-7, 2003.

Jones, Norah. *Come Away with Me*. Blue Note 2435-32088-2, 2002.

Lee, Laura. *Greatest Hits*. HDH Records. Hot Wax 80931-0303-2, 1972.

McDonald, Michael. *Motown*. Universal Records/Motown 02498-01133, 2003.

Moore, Sam. *Plenty Good Lovin'*. EMI Music 8026-4-22003-2-5, 2002.

Nesby, Ann. *Put It on Paper*. Universal Records 440-017-391-2, 2002.

Pendergrass, Teddy. *Teddy Pendergrass*. Philadelphia International 7243-8-27630-2-4, 1977.

Porgy and Bess: Original Broadway Cast. MCA 0881-10520-2, 1992.

Rawls, Lou. *Portrait of the Blues*. Manhattan 7777-99548-2, 1993.

Redding, Otis. *The Ultimate Otis Redding*. Warner 7599-27608-2, 1987.

Reeves, Dianne. *That Day. . . .* Blue Note 2438-56973-2, 1997.

Rivers, Johnny. *Greatest Hits*. CEMA Special Markets 7777-57410-2, 1991.

Robinson, Smokey, and the Miracles. *The Ultimate Collection*. Motown 31453-08572, 1998.

Simon, Paul. *Still Crazy after All These Years*. Columbia 7599 25591 2, 1975.

Sisters of Glory, The. *Good News in Hard Times*. Warner Brothers 9362-45990-2, 1995.

Snow, Phoebe. *Against the Grain*. Columbia 5456, 1978.

————. *I Can't Complain*. House of Blues 51416-1352, 1998.

————. *It Looks Like Snow*. Columbia CK 34387, 1976.

————. *Natural Wonder*. Eagle 26992-00162, 2003.

————. *Never Letting Go*. Columbia 7464-34875-2, 1977.

————. *Phoebe Snow*. 1975 Shelter Records. The Right Stuff 2438-31972-2, Reissue 1995.

————. *Rock Away*. Mirage WTG 19297, 1981.

————. *Second Childhood*. Columbia CK 33952, 1976.

————. *Something Real*. Elektra 7559-60852-2, 1989.

————. *The Very Best of Phoebe Snow*. Columbia 7464-62241-2, 2001.

Stone, Joss. *Soul Sessions*. S-Curve Records 24354-22342, 2003.

Supremes. *The Supremes Sing Holland-Dozier-Holland*. Motown 650, 1967.

The Blues: A Smithsonian Collection of Classic Blues Singers. RD 101 A423981, A423986.

Washington, Dinah. *The Best of Dinah Washington*. EMI 0777-7-99114-2-4, 1992.

————. *Dinah Washington*. Verve Records 314-538-635-2, 1999.

————. *Dinah Washington's Finest Hour*. Verve Records 314-543-596-2, 2000.

————. *What a Diff'rence a Day Makes*. Mercury SR 60158, 1959.

Williams, Hank. *Timeless*. UMG Recordings 088-170-239-2, 2001.

Wilson, Jackie. *Reet Petite: The Very Best of Jackie Wilson*. Crimson 033093-005923,

Wright, Syreeta. *Stevie Wonder Presents Syreeta*. Motown 31453-0402-2, 1974.

index

Emerson, Ralph, xviii, 83, 93, 95–96, 113, 124, 131
Emotions, the, xxiv–xxv
En Vogue, 75–76
Escott, Colin, 63–65, 120
Esquire, 148, 167, 198
Eubanks, Kevin, 185
Everett, Betty, xvi, 197
"Every Beat of My Heart" (Gladys Knight and the Pips), 216–17 n.8
"Evil Gal Blues," 18

Faith, Percy, 64
Farley, Christopher John, 43
Feather, Leonard, 33; on Aretha Franklin's artistic similarities to Dinah Washington, 33
Fire in My Bones (Hinson), 88–90, 127–29; and overarching frames of religious performances, 89–90; and unity of gospel sets, 89–90
Fitzgerald, Ella, 17, 25, 31–33, 148, 178, 181–82, 187, 214–15 n.3
Fitzgerald, Jon, 188–92
Flack, Roberta, and Donny Hathaway, 12
Floyd, Eddie, 165
Fontane Sisters, 63
Forte, Allen, 176
"For the Good Times" (Green), 119
Four Tops, the, xvi, 28, 188, 207–9
Franklin, Aretha, xv, 8–10, 17–18, 25–78, 83, 138, 159, 197, 209–12, 213–14 n.1, 215 n.4, 218 n.11; cover of "Bridge Over Troubled Water" by, xvi–xviii, 6; cover of "Respect" by, xxvi, 8–9; critical derision of work by, for Columbia Records, xxiii–xxiv; and fear of flying, 50; reaction of, to Dinah Washington's death, 39–40; replacing Phoebe Snow as singer of *A Different World* theme, 156–58
Franklin, Carolyn, 44–45, 51–52

Franklin, C. L., 25, 29, 37–49
Franklin, Erma, 44
Frith, Simon, xix, 5–6, 7, 8–10, 21, 86–87, 90, 96, 127, 219 n.2; on bad vs. good song covers, 8–9; on listeners' creative responsibilities, 8; on "the performing body," 86; on singers' interpretations of songs, 8; on singers' invented images, 8; on songs as mini-musicals, 86–87
"From His Woman to You" (Mason), xxi–xxii
Funk (Vincent), 75
Funk Brothers, the, 189–90
"Funny How Time Slips Away," xxiv, 19, 83, 121, 125–26

Gamble, Kenneth, 30–31, 139, 158
Gaucho (Steely Dan), 74
Gaye, Marvin, xx, 30, 86, 108, 110, 188, 214 n.2, 218 n.10, 222–23 n.7
Garfunkel, Art, xvi, xxvi
George, Nelson, 53, 74, 75, 77, 84, 167, 221–22 n.4
Gerard, Charley, 162–63
Gershwin, George, 6, 7, 20, 141, 142, 176–80
Gersten, Russell, 216–17 n.8
Get It Right (Franklin), 41
Gibson, Don, 9
Gilroy, Paul, 159–62
Glen Miller Story, 198
"Going Down for the Third Time" (Supremes), xxiv–xxv, 174, 188–92; Phoebe Snow's cover of, xxiv–xxv, 20, 192–96
"Going Home" (Snow), 207–9
"Gone at Last" (Paul Simon and Phoebe Snow), 137–38, 151–52, 173
Go Tell It On the Mountain (Baldwin), 11
Goodman, Benny, 140
Good News in Hard Times (Sisters of Glory), 158

Michael Awkward

is the Gayl A. Jones Collegiate Professor
of Afro-American Literature and Culture at
the University of Michigan.

Library of Congress Cataloging-in-Publication Data
Awkward, Michael.
Soul covers : rhythm and blues remakes and the struggle
for artistic identity (Aretha Franklin, Al Green, Phoebe Snow) /
Michael Awkward.
p. cm. — (Refiguring American music)
Includes bibliographical references and index.
ISBN-13: 978-0-8223-3980-9 (cloth : alk. paper)
ISBN-13: 978-0-8223-3997-7 (pbk. : alk. paper)
1. Soul music—History and criticism. 2. Franklin, Aretha.
3. Green, Al. 4. Snow, Phoebe. I. Title.
ML3537.A95 2007
781.644—dc22   2006034550